*Media and the Transformation
of Religion in South Asia*

This project was sponsored by the Joint Committee on South Asia of the Social Science Research Council and the American Council of Learned Societies.

Media and the Transformation of Religion in South Asia

edited by
Lawrence A. Babb and
Susan S. Wadley

University of Pennsylvania Press

Philadelphia

Library of Congress Cataloging-in-Publication Data
Media and the transformation of religion in South Asia / edited by
Lawrence A. Babb and Susan S. Wadley.
    p.   cm.
  Includes bibliographical references and index.
  ISBN 0-8122-3304-2 (hdbk : alk. paper). — ISBN 0-8122-1547-8
(paper : alk. paper)
   1. Asia, South — Religion — 20th century.   2. Mass media — Religious
aspects.   I. Babb, Lawrence A.   II. Wadley, Susan S., 1943–
BL1055.W33   1995
291.1'75 — dc20   95-13168
                                          CIP

Contents

Illustrations

A Note on Transliteration

In most of this volume italicized technical terms and other materials from Indian languages have been transliterated according to standard conventions. However, the transliteration of Urdu terms and texts in Chapter 6 is based on the standard dictionary by Platts (*A Dictionary of Urdū, Classical Hindī, and English*). The names of castes and other groupings are not italicized but are given with diacritics (e.g., Rājpūt, Vaiṣṇava). Throughout the book, personal names are given without diacritics, as are words that are well-known in English spellings, such as place names (Delhi, Bombay), and the names of deities (Rama, Vishnu, Krishna).

Lawrence A. Babb

1. Introduction

Is South Asian religious culture changing? Of course it is, which is hardly news; common stereotype notwithstanding, South Asian religions have been ever-changing. What *is* news is that the nature of the religious change itself may be changing. Religious evolution in South Asia has entered a new phase. Over the past couple of centuries South Asia, like most of the rest of the world, has seen a complete revolution in the means available for the propagation of information, a revolution that began slowly and now seems to have begun a phase of self-induced acceleration. Beginning with the surprisingly early (sixteenth century) introduction and somewhat belated spread of printing technology, and continuing into recent times with the introduction of television and video recording, new communications media have profoundly altered the circulation of symbols, including religious symbols, in South Asian societies. This, in turn, has affected the quality of religious life in South Asia in important and sometimes startling ways. The studies in this volume describe and trace the implications of some of the most recent of these changes.

Media and Religious Systems

Understanding the impact of communications technology on religion requires looking at religious tradition from a somewhat unusual perspective. It is possible to say that if one takes an extremely inclusive view of what a religious tradition is — a view, that is, that includes its total range of manifestations in belief, patterned behavior, written records, ceremonial performances, iconography, traces in human memory, and so forth — then one can visualize any particular religious tradition as a sort of "system" that retains and transmits information. The information is encoded in the form of symbols that can be propagated in various media: speech, writing, ritual gesture, iconography, and others. Thus conceived, a religious tradition can be regarded as a reservoir that *retains* such information, which is deposited in human memory, books, durable artifacts, carved images, and so on.

But a tradition actually lives only insofar as it informs the thoughts, feelings, and conduct of persons belonging to a community of some kind, which is simply to say that its content must be socially *transmitted* as well as retained. This aspect of a religious tradition is its most visible surface. At one level, a tradition's transmission of its content is diffuse and pervasive; it occurs constantly in the talking, acting, and reacting of persons in ordinary social life. The most focused transmission, however, occurs mainly in what have been called "cultural performances": the rituals, discourses, tellings of myths, recitations of texts, and the like that we normally consider manifestations of "religion." In such performances the channels through which information is conveyed are various. Verbalizations are often basic, as are the visible symbolizations of ritual and iconography. But the scent of incense can also carry a message, as can the taste of a food offering retrieved from the altar and consumed by devotees.

Utilizing this general perspective, one can construct a model of a religious tradition's career in the flow of time based on the notion of information transmission. Often borne by the verbalizations and other performances of religious specialists, symbols are propagated to "audiences." Members of such audiences, however, are performers themselves; indeed, everyone in the system is both performer and audience, depending on the context. The most important factor determining the direction and relative amplitude of information flow is the social structure in which the tradition is embedded. Exchange is dense within groups and attenuated by group boundaries. Social hierarchy may retard the transmission of symbols in some directions, while the existence of specialists in symbol-propagation (such as priests) may strongly augment the flow in other directions. Actors, moreover, are not mere transponders; individuals give their own personal stamp to the religious symbols in which they traffic, and in this sense the system can never be, at any given time, quite what it was before. When symbols pass through such "sticky" media as writing, they tend to eddy backward into relatively stable social memory. Thus, the content of tradition can accumulate and grow. But nothing is truly fixed; time inevitably deposits new layers over previously stored materials, and each generation finds its own new ways of construing the deposits of the past. Therefore, as symbols circulate through such a system, the system as a whole is not only socially reproduced but also altered.

This model provides us with a general (and admittedly roughly sketched) frame of reference for understanding the impact of new communications media on South Asian religious traditions. What do we mean by new communications media? We mean new techniques for the transmission of information-bearing symbols. These are techniques that in one way or another enhance the capacity of symbols to be projected from one place to another. This is precisely what the new media considered in this volume have done; in various ways and by different means they have greatly increased what might be called the *mobility* of religious symbols in South Asia. If a religious tradition can be viewed, as suggested above, as a system that retains and transmits information, then we can say that the principal effect of new communications media has been to attenuate the barriers that inhibit the projection of symbols and to dilate the channels through which symbols move. To move beyond this simple formulation, however, is to confront a number of interesting complexities. The mobility of symbols turns out to be a more subtle matter than one might suppose.

It is not, for example, a matter of mere *spatial* mobility, or at least not in any simple sense. From a pure engineering standpoint, technological advance in communications tends to be seen primarily as a means of overcoming physical distance, and it is true that the media considered in this volume have this characteristic. Printed words and pictures, audio recordings, videotapes, and the like can be transported easily over great distances, and to the degree that they can be reproduced cheaply, they can be disseminated to large populations. Moreover, when words, music, and visual images are carried as modulations of electromagnetic radiation, they are not only projected over great distances at high speed but something approaching saturation coverage is at least a theoretical possibility. Within South Asia, these basic facts have had much to do with the impact of new communications media on religion.

But physical distance, as such, is not necessarily the main consideration; at least as important is *social* distance. As the great anthropologist E. E. Evans-Pritchard showed long ago, the human landscape is one in which spatial relationships are deeply modified by social structure. The distance between one point and another is magnified by social and cultural barriers and diminished by social interaction and cultural similarity. These effects have been cleverly parodied by the "New Yorker's Map of the United States" in which a vastly expanded Manhattan and West Coast are separated by a shrunken Midwest. The studies in this volume show that new media have not only given religious symbols greater spatial mobility but have significantly enhanced their *social mobility* as well. That is, new media have increased the capacity of religious symbols to penetrate social barriers and to bypass social bottlenecks that have inhibited their propagation in the past. Generally speaking, this has probably been the most important effect of new communications technologies on South Asian religion.

Another way to put this is to say that the increased social mobility of religious symbols has had a socially "disembedding" effect on religious traditions. The pattern of religious belief and practice prevailing in the past was one in which religious life was tightly interwoven with the social structure (and often the social microstructure) that provided its context. Family, lineage, clan, caste, village, neighborhood, and so on, were the primary social settings in which religious observance occurred and the main background of reference against which religious consciousness was formed. To participate in ritual and ceremony was, to a significant degree, to enact an identity as a particular *kind* of person belonging to one or more of the many groupings that are the fabric of South Asian social life. In this sense, parochial groups can be seen as "pools" in which the flow of symbols has recirculated. Moreover, the movement of symbols through the wider system was closely linked to the roles of religious specialists, such as Brahman priests, mendicant teachers, and others. One can say that it was precisely these specialists who made possible the internal communication of South Asian religious traditions; but from another point of view they represented, as necessary mediators, a relatively narrow aperture for the downward flow of a vast and rich "great" tradition. These patterns still obtain, but the essays in this volume suggest that they are eroding because of the influence of new communications technologies, and this may foreshadow truly fundamental changes in the structure of religious tradition in South Asia.

These same essays indicate, however, that along with their ability to increase the mobility of religious symbols, other features of new communications media need to be considered if we are to understand fully their role in modern religious change. Another factor of great importance is the extent to which the mechanical or electronic exigencies peculiar to a given medium may affect the content transmitted and the way that content is perceived by audiences. A complex myth presented in comic book format, for example, is likely to be greatly simplified; simplicity is obviously inherent to this medium. A televised performance of a religious drama may well adhere to traditional performance conventions to an impressive degree, but it will inevitably abstract the performance from the social and ritual contexts that, in traditional settings, invest the experience with its full range of meaning to audiences. Some of the materials presented in this book, however, suggest that these distorting effects need not always be large.

Economic considerations are also crucial in determining the impact a new medium is likely to have on tradition. For example, if the medium is one in which the production costs are high, then producers are likely to be motivated to minimize risk to their investment by avoiding experimentation and concentrating on products that will appeal to the widest possible audience. The result will be standardization. If, on the other hand, production costs are low, then producers can afford to seek specialized niches in a more general audience, and the result will be an accentuation of variety. The studies in this book suggest that both tendencies have been operating simultaneously in South Asia.

Standardization is a central issue in the study of the impact of modern media on religious culture. One might have hypothesized that the increased mobility of symbols afforded by new technologies would inevitably lead to homogenization and uniformity. One would then envision a future South Asia quite different from the one we currently observe: a South Asia in which rich cultural and subcultural variety have been smeared into dull uniformity by modern media. But this outcome seems highly unlikely. Some media, such as film and television, do have a strong propensity in this direction. As we shall see, however, other media — good examples are chromolithography and audio cassettes — seem to be able to register the variety of South Asian tradition even as they also project more unifying religious visions. Moreover, we shall also see that some of the newer media have brought new forms of religious expression into being, forms that actually add to the diversity of the South Asian religious scene.

The time frame for the studies included in this volume is the twentieth century, with an emphasis on recent decades. All the studies therefore deal with what might be called the "second wave" of modern change in the media through which religious culture has been transmitted in South Asia. The first such innovation, revolutionary in its effects, was the printing press. First brought to South Asia by the Portuguese in Goa, and later extensively used by missionaries to propagate the Christian faith, print technology became a factor in the transmission of Hindu and Muslim religious traditions in the nineteenth century. By the late 1800s and early 1900s the printing of religious materials had begun to give rise to many of the trends noted by the studies in this volume: the increased spatial and social mobility of symbols, the social disembedding of tradition, and so on.

Our concern in this volume, however, is with newer media that seem to be bringing about — as printing itself did in an earlier era — profound changes, and potentially revolutionary changes, in the structure and content of Indian religious traditions. We have grouped the chapters into three general sections. Section 1 deals with printed pictorial images — religious poster art and comics — and these forms may be said to represent innovations on an older printing base. Sections 2 and 3 are concerned with audio recording and moving visual images respectively, and these are distinctively twentieth-century phenomena.

Printed Images

SACRED PICTURES

Central to religious observance in the Hindu tradition is *darśan,* the auspicious seeing of a divine being. Given that fact, it is hardly surprising that the mechanical reproduction of pictures of deities (and other sacred entities) has become one of the most ubiquitous manifestations of modern religion in South Asia. Oddly, however, this phenomenon has been little studied by scholars, and the two chapters on this subject included in this volume are thus pioneering studies.

H. Daniel Smith's chapter presents unique new data on the production and marketing of "god posters" and on their use in domestic and other settings. It is clear from Smith's materials that chromolithographic technology (that is, technology for the reproduction of colored pictures) has greatly increased the spatial and social mobility of iconic symbols in South Asia. Among other things, this has contributed to the spread of certain devotional cults and has made it possible for otherwise localized "personality cults" of holy men to develop and maintain wide networks of support (an issue also raised by John Little in Chapter 10). The overall result, however, has not been religious homogenization. Although pan-Indian deities are prominent in religious poster art, regional deities are also represented. Moreover, Smith shows that this genre has been the source of religious innovations that enrich the variety of ways in which tradition can be expressed. Poster artists, for example, have portrayed well-known deities in new combinations. The relative fluidity of this medium (by comparison with more convention-bound temple iconography) seems to permit an unprecedented degree of iconic experimentation, which, in turn, has generated and supported new syncretisms. This same fluidity is even more marked in the combinations and permutations of deity posters found in domestic shrines and in other micro-settings. Here iconic symbolism responds directly to the religious imaginations of individuals and small groups, and the result is a pattern in which subcontinental traditions, reflected in standard images, can be manifested in endlessly local ways.

Smith's materials also show that religious poster art has contributed to the growth of a new "omnipraxy." This is a populist version of tradition; it is inconspicuous, casual, informal, and unmediated by specialists. At its heart are the simplest possible ritual gestures performed before inexpensive lithographed images, and it is often found in what might seem to be quite mundane and ordinary settings. Such minimalist rituals have probably always been a part of the South Asian religious scene, but the pervasiveness of popular religious art surely has something to do with current high visibility of the pattern.

In his examination of the life and oeuvre of C. Kondiah Raju (1898–1976), a figure second only to the celebrated Raja Ravi Varma in his influence on Indian popular art, Stephen Inglis dispels the widespread notion that religious poster art is devoid of genuine esthetic expression and alienated from its cultural surround. Here was a true master artist, who all his life regarded his art as an activity deeply responsible to religious tradition. Inglis shows how, to this day, the genre he created retains traces of painted scenes used in traditional drama, which was the milieu from which Kondiah came. His relationship with his pupils was of the traditional master–disciple sort. This has been the case with most artists in this genre, and the resulting phenomenon of artistic "lineages" — echoing the theme of disciplic succession in South Asian religious traditions — has been an important factor in the standardization of popular images of deities. Images tend to be recycled within lineages, and when this is combined with the enormous reproductive power of photo-offset printing, the consequences can be startling. As Inglis shows, the artistic (and spiritual) insights of one man, a lineage-founder like Kondiah, can be "amplified" in such a way as to become normative within the tradition. Indeed Kondiah's renditions of certain deities have become the way these deities are actually visualized by South Indians.

The pictorial standardization of images of some deities has become quite marked, and Inglis suggests that we are witnessing the emergence of a "national aesthetic" in which the universality of certain images draws Hindus everywhere into a common vision of the divine and its manifestations. So authoritative have certain standardized images become that, when displayed in temples, they seem to have the function of authenticating the "real" three-dimensional icons within. Mass-produced popular images have also made the Hindu world smaller, both spatially and socially. Pilgrimage can become vicarious for those who must remain at home. People can become devotees of deities from whose temples they have been traditionally barred.

Inglis joins Smith, however, in stressing the potential of popular art to support religious variety. Standardized images are often combined in permutations that reflect the religious microdialects of families and individuals. Religious and secular images are often displayed together in domestic settings, which suggests that popular art has enabled Hindus to engage in an entirely new kind of iconic commentary on relationships between divine beings and events and figures in the contemporary world. It can be argued, therefore, that popular religious art has not only fostered certain universalizing trends, but has also enhanced and diversified the total range of meanings that can be expressed through iconic imagery.

COMIC BOOKS

In what is surely one of the more astonishing vignettes reported in South Asianist scholarship, in Frances Pritchett's chapter we learn that Anant Pai, founder of the famed and ubiquitous *Amar Chitra Katha* comic book series, once overheard two high government officials settle an argument about some point in the *Rāmāyaṇa* by referring to one of Pai's comics. Whatever else one might make of this, it seems clear that something quite new has entered the enculturation process of at least some members of India's most important elites. Comic books are easy to overlook; the form itself has generally inspired little respect among aficionados of high culture and has been regarded by many as deeply unserious. And yet it is clear that in societies like the United States comics register trends in popular culture with great sensitivity. In any case, comic books in India should be taken seriously, for they may well be among the more important channels of contact between English-educated, middle-class children and South Asian religious traditions.

Pritchett's study is an introduction to the religious comic book in India and an exploration of the institutional subculture of *Amar Chitra Katha* as expressed in the organization and content of the series. The series' world view, Pritchett shows, has largely been an expression of the outlook of one man, Anant Pai. In turn, Anant Pai's outlook is a reflection of the ideals and social vision of India's modern urban middle class, and in this sense the series as a whole may be considered a kind of anthology of the religious and social attitudes of India's most influential elites.

The stated aim of the series is to provide children with a comprehensive understanding of India's "cultural heritage." As Pritchett points out, however, the series actually presents a highly selective version of this heritage; some groups and traditions receive much less or much more attention than others. Women and Muslims, for example, are quite egregiously underrepresented in the "Makers of Modern India" series. There is, moreover, a strong Krishnaite emphasis in the series' presentation of the Hindu tradition. Still, the series treats Krishna's "cosmos-embodying form" with special favor, and this stress on cosmic integration resonates with the series' overall social vision in which the accent is on inclusiveness and communal harmony. These emphases are unexceptionable, but they are also coupled with a tendency to "airbrush" away all traces of communal conflict, which can result in distortions of reality. Thus, for example, Hindus and Muslims are never presented as hostile, and all traces of anti-Muslim sentiment have been expunged from the series' version of Bankim Chandra Chatterji's *Ānanda Maṭh*.

The series must struggle with a truly basic contradiction. Inherent to the comic book form is simplification of content. This means that when complex materials from the Epics or the *Purāṇa*s are presented, they must necessarily be impoverished, and sometimes drastically so. This, however, is in conflict with the high seriousness of Pai's stated purpose. He believes (quite accurately) that the series is, for many children, an important conduit to India's traditions; and this has naturally given rise to a great concern for "authenticity" and accuracy. Pritchett points out that, unlike the *kissā* and related genres, the purpose of the series is finally to instruct, not to entertain. But if comics are to instruct they must also entertain, and in recent years the series seems to have drifted away from that basic insight. The series has increasingly relied on blocks of dense text, often complete with authenticating scholarly notes. This tendency may leave *Amar Chitra Katha* vulnerable to its competitors. But whether *Amar Chitra Katha* or some other similar series dominates the field, it seems likely that the religious comic book has arrived in India to stay.

John S. Hawley compares hagiography in the *Amar Chitra Katha* series with the way saints' lives have been portrayed in centuries past, and the differences are instructive. In consonance with its middle-class outlook, the series tends to de-emphasize "superstition," violence, social conflict, and sexuality; it stresses instead social harmony and "national integration." In general the series presents softened and less provocative versions of great religious figures. Mirabai, for example, is represented by tradition as someone who defied family and social convention, but Pai's Mira is a Sita-like "ideal Hindu wife." Kabir appears primarily as an apostle of Hindu-Muslim unity, and the theme of reconciliation is a dominant motif in the presentation of various other saints' lives. The series stresses a network of connections between North Indian saints; and sectarian rivalry is downplayed, as are the links to Brahman status that some older traditions assign to many of these figures. Hawley shows how the series has treated Ravidas, a saint of the untouchable Camār community, with special delicacy; the result is a distinctly denatured Ravidas whose principal message is a devotionalist vision (with an *advaita* flavoring) of nonhierarchical social integration.

Emerging in the ever-growing *Amar Chitra Katha* corpus is a kind of "canon," one that in recent times has begun to incorporate the contributions of multiple individuals and groups. Although Anant Pai remains its guiding spirit, the content of the series has increasingly been negotiated with important communities and institutions in Indian society, and the series has now become something approximating a national institution projecting a coherent (and some would say misleading) view of Indian nationhood. Hawley suggests that this image of national integration is one in which the distinction between "Indian" and "Hindu" is becoming ominously fuzzy.

Audio Recording

The ubiquity of popular art has been noted, but it seems fair to say that no modern communications medium is more intrusive in modern Indian life than recorded and electronically amplified sound. Urban India, many would say, is acoustically polluted, and even if this harsh judgment is rejected, it might still be conceded that the impact of recorded music is large indeed on the sensory environment of most urban people. Somewhere in the cacophony, and perhaps an increasingly important part of it, is recorded religious music. The two studies included in the second section of this volume treat the career of recorded *qawwālī* and the more general impact of cassette technology on recorded religious music.

In her fine-grained analysis of recorded *qawwālī*, Regula Qureshi points out that recording technology has a powerfully decontextualizing effect on religious music. No longer does a community share the listening experience as a ritual event; listeners instead become anonymous individuals who interact neither with each other nor with performers. Between the creator of music and listener, market relations obtain; the music is deper-sonalized, standardized, and altered in response to the mechanical and elec-tronic requirements of recording technology. But in the case of *qawwālī* this dismal picture may not apply completely, for the altered product has re-turned to its source in ritual observance and may be enriching that source.

Qawwālī was particularly well placed to become a recorded genre: it was never seen as "sacred music," its performers lacked special religious status, and its heritage has always stressed the propagation of Sufism to all hearers of whatever community. Its very unorthodoxy, that is, shielded it from the ire of the orthodox. The earliest recorded *qawwālī* was marketed mainly to urban Muslim business communities, especially in Bombay, and it was strongly influenced by the then-developing conventions of film mu-sic. From the 1940s onward, "narrative *qawwālī*" came to the fore, a form well suited to the expressions of nationalism and cultural ecumenism that were common in the *qawwālī* of the period. A completely secularized ver-sion of the form ultimately emerged in films, where it was utilized to sug-gest a "Muslim" atmosphere. The post-Independence trend in India was for recorded *qawwālī* to continue to emphasize religious inclusiveness; in Paki-stan, not surprisingly, Muslim elements were re-emphasized.

In today's Sufi assembly, traditional performers must respond to au-diences whose tastes have been formed by listening to recorded *qawwālī*. But because the acceptability of a given piece depends on whether it passes muster with the performance's religious leader, the Sufi assembly is in no danger of being swamped with musical kitch. What we see instead is a con-trolled interchange in which recorded "entertainment" *qawwālī* enriches the repertoires of traditional performers, but in a way that is responsive to traditional religious imperatives. Precisely because recorded and traditional *qawwālī* have maintained this sort of contact, it is possible for *qawwālī* to be a musical idiom that at once entertains, expresses devotional Islam, and supports a sense of mutual identity among South Asian Muslims.

There is simply no doubt that the audio-cassette technology discussed by Scott Marcus has begun a revolution in the dissemination of recorded sound in South Asia. Marcus begins his analysis by developing a portrait of traditional performance contexts for music: he provides examples of perfor-mances that are either fully embedded in traditional contexts or only partly dislodged. Contrasting with these, and exemplary of the full impact of recording technology, is a superhit *bhajan* recorded by Anup Jalota. Here we see all of the earmarks of a big-time commercial recording: a nearly complete absence of performer–audience interaction, the loss of traditional performance contexts, and the esthetic responses of producers to what they believe to be popular taste. Such recordings enable millions of listeners to share a musical experience of a sort in the absence of any real contact with one another, but this experience can nonetheless support a sense of a common devotional bond.

The extraordinary impact of cassette technology on the recording industry in India, Marcus shows, is largely a consequence of the economics of production and consumption. On a per-song basis, cassettes are cheaper for consumers than records, and they can be produced in one-room factories. These circumstances have resulted in a democratization of the world of recorded music; specific categories of religious music that had rarely been recorded before are now available on tape, and regional music genres, largely ignored by the big recording firms, are now being recorded. *Bhajan*s associated with particular rituals are now available on cassette, as are songs associated with the cults of certain holy men (such as Satya Sai Baba). Tapes of religious discourses have also come into prominence. Another effect of the economics of cassette production has been the end of the complete domination of the industry by film music; so cheap are tapes to produce and buy that the impetus of a hit film is no longer necessary to generate sufficient sales to recover producers' investments. The latest "craze" in nonfilm recorded music is, in fact, devotional music, which is challenging film music for sales supremacy and which producers tend to favor because of the relative stability of the market.

These developments, Marcus notes, have affected the structures through which tradition is transmitted; it is now possible to listen to the *satyanārāyaṇ kathā* without a priest or to hear a *bayān* in the absence of a *mullāh*. And although the recording industry tended in its earlier phases to foster standardization, the economies made possible by cassette technology have enabled an expanded and diversified recording industry to reflect South Asia's cultural and religious variety.

Moving Images

It is likely that, of all the senses, the visual sense is the most consequential in the interaction of human beings with their environment. The immediacy of visual images in our perceptions of the world probably has much to do with the enormous popularity and impact on popular culture of film and television everywhere in the world. These are technologies that convey moving images, and when such images are combined with sound, the result is the closest approximation to actual experience of the real world yet provided by media technology. Even when the content conveyed is known to be fictional, the sense of verisimilitude is great. Moreover, these media have the potential to reach mass audiences, an especially significant fact in regions like South Asia where literacy rates are low. Film and television can convey quite complex messages that would otherwise be inaccessible to nonreading audiences. These characteristics have important implications for the role of film and television in the propagation of religious symbols.

India's film industry is a true colossus, and there have been links between Indian film and religion from the medium's earliest days. It was in fact religious films — the so-called mythologicals — that first generated an audience for cinema in India. Moreover, the impact of film on religion has been quite conspicuous; a good example is the film-generated cult of the goddess Santoshi Ma. Nevertheless, Steve Derné's study of Hindi film shows that the relationship between film and religion in India is more complex than is commonly supposed.

One of the most startling facts reported by Derné is that the classical religious film, the mythological, is very much on the wane: in the 1970s only 5 percent of films produced belonged to this category. The reason seems to be that films of this type appeal mainly to rural audiences and also to urban women, groups of relatively infrequent filmgoers, which obviously depresses profits. Derné argues, moreover, that religious films have been a remarkably feeble source of innovation in the content of religious tradition. The reasons for this are several. The costs of film production in India are extremely high, so producers are reluctant to take creative risks and are strongly inclined to produce films that will appeal to groups at all levels of society and that will be accessible even to people whose Hindi is weak. This means that the content of all films, including religious films, tends to be formulaic, predictable, uncontroversial, and simple. The demands of censors are a further impediment to experimentation and deviation from culturally conservative formulas. In religious films, Derné argues, these factors have resulted in a genre that stresses the most widely shared and least controversial aspects of religious tradition. Derné also suggests that even when films do innovate religiously, the results are not likely to have much impact on viewers. Film in general is held in low esteem in India, and audiences are not likely to view film as an authoritative guide to how they should behave or what they should believe.

At a quite different level, however, religion has had a profound influence on Indian film in general, with results that may be quite momentous. Derné's most important finding is that ostensibly secular films are in fact strongly influenced by religion. In part this is a matter of form. Derné's data indicate that entertainment films of all kinds are shaped by the conventions of folk drama, which traditionally presents mainly religious material. The punctuation of plot line by song and dance, the extravagant speeches, the utter predictability of the plot, the black-and-white moral oppositions between characters — these are well-known features of Hindi cinema, and they derive from various traditional dramatic genres. But more important yet, Derné shows that characterization in secular films draws heavily from Hindu-mythical stereotypes: women appear as dutiful and long-suffering Sitas or vengeful Kalis, men as virtuous Ramas or villainous Ravanas, and so on. Some filmmakers are apparently quite self-conscious and deliberate in the use of such mythical models.

This may be the real news as far as religion and film is concerned: that behind the backs of nearly everyone a distinctly religious imagery has found its way into India's most influential entertainment medium, an imagery that may be defining a semi-secular national culture embodying values, especially those pertaining to family and social life, that are Hindu to the core.

Of all the communications media recently introduced in India, television is generally believed to have the most comprehensive impact on audiences and the most far-reaching effects on the materials transmitted. Although television has been a part of the Indian scene for some years, the full potential of the medium is only now being realized. It seems likely that the 1987–88 presentation of Ramanand Sagar's serialization of the *Rāmāyaṇa* will ultimately be seen as a watershed event in the history of Indian television. For the first time the medium was utilized for the transmission of a major cultural text. The result was something approximating a national obsession: the program attracted huge audiences and touched off an anguished debate about the possibilities and limitations of television, and indeed about the nature of the *Rāmāyaṇa* itself. But as the volume of strident criticism (mainly from the English-language press) increased, a vast audience of ordinary men and women continued to find the series both entertaining and spiritually uplifting. If some cultural critics found the series in some sense "inauthentic," most viewers were unconcerned; for them, it seems, Ramanand Sagar was the "Tulsidas of the video age."

What was the meaning of this phenomenon? Many — both in India and elsewhere — are predisposed to believe that television possesses something like a Midas touch in reverse: it corrupts and debases all with which it comes in contact. But as Philip Lutgendorf's contribution to this volume shows, such a view would be too hasty in the case of the televised *Rāmā-yaṇa*. Most features of the program criticized by the English-speaking literati turn out to be entirely "authentic" reflections of the performance traditions and religious culture from which the program drew. In the televised *Rāmāyaṇa* may be seen elements of traditional *kathā* and *rāmlīlā*, and central to the audience's experience is *darśan*, sacred seeing. Nor, as it turns out, is there any convincing evidence that the televised version is displacing other versions. The televised *Rāmāyaṇa*, Lutgendorf argues, must finally be seen as an "independent *Rāmāyaṇa*," a culturally authentic retelling that incorporates older performance traditions and that utilizes the potential of the new video medium in highly distinctive ways.

A significant recent innovation in media technology is the videocassette recorder (VCR). This could be regarded as an "add-on" to television, but in fact its characteristics as a medium are quite different. VCR technology may be to film and broadcast television what audio cassettes are to pressed records: the basic principle is the same, in this case the propagation of moving images, but the costs of producing a "receivable" image are drastically lowered, which allows groups or individuals with limited resources to use the medium in their own way. In middle-class India, as elsewhere, VCR technology seems certain to revolutionize patterns of home entertainment, and judging by the ubiquity of video parlors in urban areas, the process is already well under way. But this technology has other potential uses, as shown by John Little's study of Swadhyaya, an extremely successful modern Hindu religious movement.

The Swadhyayees make extensive use of videotapes of the discourses of the movement's founder, Pandurang V. Athavale. At first glance, the most significant use to which these tapes are put would seem to be recruitment to the movement, but there may be less to this than meets the eye. Little shows that although Athavale's tapes are certainly extensively employed in proselytizing, the movement's obvious success in this endeavor is more likely rooted in the time-honored strategy of utilizing preexisting social networks. Little's analysis suggests that the real significance of the tapes lies in the role they play in maintaining what might be called the movement's "spiritual cohesion."

The tapes are a central part of the ritual observances of the movement wherever they occur, in India or abroad, and the evidence presented shows that devotees believe that viewing these tapes is a true devotional encounter with a sacred being. The tapes themselves are regarded as sacred objects.

They transmit traditional religious discourses, *pravacan*s, and, when they are played, all the framing devices of ritual performance are present, from opening benediction to closing *āratī* ceremony. It is well known that in India (and elsewhere too) books can be regarded as vehicles for the transmission of sacred power as well as mere information. What we see in Little's materials is that copper, silicon, and magnetized tape can also retain and convey sacred power.

Swadhyaya is a typical example of a type of religious movement common in India; the key to its structure is a highly personalized tie between a group of devotees and a single, focal, charismatic individual. Movements of this type often suffer from a limitation that seems inherent to their structure, namely, an inability to project a sense of the charismatic leader's presence to large numbers of devotees over great distances. In the case of Swadhyaya, these limitations have been overcome by the use of video technology. The tapes have allowed the movement to utilize a highly traditional ritual format in a way that allows the central, sacred figure to be multilocational. Like Krishna, Athavale can be multiplied and yet remain whole and entire to each of his widely scattered local congregations. This is a highly significant development and may portend a modern florescence of movements of the Swadhyaya type, released by technology from the prison of the social structures through which religious culture has been traditionally transmitted in South Asia.

Trends

What do we learn from these studies overall? The most important general lesson is probably that modern media have had multiple and, in some respects, contradictory effects on religious belief and practice in South Asia. All of them have dramatically increased the spatial and social mobility of religious symbols in South Asia, although different media have clearly done this to different degrees and in different ways. And this feature of modern media has, in turn, given rise to a range of effects that all fall more or less under the labels of standardization and homogenization. Pressed records, film, and television seem to exemplify this trend best, but all the media considered in this volume have, in one way or another, contributed to an ever-wider dissemination of a limited number of key symbols or images. This has made South Asian societies smaller. Standardized images transcend older cultural and social boundaries, making it possible for people to share social, national, and spiritual identities in ways that they never did before.

Closely related to the above is the social disembedding of religion. All the media considered here have lifted religious belief and practice out of older, parochial contexts, and, to the degree that this has happened, religious symbols increasingly become "for" everyone in general rather than someone(s) in particular. We also note that, as part of this process, modern media have begun to render problematic the roles of traditional specialists in symbol transmission, but it is certainly not yet the case that these specialists are redundant. Whether the general abstraction of religious symbols from traditional contexts is seen as liberating or as a compromise of authenticity depends, perhaps, on one's point of view.

But standardization is in no sense the end of the matter. When the economics are right, modern media in South Asia have reflected, and even celebrated, regional and other kinds of diversity. Some newer media—perhaps preeminently poster art—have opened up new possibilities for the expression of the unique religious sensibilities of groups and individuals. Video and audio cassettes have a great potential to leaven the religious mix with a profusion of new cults and sectarian movements. The materials presented here, in sum, should give comfort to those who fear that new media will reduce South Asia's rich religious heritage to a plastic homogeneity. If there is a tide in the direction of uniformity, there is also a strong countertide.

Acknowledgments

The original impetus for this book was a decision in the mid-1980s by the Joint Committee on South Asia of the Social Science Research Council and the American Council of Learned Societies to investigate issues facing South Asia since Independence in 1947. This led to the formation of a subcommittee (L. A. Babb, Richard Eaton, John S. Hawley, Philip Lutgendorf, and Susan S. Wadley) that proposed a series of conferences on religious change in South Asia. A conference on religious change and the media was held in Monterey, California, in the spring of 1989, and this book derives from that conference, although in vastly modified form. Chapter 9 was originally written for the conference; a longer version of it appeared in TDR (The Drama Review), Summer 1990. We thank the National Endowment for the Humanities and the Joint Committee for their sponsorship of the original conference. We are particularly grateful to Toby Volkman for her assistance in putting the conference together and for her invaluable input into the conference itself. The Joint Committee, Syracuse University, and Amherst College aided in the production of the final manuscript.

Section 1

Printed Images

Susan S. Wadley

Introduction

The printing press has a far longer history — on a world-historical stage and in India — than the other communications media considered later in this book. The press first came to India shortly after the Portuguese landed in Goa, and its early use in southern India was closely tied to Portuguese, Danish, and French attempts to win Christian converts. The advent of the first press, though, was unplanned: in 1556, the Portuguese sent a printing press, by way of Goa, to missionaries hoping to win converts in Abyssinia. But when the emperor there changed his mind about welcoming the Christian fathers, the press remained in Goa. In 1556, the first book published on Indian soil, the *Doctrina Christiana,* was printed. Twenty-two years later, a printing press on the Malabar coast issued a translation in Tamil script. This translation, many believe, marks the first printing of Indian script in India. Thus, barely one hundred years after the Gutenberg Bible was published, printing had made its way to India.

The early presses were found first on the coast of western India and later moved around the tip of Cape Comorin to the east. The Danes opened an important press at Tranquebar, where a settlement was founded in 1618. In 1706, two young Protestant missionaries, Ziegenhalg and Plutrarch, arrived in Tranquebar. With support from the Society for Promoting Christian Knowledge, they received a printing press in 1712. Soon they were making Tamil fonts and publishing tracts and scriptures in Tamil. Ziegenhalg also wrote an early Tamil dictionary. The group in Tranquebar helped establish the Colombo Press for the Dutch East India Company. By 1736, the Dutch were publishing official proclamations in Sinhalese. In 1737, a Sinhalese prayer book was published, followed by a Confession of Faith in 1738 and a complete Tamil Bible in 1741.

Printing was slower to emerge under the British. The first press in Madras resulted from a 1761 battle with the French at Pondicherry, whose loot included a printing press. The East India Company Press was used to print government proclamations and alphabets and calendars for the missionaries. Later grammars and numerous Christian religious tracts were published by various presses in Madras. It was not until the early nineteenth century, however, that printed editions of Hindu religious texts became available.

Printing came even later to Calcutta, with the arrival of William Carey, a Baptist missionary, who obtained a press in 1798. But government censorship compelled him to move to Serampore, then under Danish control. From there the first Indian language monthly was published in 1818 and the first weekly a year later. The Serampore press sought to present the scriptures in as many languages as possible to as many people as possible. A Bengali Bible was issued in 1800–1801, with some 212,000 items in forty languages published between 1801 and 1832. In addition, the need for Hindu scriptures for students at Fort William College led to the production of Hindu texts in Indian languages in the early 1800s. But censorship and paper shortages continued to plague all the Indian presses, despite efforts by Charles Metcalf, acting Governor-General in 1835, to remove the more stringent censorship laws.

Nevertheless, by the late 1800s, printing presses had sprung up in district towns throughout India, with increasing numbers being privately owned by Hindus. That the major output of these presses was initially religious works is not surprising, given the models presented by Christian missionaries. The printing press became a vital instrument in the religious changes that enveloped South Asia in the late 1800s and early 1900s.

When one thinks of printing, one inevitably thinks of the printed word. It was, in fact, primarily through the medium of the printed word that the printing press exerted its extraordinary impact on practically every aspect of life in India, including religion. This is an impact that has been described and analyzed in an abundant scholarship. Our concern in this section of the book, however, is not primarily with the printed word but with types of printed images that are not at all well explored — or even described — in South Asian cultural studies.

The first of these media is religious poster art, which is treated in essays by H. Daniel Smith and Stephen Inglis. Image-making in India has a long and complex history of its own.[1] Before 1900, India had several chromo-lithographic presses, including the Ravi Varma Fine Art Lithographic Press in Bombay and the Calcutta Art Studio in Calcutta. The press of Hem Chander Bhargava and Company in Chandni Chowk, Delhi, has been continuously printing lithographics of religious subjects since 1900. The twentieth century has been a particularly rich and dynamic period in the production of new forms of images, as other chapters in this volume confirm.

Religious poster art represents a particularly interesting example of this process. The two chapters approach the subject from complementary perspectives. Smith's essay lays the groundwork for understanding the marketing, subject matter, and range of uses of the genre. Inglis traces the development of a regional style through a case study, the work of an influential South Indian artist. Together the authors provide a framework for the appreciation of the "god poster" phenomenon as a significant visual form in Indian art and religion and suggest new directions for the study of art and religion in the age of mechanical reproduction.

Comic books are far more recent on the Indian scene, and as far as we know, comic books based on religious or mythological themes have become predominant as a direct result of the cultural (and commercial) entrepreneurship of a single individual, Anant Pai, who founded *Amar Chitra Katha* in 1967. Since then, religious comics have become a staple of middle-class Indian childhood — both in India and abroad. Frances Pritchett's and John Hawley's contributions to this volume represent unique scholarship on the *Amar Chitra Katha* phenomenon, giving us insight into the religious education of India's urban middle class.

Note

1. My thanks to H. Daniel Smith and Stephen Inglis for their contributions to this section.

H. Daniel Smith

2. Impact of "God Posters" on Hindus and Their Devotional Traditions

A popular genre of religious art in India today is known variously as "framing pictures," "calendar art," and "god posters."[1] The different names that have been used for this genre arise from the fact that they refer at once to color prints produced for framing to serve as wall decorations, to artistically rendered illustrations used to grace hanging calendars, and, most typically, to polychrome lithographs that depict Hindu gods. As genre pieces, they are found everywhere—in homes, in temples and shrines, in offices and shops, in schools and public halls. Because they are mass produced, they are sold cheaply (sometimes even distributed free) and hence are within the reach of all who want them. Yet their value goes far beyond their price. God posters are usually displayed in places of honor, often wreathed with flower garlands out of respect for the divine presence they disclose to devotees. The ubiquity of the god posters in South Asia is indisputable, but art collectors and connoisseurs, as well as educated, Westernized Indians, dismiss them as kitsch and question their "art." Yet god posters are adored by the masses, and, accordingly, their popularity makes them telling artifacts of contemporary Indian popular taste and popular religion.

Since this is an area of research in which both empirical and analytical precedents are practically nonexistent,[2] I will suggest how the genre including god posters has served to influence change in patterns of Hindu devotionalism by first considering its accessibility to the masses, then briefly looking at what the god posters in general portray. Only then can I characterize some of the more obvious transformations they seem to have effected. Thus this chapter addresses three questions: Where are god posters marketed? What do god posters look like? And how are god posters treated?

Where Are God Posters Marketed?

The accessibility of god posters needs to be addressed from two different perspectives: that of the numerous, local, retail merchants from whom the consumers purchase god posters and that of the wholesale distributors who supply those merchants — the same wholesalers who are most often also the manufacturers of god posters. Taken together, the retail and the wholesale sectors lead one to answer the question, "Where are god posters marketed?" with the response, "Just about everywhere."

The ordinary consumer of god posters or framing prints[3] usually purchases them at a nearby retail shop, located in cities and towns throughout India. Shops are found in two typical locales. First, as the subjects of the prints are often supernaturals of various kinds — gods, goddesses, and saints — the god poster and framing picture merchants are found chiefly in shops, stalls, and, increasingly, on the sidewalks themselves along thoroughfares leading to and from temples, shrines, and personality-cult sites. Second, since the proprietors of the shops also often deal in glass as part of their services to "frame" the prints they sell, the retailers are found in or near the glass bazaars of any given city or town (see Figure 2.1). In either case, the merchant sells the images either simply as prints (in which case the price is usually very modest: depending on size, Rs. 1.50 to Rs. 12.50, or from slightly under a dime to around 75 cents) or as a glazed and framed item suitable for hanging.

As retailers stock what sells, a simple inventory of the god poster subjects stocked by any merchant is a useful index to region-specific religious interests. Unique subjects are sometimes seen marketed in remote areas — often supplied by small, local presses and artists. More conventional inventories featuring widely recognized figures are noted among retailers who serve large, urban clienteles. In addition to Hindu subjects, depending on local demand, Muslim, Sikh, Christian, and other religious themes are often displayed alongside national heroes, political personalities, film stars, photo-real depictions of babies and animals, as well as sports figures and pinups.

Specimens of all these subjects are available in various, standard sizes, from 28″ × 20″ down to billfold size. Merchants also began offering postcards of selected subjects in the mid-1980s. Lamination, or the glossy, plastic coating of a color print on heavy paper, is an option fast becoming standard in all sizes. However, formats popular in one locale are not always universally marketable.

The stock of most merchants turns over with remarkable regularity. Because their clienteles often demand new designs, the local retailers try to keep one step ahead of their customers. The merchants anticipate the busy "holiday season," or August/September through February/March, when the public purchases god posters to use in Hindu festivals such as *jan-*

Figure 2.1. "Framing Picture" Shop. Proprietor of "framing picture" shop in Nasik, surrounded by display of his wares, prepares wood frame. Note that his inventory of supernaturals and saints, while suitably catholic in scope, still reflects regional tastes. Photo by H. Daniel Smith.

amāṣṭamī, daśahrā, divālī, śivrātrī, rāmnavmī, sarasvatī pūjā, and so on. The Hindu New Year in late March or early April is another popular time for purchasing the prints.

The retailers get their stock, in turn, from wholesalers who are often, but not invariably, also the publishers of the popular god posters or framing pictures. Deriving their livelihood from the reproduction and dissemination of color lithographs such as god posters is a symbiotic subset of workers: publishers, paper manufacturers and vendors, chemical technicians and suppliers in the color films and printers' ink industries, photographers, specialists who retouch color-separated negatives, photo-offset platemakers and their suppliers, printing press staffs, and wholesale distributors. I focus my attention here on the publishers.

Publishers of Hindu god posters are found today in all regions of India, not only clustered in major cities, but also scattered in smaller towns, notably at or near renowned places of pilgrimage. The greatest concentrations—and the publishing firms with the largest volume of production—are found in Bombay, Delhi, Calcutta, Madras, and Sivakasi (a town located southwest of Madura in Tamil Nadu).[4] Some operate only on a regional basis, others nationwide, while a few serve bulk overseas customers.

The publishing houses are typically family-run enterprises. A few have been in operation for three or more generations; many more have shorter histories. Some do nothing but Hindu god posters; others produce prints not only for Hindus but also for Muslims, Sikhs, Christians, Buddhists, Jains, and others. Most produce god posters as a sideline to a much more extensive printing program. A few deal in god posters and other printing ventures alongside yet other income-generating schemes. Cost containment is the name of the game for the highly competitive producers of god posters, who vie with one another year after year to provide retailers with novel designs.[5]

As production costs mount, so do the publishers' problems. Some try to salvage their profit margins by using cheaper, lighter-weight paper stock. This practice has its trade-offs: on the one hand, the less durable paper has built-in obsolescence that will require earlier replacement; on the other hand, flimsy stock is not attractive to discerning buyers. Likewise, the option of cutting back on the number of color separations per press run requires simpler designs and necessarily results in the bolder color combinations that some consumers find crude yet others find direct and eye-catching. Other efforts to increase initial press runs, or to recycle popular designs with only minor, cosmetic changes, or to find other ways to cut costs, often resulting in callous exploitation of artists, technicians, and other personnel who contribute at various stages to the production process, all present problems. In recent years of spiraling production costs, labor unrest, and industry-wide tax disincentives, several publishers have simply gone out of the business of producing god posters, among them some once well-established firms.[6]

That some publishing houses have ceased producing god posters suggests that the god poster industry has already peaked in this generation and is undergoing a subtle transition toward what may be the next phase of providing images for the masses. Threatening the basis of the god poster industry is color photography, with its potential for mass-producing richly hued prints at competitive prices. Already, studio stills of scenes from the extraordinarily successful television series based on the *Rāmāyaṇa* and the *Mahābhārata* have demonstrated that the characters created by the filmmaker Ramanand Sagar are very popular, as are even painted images of the stars of the Sagar Ram epic (see Chapter 9 by Lutgendorf in this volume). Yet along with the success of these prints, my own impression from my Indian contemporaries is that significant numbers of god poster buyers would (assuming per-unit costs were approximately equal) much rather have a color photoprint of Rama's sacred image in his shrine at Ayodhya than a filmmaker's or an artist's representation of him, no matter how realistic or, for that matter, imaginative. Likewise, no doubt many buyers would also prefer an actual color photoprint of Satya Sai Baba producing *vibhūti*-ashes to a stilted pose of him rendered by an artist; the same can also be said of quality photoprints of temples and locales meaningful to pilgrims, such as the *gopuram* (or *vimāna*) of Srirangam, or a panorama of the seaside sanctuary at Dwarka, or the Ram-ghat at Nasik, the "Triveni" at Allahabad, or the source of the Godavari River in a remote mountain cave. Such photoprints are beginning to appear in today's market. Their per-unit price currently prohibits purchase by all but the most prosperous, who are already sophisticated enough as amateur photographers themselves that they demand a quality product or else they will not buy at all. The current artists, when questioned about the threat of photography to their painting guild, do not seem aware of the possible encroachment of this rival format into their preserve. And the publishers who have ventured into color photoprints have not yet taken quality control seriously enough for their products to have posed serious threats to the established industry that merchandises traditional god posters.

There may be a limit, however, to this market, even in a consumer economy as image-rich as India's. If, as several contributors to this volume suggest, other imaging formats are increasingly being made available in postmodern India — for example, burgeoning lists of comic book titles, expanded broadcasting schedules of television programs targeted to increasingly massive audiences, proliferating opportunities to rent or buy videocassettes — a glut could result. Eventually, something may have to give in this new system of competing image-marketing. Some early warning signs are that it could well be the god poster industry.

But for now, the production and distribution of god posters appears to be a growth industry. As a result, the markets are flooded with mechanically reproduced images. Stephen Inglis points out in Chapter 3 of this volume that it is not necessary to join the chorus that laments the multiplication of such imagery. On the contrary, he suggests, it may be crucial to view the god posters in contemporary India as occasions for religious Hindus to regard the sacred as enhanced in power, rather than diminished, because of its ubiquitous presence. The accessibility of those potent images to the masses appears to have stimulated complex, diverse, and fluid religious responses as they are assimilated into a cultural setting that has itself always been adaptive and dynamic.

What Do God Posters Look Like?

Their subject matter contributes as much to the look of framing pictures and god posters as their physical characteristics specified above. Demographically, Hindus constitute more than 80 percent of the total population of contemporary India. It is not surprising then that, within the god poster genre, Hindu subjects now and historically comprise a majority of the designs on the market. Muslim, Sikh, Christian, Jain, Buddhist, and other communities each, and in toto, represent significantly smaller markets, and the function of framing pictures in those religious traditions is considerably more ambiguous than what prevails in Hindu circles.[7]

The specific subjects celebrated in Hindu god posters fall into three groupings. The first of these, "supernaturals," is also the largest and most obvious, containing all available representations of gods and goddesses, along with other composite, abstract, and occasionally archaic divinities. Subcategories under this heading most naturally surface along generic, sectarian lines (Vaiṣṇava, Śaiva, Śākta, etc.), but occasionally special subcategories must be constructed to accommodate extraordinary specimens. The second category, "saints," comprises depictions of human beings of the legendary past and of subsequent historical periods up to the present. Most of the portrayals within this second grouping are imaginary renderings based on canonical models; but portrayals of the most recent personalities appear in many cases to be based on photographic records that god poster artists enhance to various degrees. The third grouping, "sacred sites," celebrates temples of repute, special shrines and *samādhi*-spots, sacred towns, mountains, forests, and rivers. A significant subset within this third category are memento "maps" of pilgrimage sites, including some charts and diagrams that suggest metaphorical, occasionally physiological, or eschatological references.

SUPERNATURALS

There are few surprises after collating publishers' lists of the most popular gods and goddesses in their marketing territories. Ganesha, Krishna, Rama, Hanuman, Shiva in his ascetic persona (see Lewis 1988), and the goddess in one of her several benign aspects are there. All of these are extremely popular cult-deities throughout India. Each poster deity appears in numerous versions, as artists from all over India try to capture what is essential in the depiction of that divinity.

Indeed, when multiple examples of a particular deity are put side by side, surprisingly consistent (and traditional) iconographic idioms emerge. Nevertheless, regional variations and the innovative inventions of individual artists stand out by comparison with supposedly — but only superficially — repetitive renditions. What is striking in regard to the depiction of popular deities like Ganesha, Lakshmi, Shiva-Mahayogi, or Sarasvati are the conventions that quite consistently converge, rather than the occasional quirks inspired by artists' license.

At the same time, the multiple examples of popular deities depicted in Hindu god posters illustrate a wide-ranging and rich iconographic field from which both artists and the public draw for the recognition of a given supernatural. Both Krishna and Rama, as well as Hanuman and a few other deities, seem to have various recognizable forms that have wide currency. In the cases of Krishna and of Rama, the varied depictions have much to do with the episodic nature of the stories that surround both. In addition, specific, popular depictions of those deities have particular regional or communal associations, as, for example, in the case of Krishna, where the god poster genre also documents the locative nature of cultic Hinduism: his depictions as the chief deity at Dwarka, at Guruvayur, at Nathdwara, at Puri, at Triplicane, and so forth.

In addition to the expected, popular deities of a pan-Indian nature, publishers' lists regularly include regional favorites — for example, in the south, such figures as Murugan, Mariyamman, Minakshi, Kamakshi and other cult-specific deities predominate. This accounts, in part, for both the wide redundancy and the wide variety found among the inventories nationwide. Further, the publishers' lists occasionally include names of unexpected, "recent" divinities, telling us something of the dynamics of contemporary, cultic Hinduism and giving us an opportunity to monitor the growth and spread of specific cults by means of sales records. Examples of such cults whose growth might be better understood if correlated to emergent god poster markets are the goddess Santoshi Ma, whose popularity as a "poster deity" beyond Hindi-speaking areas is obvious; the god Ayyappan, whose marketability beyond a certain radius of his primary shrine in Kerala is likewise striking; and the goddess Vaishno Devi, whose immediate recognition outside a limited range beyond her primary shrine in Jammu in recent years is also telling.

Indeed, the incidence and popularity in varied geographical and demographic markets of any particular cultic figure — be it Vishnu in one or another of his *avatāra* forms, Shiva or the goddess in one of their respective manifestations, a figure like Satyanarayana or, indeed, any saintly personality — present informative data about that identity both as a contemporary cultural phenomenon and as a merchandising artifact. Even combinations of figures in god posters, such as what has elsewhere been dubbed a "new Trimurti" (Ganesha / Lakshmi / Sarasvati) in so-called "Diwali Puja" broadsides (Smith [forthcoming]), or the Shiva-*liṅga* shown in a site-specific location, or a particular, regional goddess accompanied by a peculiar *vāhana,* can trace out emergent dimensions of Hinduism in a postmodern period. By the same token, god posters can detail the absence or decline of deities as inhabitants of the popular Hindu imagination.

Included in this category of "supernaturals" are compositions that combine one or more deities in a single, visual statement, as, most obviously, in renderings of the traditional *trimūrti* (Brahma, Vishnu, Shiva) or in other pairings and groupings of recognizable divinities. This is where must be clustered also a number of miscellaneous, aniconic depictions (*liṅga*-forms, *yantra*-designs, *stotra*-texts, etc.), imaginary beasts (Kamadhenu, Gomata, and other composite forms, as well as singular portraits

mantra of use of Brahma
satru

of *vāhanas*), and celestials (*navagrahas*) as well as specific renderings of Surya, Gayatri-devi, Shani, and others.

Therefore, this grouping becomes the largest of the three, given the major gods and goddesses found in solo portraits, in their various manifestations with and without consorts, and with and without companions.

SAINTS

While Hindu deities regularly feature multiple body parts, the representation of saintly, human figures is characterized by more subtle iconographic markers of their referents' exalted status. Almost invariably the saintly figures have one head, two eyes, one torso, two arms, and two legs. What sets them apart from one another are characteristic manual signals or symbols held in one hand or the other — or both — and distinguishing details that adorn or surround the figure. Also, a significant posture (standing, moving, or sitting) is often employed to provide another range of visual cues to identity and yields another sort of index to spiritual powers ascribed to particular personalities. In addition, dress and color codes convey distinctive, symbolic information. Accoutrements to suggest a spiritual commitment — for examples, a *daṇḍa*-staff with one or two or three component shafts, or a bordered or borderless garment, or the presence or absence of an *upavīta*-cord, or a peculiar coiffure, or a book composed by or associated with the individual and intentionally inserted into the composition — may all draw attention to a career claim associated with that person. The setting that surrounds the figure, or from which the figure stands out and apart, is also revealing. Sometimes episodes from the individual's life surround the figure in decorative vignettes, or the figure is itself displayed performing a characteristic deed drawn from the hagiography that all devotees of the figure know well.

sectarian

Many times, the saintly figure will be portrayed worshipping a special manifestation of the divine known to have been dear to him or her, or depicted in or near a temple that serves also as a signifier. As well, cosmetic *puṇḍra* symbols will confirm a devotional attachment. Sometimes a secondary figure, or a cluster of admirers or disciples, will enhance the portrait of the charismatic subject. Therefore, it is rarely necessary to resort to the label of a saintly portrait for identification.

With personalities of more recent times, especially those who in their lifetimes have been photographed, the saintly portrait may well be based on a photographic likeness, or will even be a color-enhanced reproduction of an original photoprint.[8] But whether ancient sages and saints or more recent personalities, the common thread is their exalted humanity, for which reason it is conventional to show either a radiant halo backlighting the head (or sometimes the full body) or a fixed, beatific expression illumining the face, or both. Saintly figures depicted in trance—an often-used convention—become a shorthand way to express their affinity with, and openness to, the divine source of all human existence.

Saintly figures represent all conditions. Some are contemplatives, some are active doers. Some are immediately recognizable by Hindus of almost any walk of life. Many more are known only within very limited social and geographic, linguistic and cultic circles. Regardless of their form and representation, nearly all saintly figures celebrated in Hindu god posters are recipients of *pūjā* worship in some truncated form at least, even though the process of their elevation to the status of apotheosized human is not well documented nor is the specific dynamic of the liturgical attentions addressed to them well understood. The saintly figures portrayed in god posters point to the remarkable diversity within popular Hinduism today, especially with regard to "personality cults."

Sacred Sites

In this smallest of the three groupings fall various kinds of schematic mementos that remind pilgrims or other practitioners of a cherished place. Subcategories here pertain to pilgrims' maps, mythological charts, and mystical diagrams. Pilgrimage maps are, further, of two types.

The first type of pilgrims' map is an idealized landscape of a place—a mountain, a temple elevation, a riverside *ghāṭ*, a reputed shrine, the tomb or *samādhi*-spot of a saint. They are generally available only at or near the site they celebrate. Usually prints of such subjects are not produced by a large, commercial press but rather by a small, entrepreneurial press in or very close to the place it promotes. There, they are purchased and taken home, where later they will remind the pilgrim of that earlier visit.

The second type of pilgrims' map is more elaborate. It is normally an imaginative rendering of a larger area that shows or suggests pilgrimage paths, usually enhanced with indications of halting places along the way to and from a destination shown on the map. The place depicted is at least of local renown.

For instance, a traveler going to Ayodhya may buy an ordinary road map, or railroad map, or state or provincial map. In addition to this, the traveler making the same trip may also, once in Ayodhya, go to a bazaar and buy an artist's rendering of an idealized Ayodhya, the map of the city as a sacred site. In that map, the usual markers may be shown, but also indicated are the locations of shrines, temples, shelters, and institutions within the city pertinent to a pilgrim's needs. This pilgrim's second map may not be drawn to scale at all but instead will contrive to present the relative importance of the religious constituents of the place by size and color or by placing those elements in terms of a design relationship (or mystical juxtaposition) to one another. Thus, in many cases, is this second type made to approximate a *maṇḍala* or a *yantra* design. In addition, there are also often various decorative or illustrative embellishments reflecting legendary associations of the place and its environs to the lore of the pilgrimage as performance. These schematic maps are not meant to be realistic, but serve another purpose — both during the journey and once that map has been brought back home — as a guide to how to experience the pilgrimage to its full extent.

Most major places of pilgrimage market pilgrimage maps of this second order of cartography in the bazaars and along the byways leading to the site celebrated. Often, in popular places like Varanasi, Ayodhya, Prayag, Rameswaram, and Hardwar, more than one version is sold, depending on the special interests and needs of pilgrim consumers.

There are two additional subcategories under sacred sites, both pertaining to *places* that have been, as it were, mapped. The first subcategory contains those god posters that present mythical illustrations of the *states* those who commit specific sins will suffer in a future hell. In some cases, the illustrations in this "*karṇī-bharṇī*" subcategory are graphic — both as to the occupations condemned and the punishments meted eternally. Smoking, drinking, fornication, and killing are only some of the acts attributed to the eternally damned. These "sins and punishments" posters are not numerous, but evidently they have found a constant market over the years, as both old and new designs are known. Typically, the posters feature grids with small squares surrounding a central figure — usually Yama, or *dharma* personified — while the surrounding squares provide spaces in which the deeds are depicted. Insofar as they are also pedagogical pieces, they serve as diagrams for self-examination and reflection.

The final subcategory within the sacred sites typology consists of god posters that illustrate yet two other realms — one interior, the other paradisiacal. Both kinds of illustrations for framing are rare. The former has to do with presenting a mystical chart of the body's interior in terms of *cakras*, and sometimes also in terms of an idealized respiratory and nervous system. Such depictions are quite clearly color-coded, presumably to conjure up occult associations for those who are informed by the traditions disclosed in the imaginative renderings. The latter has to do with celestial and heavenly charts. In specimens of this subcategory, the viewer sees the mystic track that is to be followed by the released spirit on its journey after death. Revealed in these eschatological projections is a symbolic universe replete with rivers, ramparts, thrones, and celestial guides that the liberated individual will encounter on the way from this world to the next.

Having described some of the subjects depicted in god posters, let us see how these artifacts are used by Hindus today in ways that transform traditional practices into new manifestations of religious expression.

How Are God Posters Treated?

When assessing the impact of god posters on Hindu devotional traditions, it becomes apparent that not all Hindus regard god posters in the same way. For some, god posters are ascribed a power beyond the material or aesthetic.

GOD POSTERS EVOKE VARIOUS DEVOTIONAL RESPONSES

To some, the prints are venerable by virtue of the subjects they portray. It is reported, for example, that in the Tamil Nadu pilgrim town of Palni (where one of the foremost shrines to the popular South Indian deity, Murugan, is located) pilgrims return home with wallet-sized god posters of the deity, to be ingested as a curative later by family members who are ill. Thus the pictures take over the function found elsewhere for sanctified food remnants known as *prasāda* (Hindi, *prasād*). On a less dramatic scale, one informant in 1988 said that visitors to his home remove their footwear before entering because god posters are displayed on his drawing room walls. By the same token, he reasoned that visitors to his brother's house down the road do not remove their footwear because he does *not* display god posters in rooms generally accessible to guests.

Along the same line, some customers and proprietors of distribution offices and showrooms do, others do not, remove their footwear before entering the premises where god posters are warehoused. Likewise, among the artists of the god posters, some commence their work with prayers or meditation, others approach their task with the brisk efficiency demanded of a competitive business enterprise. What accounts for these behavioral differences?

One reason for not removing shoes may be that the god posters involved had not yet been consecrated for the purposes of worship. But, while such a qualification no doubt applies to temple icons, the situation is considerably more ambiguous in regard to god posters. As indicated below, they seem not to require "establishment" (*pratiṣṭhā*) in the same way, if at all, to render them suitable instruments of worship. More about that in a moment. But first, some other observations.

Many devout families display god posters in their homes for devotional purposes and in places of honor, often freshly garlanded or with traces of *pūjā* paraphernalia in view. For many others, however, the framing pictures — even when they depict personally favored supernaturals or saints — function strictly as decorations. Their casual placement, or their combination with other, secular decorative objects, in many cases argues for their nonreligious function. Indeed, a whole range of god poster subjects depicts the principal figure(s) in an attitude or setting that is more appropriate to instruction or conducive to the recollection of a narrative than to homage (e.g., Dasharatha remembering his fateful encounter with the blind ascetic's son, Krishna abducting Rukmini, Rama with Sita in their peaceful forest hut, Shiva as ascetic approaching Annapurna). Adding to the view of god posters as secular objects is their recent emergence in a postcard format suitable for mailing or, even more recently, in the form of adorning magnets to post on refrigerators — which are certainly examples of quite casual treatment.

Typical placements of god posters are indicative of the power they are believed to represent among contemporary Hindus. The fact that a framed picture of Lakshmi is often to be found above the cash register in places of business, or that a billfold-sized depiction of her is found tucked away in many a wallet, certainly amplifies what is already known about her identity as Goddess of Wealth and Dispenser of Fortune. Similarly, Sarasvati's presence in a school corridor or over the circulation desk in a library reflects her association with learning and books. Likewise, the depiction of Nataraja in a theater or, more especially, in a dance academy, and the display of Shiva and Parvati's wedding — or Rama and Sita's — in a marriage hall, are markers of cultural customs made all the more telling because technology has made the images so ubiquitous today.

A New and Pervasive "Omnipraxy" Among Those
Who Most Treasure God Posters
The same technology that gives rise to the ubiquitous god posters phenomenon also is responsible for new forms of ritual response to the images.

For those who see in god posters a positive theophany — that is, among those for whom the god posters function as "real" images — many unprecedented, remarkably widespread and democratized, even innovative and idiosyncratic, rituals have crept into common usage. In fact, contemporary Hindu India has witnessed what might be termed a new and pervasive "omnipraxy," as exemplified by the shopkeepers and taxi drivers who daily offer flowers and incense to framed pictures of deities before whom they stand simultaneously as *pujārī* priest and as devotee; or the unmarried women, bachelors, widows, and widowers (among others) who pay homage to garlanded portraits of *iṣṭadevatā*s or, just as often, to personality cult figures; or the housewives and the infirm who do *yātrā* (pilgrimage) to distant sites all the while remaining stationary in front of a pilgrimage map. As a popular art genre, the poster gods have fostered a democratic devotionalism, a populist piety, of extraordinary proportions in the present age.

Yet, very little of the dynamics of this devotionalism has been reported. Who knows the exact ritual — if, indeed, there is an "exact" ritual — performed by devotees such as taxi drivers before the framed pictures or decals of the deities on their dashboards (see Figure 2.2). Much of what is vital to the everyday devotional Hinduism of the masses remains a mystery to all but those who themselves practice it.

The study of god posters is complex and fluid, a condition exacerbated, in my case, because of a relatively brief period in the field.[9] Still, study of the god poster phenomenon and its transforming potential on ritual activities and ways of "seeing" theophanies presents a unique opportunity for researchers to trace out emerging trends in contemporary Hindu culture and devotional practices. The observations and trends identified below are a first step in this vein.

God Posters, the Masses, and Omniprax Pūjā

In brahmanical Hinduism, manmade images of the divine are considered to be mere mundane objects until they have been sanctified by the divine presence, invoked through a series of ritual acts known collectively as *pratiṣṭhā*.[10] Once consecrated, the images are believed to be transformed into appropriate mediums through which the supreme being may be seen and honored with *pūjā* offerings.[11] Exactly what, if anything, is required for consecration of god posters may be as simple as the utterance of a voluntary prayer of invocation or merely the presence of an intention to worship. In any case, it is very doubtful that whatever is done entails the paid services of a professional.

God poster *pūjā* in the home setting is both simple and streamlined

Figure 2.2. Rickshaw with God posters. Over the shoulder of autorickshaw driver can be glimpsed a framed display of deities that adorns the dashboard (left to right — Shiva with Parvati and Ganesha; the goddess astride her feline mount; Hanuman carrying Rama and Lakshmana on his shoulders). Photo by H. Daniel Smith.

compared to the relatively demanding liturgies expected of the orthoprax householder who honors an established domestic icon during *grhārcana* worship.[12] While the extensive rituals of the latter are scarcely standard throughout India, they nonetheless offer a pattern by which we identify divergent practices among the ways Hindus recognize divinity in their lives. Worship techniques featuring god posters are neither gender- nor class-exclusive. Nonspecialist males and females assume central roles, with remarkably economical rituals. What one sees is, at most, the touching of the glazed surface of the picture, on special occasions, with *kuṅkuma* powders; the lighting of incense, usually in stick form, which, when lit and circled in front of the deity's depiction, serves also for the waving of a separate, second flickering flame or lamp; and, finally, the decoration of the picture frame with a garland of flowers or sprigs of leaves. Foodstuffs are not normally offered; the flowers that festoon the god poster or that are placed on a shelf in front of the picture appear to replace food-offerings. A period of meditation may follow, but more often than not, the preceding gestures are completed by a formulaic repetition of the deity's name or perhaps also by some spontaneous prayer of petition or intercession.

GOD POSTERS AND ACTS OF VESTING:
EMBELLISHING AND SUCCESSIONING

Aside from the framing and thoughtful placement of "broadside *bimbas*" (images printed on one side of a piece of paper) in their various settings, it is clear that in the home setting, at least, some practices have developed that may be noted as folk traditions.

In traditional, orthoprax forms of image worship, the deity is "dressed" as one part of the ministrations accorded the divine presence. This act is repeated daily, or whenever *pūjā* is performed (cf. note 12, above, *alaṅkarāsana*). In the same tradition, some framed god posters display figures that have been permanently "dressed" and "decorated" before the glazing of the frame was put in place. In the past, this was a job performed primarily by women, who would appliqué bits of cloth to the two-dimensional figures, highlighting them with metallic threads, beads, semiprecious stones, and, more recently, sequins and glitter. Nowadays, retailers themselves (e.g., Vijaya Glass House in Madurai) sell such elaborate god posters, finished and framed, to customers who are unable to produce the desired effect themselves.

Recently, another tradition has emerged in the relatively short history of the god poster genre. In some families, especially as extended families *why surprising?*

fragment into smaller, nuclear units, particularly beloved god poster specimens are being passed down from generation to generation. For example, a
mother who has inherited a framing picture from her mother — more than
likely, one that has been decorated with pieces of cloth as described above —
will, in turn, take special care in selecting which of her children will inherit
it from her. The passing down of such cherished family heirlooms is not
unlike an older custom in certain families in Tamil Nadu who display collections of semireligious objects and family mementos during *navarātrī* season. Those, too, evidently have special sentimental value. In the case of the
inherited framing pictures, it is not yet clear what status and disposition the
inherited object will be given in its new setting.

God Posters and Associational Epiphanies

God posters are often displayed in settings with images of other deities.
These clusters of god poster figures, whether in shrines or wall arrangements, at first may appear idiosyncratic but later may reveal volumes about
devotional practices of both individuals and groups. Stephen Inglis, in
Chapter 3 of this volume, describes the *pūjā* area in the home of the South
Indian artist M. Ramalingkum. Inglis shows how Mr. Ramalingkum's particular juxtaposition of images serves to represent for the artist the forces
that have shaped his life.

Nothing seems alien to the domestic shrine, where sacred souvenirs,
liturgical paraphernalia, and family memorabilia are displayed along with
photographs of departed elders, portraits of luminous personalities, and
icons or printed images of *gṛhadevatā*s, *iṣṭadevatā*s, *kuladevatā*s, and *grām-
adevatā*s. The god posters deployed may be old or new, framed or not,
touched with *kuṅkuma* or pristine. Combinations of divinities vary greatly
from home to home and even among different households maintained by
members of the same family. In every case, the particular combination of
sacred images employed has a powerful association to those who worship at
that shrine.

In shops, the workplace sanctuary, though simple and chaste compared to the crowded home shrine, is a carefully maintained display of
the proprietor's chosen god(s), occasionally complemented with, or substituted by, a saintly portrait or two, perhaps also with a likeness of a de-
ceased predecessor in the firm. Office shrines are even more streamlined as a
rule and are often the preserve of staff menials rather than white-collar
workers (who, in many cases, maintain allegiance to the deities at their
home shrines). In any event, these streamlined altars also reveal the same

penchant for aligning two or more supernaturals in apparently casual, though no doubt conceptually significant, juxtaposition.

The assemblages effected in public shrines and temples reveal endless combinations and permutations of divine representations. What is most ordinarily encountered is replication of the main, divine image housed in the place with other, affiliated figures placed at the discretion of, and for reasons clear to, the chief resident *pujārī* priest. A sanctuary housing a Shiva-*liṅga* might display, in addition to "established," subsidiary icons (such as Nandi or Hanuman), printed representations of the *liṅga*-form (either generic or specific ones from celebrated shrines) of Shiva in other manifestations, of his divine consort(s), as well as of saints of related repute. Or a shrine sacred to Rama might house prints depicting one or more episodes from his earthly career along with printed likenesses of Hanuman and other supernaturals and devotees (see Figure 2.3).

In examining the combinations of god poster figures, it is difficult to comprehend at first sight the significance of the easy alliances made between Shiva and Rama, or between some local goddess and Hanuman, let alone the many triads of supernaturals brought into fresh associations in this era of image accessibility and of serendipitous omnipraxy. However, sustained exploration of the significance and frequency of the alliances between deities and the popular perceptions regarding what "happens" when certain gods are assembled together in home, workplace, and public shrines will bring another dimension to the study of contemporary Hindu devotionalism.

SYNCRETISTIC GOD POSTERS AS VISUAL "TEXTS"

oxymoron or not?

At still another level of inquiry are the combinations of deities found ready-made in god posters. The designs may be the artist's own invention or perhaps are commissioned by a publisher. Assuming that both painters and publishers possess some insight into public tastes, such combinations may represent significant new alignments of cults. Vaishno Devi depicted with Hanuman and Bhairon flanking her certainly reveals a good deal about the syncretistic nature of the Vaishno Devi cult; it also speaks volumes about how the historian of religions must henceforth "see" both Hanuman and Bhairon in relation to each other. Similarly, combinations of region-specific deities, such as Ayyappan and Guruvayurappan, in the same god poster may offer tacit comment in regard to regional chauvinism. It also points to the permissiveness that relates supposedly different deities in the ambiance of a syncretistic, living, and evolving Hinduism. In fact, the many combina-

Figure 2.3. Shrine with God posters. Leafy setting in a small shrine recalls the forest idyll of Rama, Sita, and Lakshmana at Tapovan, near Nasik. Note that the three central figures are supplemented by framed images of other supernaturals and saints of local repute. Photo by H. Daniel Smith.

tions of goddesses are most instructive, especially in light of the claim made by some firms that *aṣṭa-lakṣmī* configurations are among their "most popular" (personal interview, February 13, 1988: Sri Kalamaigal Industries, Madurai).

It may be that there is a syncretizing process unfolding that is reflected in the many god poster designs marketed today. In the past, there have surely been precedents to provide guidance for recognizing the collapse of formerly autonomous cults into compelling, new, larger alliances of supernaturals. The most striking example in the south may be the absorption by resort to the fiction of "marriage" of an autochthonous goddess cult (a good example, Minakshi) into an expanding, Shiva-centered movement. Elsewhere and earlier was the dissolution of what must have been autonomous hero-cults and their reconstruction within the larger ambit of *avatāra*-descents of a universal, all-pervading Vishnu. And, even earlier, was the merging of prehistoric, zoomorphic presences with other, overriding powers, the former becoming the *vāhana*s (vehicles) of the latter. Iconographical clues comprised a large degree of the evidence then, and a responsible study of the god poster phenomenon today takes such clues seriously, treating god posters as visual "texts" to be interpreted systematically. And, just as in the study of other historical situations, the isolated clues here must be considered in a larger context.

GOD POSTERS + PERSONALITY CULTS = "PERSONALITY POSTERS"

The preparation of portraits of prestigious personalities has a long tradition in Indian art, from the earliest depictions of rulers, donor figures, heroes, and saints well before the early centuries of the current era. *Āgama* texts of the late puranic period, as well as *Purāṇa*s themselves and *śilpa-śāstra* anthologies of a slightly earlier time, confirm that there has been a sustained concern for the production of *bhakta* images for more than a millennium in Hinduism itself. Later on, it had been widely accepted that Ramanuja (d. 1137) personally approved of four different images of himself—among them one that can be seen even today at a temple marking his birthplace at Sriperumbudur, not far from Madras. Portrayals of Hindu saintly figures are nothing new, and today they are a substantial subcategory of the god poster genre. What is new is their wide availability to new publics in this format and their portability—factors affecting their impact on contemporary, devotional Hinduism.

At the most obvious level, the diffusion of the images helps to maintain far-flung networks of personality cults (on which point see also Chapter 10 in this volume). While the founder or exemplar may not always be able to travel to cult outposts, and may long since be dead, the image serves to carry that personality's message and sense of abiding presence and power. Personality cults that were once confined to a particular geographical, linguistic, or cultural region now have the potential, through the dissemination of powerful visual imagery, to breach parochial barriers. The accessibility and portability of god poster images of saintly figures has much to do, then, with the spread and maintenance of the cults associated with them.

Not surprisingly, the new omnipraxy is further sustained as the portraits of beloved personality cult figures are honored. When, by whom, and how such "worship" is conducted are legitimate queries to pursue further. Predictably, what will be exposed are such matters as particulars on hitherto little-known personality cults; new calendric schedules not noticed before; new religious specialists; new forms of lay participation in liturgical domains yielding to new and streamlined forms of *pūjā*. For instance, street processions have always been organized for varieties of purposes by diverse groups. Often today, however, at the core of the cavalcade will be not a temple icon, or a bier, or even a living agent, but rather a god poster of a saint like Madhwa (from the medieval period), or Chaitanya or Raghavendra (from a later age), or Shirdi Sai Baba (of more recent times). The occasion may be the commemoration of a birthday of such a personality cult figure or of a *samādhi* date. And those who flow with the parade represent a cultic identity by no means new per se in Hinduism but arguably more dispersed geographically, varied demographically, and heterodox ideologically than ever before.

On the domestic scene, several striking observations can be made about the visibility of personality portraits. One is the combinations found that reveal specific saintly figures in a dialogue, as it were, with an already established (or, at the other extreme, imaginatively juxtaposed) colloquy of gods and goddesses. What connections may be inferred from these new combinations? Another is that, as often as not, the saintly figures are ignored for long periods of time. They appear to serve as occasional mascots, if that, or on a par with family photographs. Only now and then, and in no discernible, regular pattern, do they receive particular honors. Lastly, when they are honored, the worship routines can be quite idiosyncratic. There may be the usual *puspa,* the *dhūpa,* and the *dīpa,* but from there on procedures may be unique to the figure attended or, more significantly perhaps, to the person performing the ritual. All told, the cultic uses of saintly personality posters present many displays of contemporary Hindu piety that beg for better understanding.

PILGRIMS' MAPS AND ARCANE CHARTS AS *YANTRAS*

A final set of examples concerns the god posters that deal with sacred sites: pilgrims' maps, mythological charts, and mystical diagrams.

In addition to their function of directing purposeful travelers on excursions to geographical sites of sacred esteem, pilgrims' maps — or what might be called *tīrtha* prints — also serve an important function back home. Once the pilgrim has returned from the journey, the map facilitates an inner, spiritual "return," substituting for the actual repetition of that *yātrā*.

What, then, may be inferred more generally from such maps and in the light of the pervasive, new omnipraxy that must also be factored in? The more idealized renditions of pilgrimage maps — which, as noted earlier, are laid out so that places of interest (visitation to which produce merit [*puṇya*]) relate to one another in a pattern reminiscent of a *maṇḍala* or *yantra* — indeed seem designed to encourage interiorization of the sacred journey. *Yantra* means, literally, a "mechanical contrivance"; accordingly, the framed souvenir of the pilgrimage provides a convenient medium through which the former pilgrim can repeat the original experience. Thus it is possible to imagine an individual motivated by the map alone to experience the essence of a pilgrimage without ever stepping foot outside the home. And, by extension, what serves as substitute for a repeated pilgrimage for one, for another might provide a surrogate for physical pilgrimage in the first place.

While the "*karṇī-bharṇī*" charts that so graphically depict the sins and punishments of the wicked serve primarily as cautionary and hortatory devices, the diagrams that delineate the path of the departed devotee after death clearly serve a higher purpose. At the very least, the latter provide occasion for eschatological reflection. In a culture in which the poetic utterances of saints have long imprinted in the hearts and minds of devotees the indelible images of a blessed afterlife in the joys of divine company, such graphic reminders as are sometimes found in some god pictures serve as welcome anticipation of that ultimate reward.

As for the mystical diagrams purporting to reveal the psychic channels within, the relatively few specimens available presumably relate to yogic lore deriving from one school or another. The best way to find out precisely just what lore they convey — as it is unlikely that traditional texts and teachings will be found to apply in detail — is to ask the individuals who purchase them or the artists who produce them directly. Given the amateur status of most yogic practitioners in a climate of omnipraxy, the variety of responses would perhaps provide key insights into contemporary "pop" yoga as the arcane accommodates to untutored interpretations.

Summary

The god poster industry is a subsidiary within the larger printing establishment in India. It employs large numbers of specialists who are all more or less gainfully employed in the creation and dissemination of a symbol system close to the heart of cultic Hinduism: the visual representation of its gods, goddesses, saints, and holy sites. As "art" the genre is eschewed by connoisseurs and collectors, ignored by mainline art critics and art historians, disdained by India's Western-educated elites, but adored by the vast majority of Hindus. The impact of the industry on devotional Hinduism in recent decades has been to make a new artifact available. Its availability in turn stimulates the invention of new, or the transformation of old, ways of "seeing" theophanies in the midst of ordinary, everyday, mundane, mortal experience. As a result, what may be called a new omnipraxy is discernible in the large number of diverse, ritual activities related directly to the god posters, the saintly portraits, and the pilgrims' maps. The impact of these innovative ways of worship — which demonstrably open up doors to new ranks of ritual specialists operating according to schedules that do not necessarily coincide with traditional calendars and performing for the benefit of individuals with populist values rather than solely for those informed by elitist norms — is difficult to gauge. Future studies of the emerging god poster phenomenon outlined in this chapter will reward us with a better understanding of institutional and personal dimensions of popular Hinduism today.

Notes

1. More accurately, "god posters" represent just one category of the diverse field of "framing pictures" or "calendar art." Other popular nonreligious subjects not considered in this chapter are animals, babies, pinups, movie stars, fruits and flowers, landscapes, patriotic themes, politicians, and sports figures. As defined

here, god posters include not only depictions of gods and goddesses, but also of saints and sacred sites.

2. In Western languages, the treatment of god posters has been limited largely to journalistic reports, both positive and negative. The subject has been taken up remarkably less often by serious and well-trained scholars. The brief list of references at the end of this chapter is indicative of the field's present state (see American Committee 1984, Blurton 1988, Ghosh 1978, Kapur 1991, Maduro 1976, Oberoi 1991, Parimoo 1975, Smith 1989, Smith n.d., Thakurta 1988, Thomas 1982, Uberoi 1990, Varma 1976, Vitsaxis 1977) — although several individuals currently working on god posters do not appear in that list. For example, Stephen Inglis, a fellow contributor to this volume, has written a number of manuscripts that await publication. He was responsible for curating an exhibition of calendar prints in 1983 at the University of British Columbia in Vancouver. Other Western scholars of god posters are Evalin Masilamani-Meyer, who curated an exhibition in Zurich a few years ago; Robert Del Bonta, who is principally interested in stylistic developments in early specimens (of which he has a fine collection) and who produced the set of slides cited in the list of references; and Katinka Kathofer, who is completing her dissertation at the University of Cologne.

3. Calendars, by contrast, are usually offered free of charge by businesses that wish to attract customers by advertising their names or wares on them. The firms' proprietors often take great care in selecting the illustration(s). Calendar manufacturers, who generally employ the same artists who produce designs for framing pictures, annually assemble large samplebooks of pictures, and business proprietors can review those and place orders through specialized stationery and office supply stores. The public is usually quite eager for the advertising calendars because they are free and because the illustrations are likely to be printed on a heavier, better-quality paper than are the framing pictures sold in bazaars. In some homes, it is evident that calendars have been very carefully combined and juxtaposed with such pictures.

4. The development of Sivakasi's printing and other industries deserves study in its own right. From production of safety matches in a sort of cottage industry, entrepreneurs diversified until the town became globally famous for fireworks and some explosives. As labels were needed for all such products, Sivakasi merchants invested in printing presses, and these were later employed for other jobs. As the printing industry developed, commercial artists and paper and chemical suppliers were attracted to the town. Eventually such diversification brought prosperous Sivakasi the nickname "Little Japan." Sivakasi now serves as a preeminent site for jobbing massive orders of color prints, and its state-of-the-art presses rival those in major cities for fast, high-quality, low-cost production. For the political background of early economic growth and entrepreneurship, see Hardgrave (1969). Inglis also has collected unpublished material on the artistic communities in Sivakasi and nearby Koyilpatti.

5. One of the oldest continuously operating firms, founded in 1900, is Hem Chander Bhargava and Company (1798 Chandni Chowk, Delhi, 110 006), which deals with the Hindu tradition and others. It accepts bulk foreign orders that are

prepaid. Those firms with branch operations are: Associated Calendars (main office at 26 Karuppanan Street, Sivakasi, 626 123; their Delhi agent is Sivakasi Pictures in the Sri Vakilchand Jain Dharmasala in Gandhi Nagar, Delhi, 110 031; their Calcutta agent is Sivakasi Emporium, 16 Synagogue Street, Calcutta, 700 001); S. S. Brijbasi and Sons (Bombay branch [established in 1950], 59 Mirza Street, Bombay, 400 003; Delhi branch [established in 1954], 32/1 Fatepuri, Delhi, 110 006), and Jain Picture Publication (Bombay branch [established 1962], 156 Dadiseth Agiari Lane, Bombay, 400 001; Delhi branch [established in the early 1980s], 5745/10 Jogiwara, Nai Sarak, Delhi, 110 006). All three deal in a great variety of images, sizes, and formats, and the aesthetic quality and quality of production vary widely. Brijbasi and Sons undertakes prepaid foreign orders. Many publishers' inventories reflect more regionally limited clienteles; those most responsive to foreign orders are: Bombay Glass House (established in 1950), Kalupur, Tankshal Road, Ahmedabad, 380 001; J. B. Khanna & Company, 10 Devaraja Mudali Street, Madras, 600 003; Lotus Picture Company, 4-A Jackson Lane, Calcutta, 700 001; Sharma Picture Publication, 175 Princess Street, Bombay, 400 002; Sree Lakshmi Agencies, 7-5-30 East Car Street, Sivakasi, 626 123; and Sri Kalaimagal Industries, 35 East Avani Moola Veedhi Street, Madurai, 625 001. This represents but the tip of the iceberg!

    6. A few are Ajanta Art Calendar Manufacturing Company (Delhi), Chinmanlal Chhotalal and Company (Ahmedabad), R. Ethirajiah & Sons (Madras), Ghosh Mazumdar & Company (Calcutta), Harnarayan & Sons (Bombay), Maharashtra Picture Company (Bombay), Picture Publishing Corporation (Bombay), Swastik Picture House (Delhi), and Takhat Singh & Brothers (Calcutta).

    7. This chapter's focus does not minimize the presence or significance of posters in non-Hindu Indian communities. See McLeod (1991).

    8. See Smith (1978:51–61) on how photography has influenced the framing picture portrayals of the "Swamy of Kanchi" (b. 1894), Satya Sai Baba (b. 1926), and Sri Ramakrishna (b. 1834).

    9. Although I have collected god posters during periods in India since the late 1950s, four months of focused research in several parts of the country were afforded in early 1988 under a senior faculty research grant from the American Institute of Indian Studies. This chapter, written shortly after return from my sabbatical, is informed largely by my observations during that period. Since then, in 1994, the Smith Poster Archive of over 3500 design specimens, field notes, and related research resources was turned over to the Bird Library at Syracuse University where it is currently maintained as a study collection.

    10. Smith (1984), Courtright (1985), Gonda (1951), Preston (1985), and Eck (1981), taken together, suggest the variety of practices and attitudes reflected within the traditions that consecrate images to make them fit for worship. A few "found" items — the *bāṇa-liṅga* for Shiva, the *śālagrāma* for Vishnu, the *svarṇabhadra* stone for Ganesha, the *svarṇarekhā* stone for the goddess, and the *sūryakānta* or *sphaṭika* crystal for Surya — are universally reputed to have intrinsic power that permits them to be worshipped immediately, even by non-Brahmans.

    11. *Pūjā* (formal acts of devotion to a revered image) forms vary according to the type of image worshipped, its location, and the disposition of the devotee. To comprehend such a complex phenomenon, see Courtright (1985:33–50), Babb

(1975:46), Eck (1981:35), O'Malley (1935:105), and Channa (1984:83–149). For visual documentation among Tenkalai Sri-vaishnavas of contemporary South India, see Smith's 1966–67 films "How a Hindu Worships: At the Home Shrine" (18 minutes) and "Hindu Temple Rites: Bathing the Image of God" (13 minutes).

12. Details of the complex rituals of domestic worship are available, for example, to the Sri-vaishnavas in Madras through Sanskrit *āgamic* texts and popular digests even more readily accessible in the vernacular Tamil and Telugu. The texts elaborate on *pañcāṅgapūjā*, or five-stage worship: *snānāsana* (bathing the image), *alaṅkarāsana* (dressing and decorating the deity while offering *dhūpa* incense and *dīpa* light), *mantrāsana* (extolling the deity with Vedic passages and poetic utterances), *bhojyāsana* (offering the deity cooked food, fruits, and nuts), and *śayanāsana* (closing the shrine doors and leaving the deity to "rest"). These procedures are to be repeated by the faithful at least once daily and may require almost an hour, and on occasion up to two hours, to complete.

References

American Committee for South Asian Art. 1984. *The Art of the Calendar Print— Popular Devotional Art of 19th and 20th Century India.* Slide set. Ann Arbor: University of Michigan.

Babb, Lawrence A. 1975. *The Divine Hierarchy: Popular Hinduism in Central India.* New York: Columbia University Press.

Blurton, T. Richard. 1988. "Tradition and Modernism: Contemporary Indian Religious Prints." *South Asia Research* 8, no. 1:47–69.

Channa, V. C. 1984. *Hinduism.* New Delhi: National Publishing House.

Courtright, Paul B. 1985. "On This Holy Day in My Humble Way: Aspects of Puja." In *Gods of Flesh, Gods of Stone—The Embodiment of Divinity in India,* ed. J. P. Waghorne, N. Cutler, and V. Narayanan, pp. 33–50. Chambersburg, Pa.: Anima Books.

Eck, Diana L. 1981. *Darsan: Seeing the Divine Image in India.* Chambersburg, Pa.: Anima Books.

Ghosh, Shalil. 1978. "In Defence of Calendar Art." *The Illustrated Weekly of India* (March 26): 32–35.

Gonda, Jan. 1951. "Pratistha." *Studia Indologica Internationalia* 1:1–37.

Hardgrave, Robert. 1969. *The Nadars of Tamilnadu.* Berkeley: University of California Press.

Kapur, Anuradha. 1991. "Militant Images of a Tranquil God." *Times of India* (January 10):12.

Lewis, James R. 1988. "The Lord Who Is Master of Yoga." *Indica* 25:93–102.

Maduro, Renaldo. 1976. *Artistic Creativity in a Brahmin Painter Community.* Research Monograph, No. 14. Berkeley: University of California, Center for South and Southeast Asian Studies.

McLeod, H. W. 1991. *Popular Sikh Art.* New Delhi: Oxford University Press.

Oberoi, Safina. 1991. "Calendar Art: Icons of Our Times." *The India Magazine of Her People and Culture* 11 (March):48–56.

O'Malley, Lewis S. S. 1935. *Popular Hinduism: The Religion of the Masses.* Cambridge: Cambridge University Press.

Parimoo, Ratan. 1975. "Pop Art and the Problems of 'Kitsch.'" In *Studies in Modern Indian Art (A Collection of Essays),* ed. R. Parimoo, pp. 105–13. New Delhi: Kanak Publications.

Preston, James J. 1985. "Creation of the Sacred Image: Apotheosis and Destruction in Hinduism." In *Gods of Flesh, Gods of Stone — The Embodiment of Divinity in India,* ed. J. P. Waghorne, N. Cutler, and V. Narayanan, pp. 9–30. Chambersburg, Pa.: Anima Books.

Smith, H. Daniel. 1966–67. *Image India: The Hindu Way.* Eleven documentary films. Syracuse University Film Rental Library.

——. 1978. "Hindu 'Desika'-Figures: Some Notes on a Minor Iconographic Tradition." *Religion* 8:40–67.

——. 1984. "Pratistha." In *Agama and Silpa: Proceedings of the Seminar held in December 1981,* ed. K. K. A. Venkatachari. Bombay: Ananthacharya Indological Research Institute Series, no. 16:50–68.

——. 1989. "Episodes of the Ramayana Depicted in India's Popular Poster Art." In *Ramayana Traditions and National Cultures in Asia,* ed. D. P. Sinha and S. Sahai, pp. 150–154. Lucknow: Government of Uttar Pradesh, Directorate of Cultural Affairs.

——. n.d. "A Contemporary Iconic Tradition: Laksmi, Ganesa, Sarasvati-An Emerging, 'New' Hindu Trimurti." In *Kalyan-Suman* (A Felicitation Volume honoring K. K. Dasgupta, ed. P. K. Mishra, New Delhi: M/S Agam Prakasan, forthcoming.

Thakurta, Tapati Guha. 1988. "Artists, Artisans and Mass Picture Production in Late Nineteenth- and Early Twentieth-Century Calcutta: The Changing Iconography of Popular Prints." *South Asia Research* 8:3–45.

Thomas, Rosie. 1982. "The Calendar Art of India." *Observer* (August 1):16–19.

Uberoi, Patricia. 1990. "Feminine Identity and National Ethos in Indian Calendar Art." *Economic and Political Weekly* (April 28):41–48.

Varma, Indra. 1976. "The Artist of the People and of the Gods." *Illustrated Weekly of India* (May 30):20.

Vitsaxis, V. 1977. *Hindu Epics, Myths, and Legends in Popular Illustration.* Delhi: Oxford University Press.

Stephen R. Inglis

3. Suitable for Framing: The Work of a Modern Master

Introduction

"A society becomes modern when one of its chief activities is producing and consuming images." By this definition, proposed by Susan Sontag (1977:153), India is very much a modern society. The mechanically reproduced image to which Sontag refers has become indispensable to the economy, politics, and religion of India and is an integral part of both public and private spaces.

The "age of mechanical reproduction" (Benjamin 1968) that has made image proliferation and the entire concept of modern media possible is relatively recent. The camera was invented 150 years ago by Louis Daguerre in France, and color lithography was perfected only three years before that. It was the interaction of these two processes and finally their combination that led to modern color photo-offset printing machines. Although the modern printed image took longer to sift through the layers of Indian society and to penetrate the diverse regions of that country than it had in Western Europe, the seeds of image communication were planted almost simultaneously. The first camera arrived in Calcutta in 1840, only a year after the device was invented, and "foul-smelling oleographs"[1] from Europe were flooding the Indian markets in the 1880s, only shortly after they became widely available in France. India had several of its own chromo-lithographic presses operating before the turn of the century.[2]

The concept of an age of mechanical reproduction and a modern mass media with all its speed, ubiquity, and commercial potential implies that the social shape and consequences of image communication will be similar regardless of where in the world it operates. Walter Benjamin argues that wherever it is introduced, "the technique of reproduction detaches the reproduced object from the domain of tradition" (Benjamin 1968:223). Many art historians of India certainly believed this. E. B. Havell, A. K. Coomaraswamy, and Vincent Smith, for example, all saw printed pictures as degenerate and as a threat to what was distinctive and culturally precious in Indian art. Richard Lannoy went even further; the popular arts in India, he proclaimed, "block individuation, alienate people from personal experience and intensify their moral isolation from each other, from reality, and from themselves" (Lannoy 1971:29).

A more particular concern of those who fear that an "image world" is replacing a "real" one is that the increasing reproduction of images is part of the desacralization of society. The argument here, as articulated by E. H. Gombrich (1950), is that the further we go back in history, the less sharp is the distinction between images and real things. In traditional societies, an image and the thing it depicts are two manifestations of the same spirit. As the reproduction of images increases, spreads, and accelerates, we are removed further and further from the world of sacred times in which the image "was taken to participate in the reality of the object depicted" (Sontag 1977:155) and image making and "consuming" were practical, magical, and sacred activities.

Recent field investigations indicate, however, that the impact of mechanically reproduced images may not be uniform in all societies and that the technique of reproduction may not necessarily result in a cultural "detachment." In India, mechanically reproduced images continue to participate in the reality of the "objects" or personages depicted, and this participation — the active association of the image with its sacred source — helps to account for the nature, popularity, and ubiquity of images in modern India.

Whether we think of technology as a curse or a blessing, we often assume, as Judith Gutman reminds us, that "technology has developed a power so completely of its own making that it overrides human participation" (Gutman 1982:2). With this in mind, I set out to identify human participation, the artist, and the creation of the image's prototype, and in so doing establish a social context for the style and development of the printed image's form. To study any art form is to explore a sensibility, and this is always a collective formation as broad as social existence (Geertz 1976); yet situating the art form in that pattern of existence always begins at a local level. I have chosen here to describe the growth and character of the printed image by focusing on the life of C. Kondiah Raju (1898–1976), an artist who had a profound impact on the development of the style of popular art in India. After presenting his annotated life story, I survey some of the sacred dimensions of the relationships between people and images in India and outline some directions in which these relationships are evolving.

The range of images in modern India is vast, and it will be useful from the outset to define the field of images referred to in this chapter. The focus is on pictures printed in color, especially those of Hindu gods and goddesses, collectively referred to as *cāmī patam,* or "god pictures" in Tamil. Although these are applied to everything from keychains to cookie tins, this chapter focuses mainly on single paper sheets in various sizes sold individually and often framed (thus commonly referred to as "framing pictures") or distributed as calendar images (see Figure 3.1). The discussion will be limited to pictures painted and printed in South India, although many of these are circulated throughout India and abroad. The more general term "popular art" is used to refer to all those art forms of modern India that have a mass audience and use mechanical reproduction in their creation and distribution.

As a typical foreign traveler in India in the late 1960s and early 1970s, I simply ignored printed pictures. They registered as a background, a colorful if somewhat garish part of the visual landscape. Ironically, the one meaningful association was to psychedelic art of North America; pictures of Hindu deities had been appropriated along with strobe lights and dayglow colors as symbolic noise. Later, while studying South Asian traditions and languages in India, I played my own deity-identification games using prints whenever they came into view, while waiting at a sweet shop or riding in a rickshaw. But it was not until I worked closely with traditional artists in the rural areas of Madurai and Ramnathapuram Districts in Tamil Nadu (in 1980–81) that the existence of these pictures became an issue that seemed to require attention in relation to the other, more ancient arts that were my primary concern. The strict lines often drawn between the handmade and the machine-made, between the arts of the elite and those of the masses, and between icon and decoration, began to blur, and what had been background slowly became foreground.[3]

Ordinary Indians were unaware of the origins and makers of these images, but the village artists with whom I worked had connections that gradually led me to many major artists working for the printing industry in South India. My informants held these "calendar artists" in the highest esteem, not only for their commercial success but also for the extraordinary influence they have on other artists in India and for the extent to which their work is a part of people's lives. These sources generally agreed that the artist who had the greatest influence on art in this century after Raja Ravi Varma was C. Kondiah Raju.

Figure 3.1. "Murugan," popular South Indian Hindu deity, by C. Kondiah Raju, lithograph, circa 1955. Photo by S. R. Inglis; by permission of M. Ramalingkum.

The Artist

C. Kondiah Raju was born on November 7, 1898, at a house on Malaiya Perumal Koil Street in Mylapore, Madras. His father, C. Kuppaswami Raju, was a practitioner of traditional Siddha medicine. Before his death in 1912, Kuppaswami made arrangements for young Kondiah to begin learning the traditional skill of the Rāju community, religious painting. He studied privately with several teachers, including a man named Murugesa Naiyakar and with N. Subba Naidu, a famous artist of Madurai. In 1916, Kondiah joined the Government School of Arts and Crafts.[4] Here he added to his traditional repertoire a knowledge of European skills of portraiture, landscape, and the techniques of perspective and color shading, using both oils and watercolors. Kondiah was evidently skilled and very successful in assessing the taste of his audience. In 1918, he stood first in the Madras state painting exams.

His first paying job was drawing maps for the State Highway Department, but this held his interest for only a short time. A spiritual tendency that was to guide him throughout his life surfaced when he joined the spiritual community (*āśram*) of Ramana Maharishi in Tiruvannamalai in 1920. At the *āśram* he had an experience that set a direction for his life. Kondiah offered to correct an imperfect portrait of the master, and the results were so successful that the Maharishi asked him to go and "share his talent with the world." Neither could have realized the impact Kondiah's work ultimately would have on the course of Indian popular art.

Kondiah's path to sharing this talent with a wider audience began when he joined a "village drama" troupe. These traveling drama companies (or "boys' companies," so called because most of the parts, including those of women, were played by young men), were a very popular part of festival entertainment by the late nineteenth century, both in rural areas and in towns and suburbs. For two decades (the early 1920s to the early 1940s), Kondiah Raju lived an itinerant life as a painter, actor, and musician, doing whatever was required of him by the troupes he was with and traveling as far as Ceylon and Singapore.[5] During this time he continued to paint and sell pictures.

In 1942, after engagements in Ceylon and Rajapalayam, the drama troupe of which Kondiah was a member stopped in the small Tirunelveli District town of Kovilpatti. The owner of the land on which they had set up to perform raised the rent, and the already debt-ridden company was forced to dissolve. Kondiah was determined to settle where he was, and a few

Figure 3.2. C. Kondiah Raju with M. Ramalingkum, Kovilpatti, 1948. Photo courtesy of M. Ramalingkum.

members of the troupe with whom he had become close friends stayed as well. For the first year they survived any way they could, selling drama costumes for the value of the silver thread and taking orders to paint metal trunks and boxes, but gradually commissions for portraits and religious paintings began to increase, notably in the early years from the Maharaja of Ettaiyapuram. Kondiah took the other members of the defunct drama troupe as his painting students, and slowly they began to receive orders as well. Eventually they all began working for the big picture-publishing companies in the neighboring printing center of Sivakasi. The small Kovilpatti group consisting of Kondiah, four fellow drama-troupe members, and others who joined later became the most potent force in the development of the popular art style in postindependence South India (Figure 3.2).

What little notice Kondiah has received in popular history portrays him as a kind of artist-saint. The media accounts at the time of his death describe him as resembling a "Bramachari whose students were like his children" (Ramalingam 1976). Although it was assumed he earned a fortune from the sale of his paintings, he distributed his proceeds and "lived like a saint, with one shirt, one vesti and one towel" (Mahadevan 1976:25). His students confirm his simple life-style and the care he took with people in need. He never married and after coming to Kovilpatti devoted his life to painting and teaching. Although his designs of Indian statesmen like Gandhi, Nehru, and Netaji were widely distributed, he reputedly was devoted to, and ultimately became best known for, his paintings of deities such as Kannan, Ganapati, and Murugan.

During his later years, Kondiah retired somewhat from his working schedule and philanthropic projects. In 1971, he turned down an offer to travel to Madras to receive a state government award for his artistic contributions. On July 27, 1976, at seventy-eight years of age, he died in Kovilpatti.

Influences

TANJORE PAINTING

Kondiah's community, the Rājus of Tanjore and Trichinopoly, was among those groups of artists with origins in the Andhra region who migrated south to Tamil Nadu since the sixteenth century, under the patronage of the Nayak and Marāṭhā kings. The work of the Rājus and related communities like the Naitus of Madurai was, and in some cases still is, the creation and renovation of wall and ceiling paintings in temples, decoration of processional vehicles (*vakaṇa*), and painting plaster sculpture on temple gates (*kōpuram*) and towers (*vimāṇa*). These groups also developed techniques for painting on panels of wood, glass, and mica, and these portable paintings of Hindu deities and saints became the earliest framed pictures in South India. They prefigure the format and use of contemporary lithographed prints.[6] "Tanjore paintings," as they have come to be called, often embossed with precious metals and encrusted with pearls and semiprecious stones, can be seen in temples, community prayer halls (*kutam*), and in the halls and *pūjā* rooms of substantial homes throughout Tamil Nadu. The styles of these paintings, while based on the correct measurements and attributes for gods and goddesses described in traditional texts, developed distinctive characteristics that ultimately influenced the lithographed image styles. Tanjore paintings were responsive to changes in popular taste and show not only the influences of the Tamil kingdoms' persistent styles but also of Muslim and European fashion. Other local and regional craft skills also had an impact on popular aesthetics. Many painters for the printing industry were heirs to a tradition of carving in ivory or wood (e.g., K. Madhavan) or metal engraving (e.g., M. Ramalingkum). The knowledge of these skills is evident in the fine sense of decorative design in South Indian prints and the elaboration of jewelry and architectural features.

EARLY POPULAR ART

The "genealogy" of Indian popular art probably can be traced back to the two decades before the twentieth century, when artists sent paintings of gods and goddesses to Europe for printing; these were then returned to India for distribution. However, most of today's painters for the popular market trace their heritage to Raja Ravi Varma (1848–1906).[7] Ravi Varma was a very successful portrait and landscape painter whose depictions of Hindu gods, goddesses, and legendary (Puranic) stories launched the popular painting industry in India and whose romantic style continues to influence Indian painters more than a century after he began his work. In response to his patrons' encouragement and the demand for his work, originally rendered in oils, Varma established India's first chromo-lithographic press in Bombay in 1891.[8]

Ravi Varma learned to paint from his uncle, Raja Raja Varma, one of a series of talented artists in his family, the Koil Tampurans of Kilimanur, Kerala. The family's position in the court of Travancore also gave Ravi Varma access to European techniques and styles, both through lithographed reproductions from Italy and Germany and possibly through contact with European artists like Theodore Jenson, who was a guest of the Travancore court and carried out several commissions in 1866.

Ravi Varma's uncle had trained with Alagiri Naidu of Madurai, a specialist in the Tanjore style. Alagiri's descendent Ramasamy Naidu was a rival of Ravi Varma's, acknowledged as an expert in portrait painting, while Ravi Varma was considered the master of "fancy pictures." Ramasamy Naidu's younger brother, N. Subba Naidu (1855–1943), was a hero to Kondiah Raju. Subba Naidu had been an earlier student at the Madras School of Arts and Crafts and had given lessons to the young Kondiah at several stages of his career.[9]

In addition to direct training, most artists keep a file of printed pictures passed down through a family or teacher as a reference source for detail or design. There are still artists in South India who have old lithographs, some originally from Europe, depicting Victorian or Edwardian beauties and pastoral scenes, as well as prints of paintings by earlier Indian artists. These continue to influence their styles.

ART SCHOOL TRAINING

The Government School of Arts and Crafts in Madras, like similar art schools run by the British in Calcutta and Bombay, offered a program combining Western classical training in high realism with some reference to Hindu and Buddhist traditions of architecture and sculpture. The teachers were fired up with a zeal to reform what they considered degenerate Indian styles and techniques, and later to revive the glorious ancient art of India. The graduates, among them Kondiah and K. Madhavan (1907–79),[10] learned techniques of shading and lettering and studied design. The emphasis in the Government College's syllabus on "commercial art" may have a considerable impact on work produced by graduates of these schools. As early as the 1880s, it was reported in Calcutta that the cheap color-lithograph representations of gods and goddesses that had appeared in the market were based on paintings turned out by "ex-students of the Calcutta School of Art" (Mukharji, cited in Nagam Aiya 1906).

DRAMA COMPANIES

Most major artists of Kondiah's generation who eventually worked for the lithograph industry developed their skills as drama scenery painters. These included K. Madhavan, who worked for Kanniya Company, for N. S. K. Nadar, and for T. K. Brothers drama companies in the 1930s and 1940s, and T. S. Subbiah (1920–), who began his career as a drama company electrician and has become one of today's most successful popular painters.

The subjects of the dramas were primarily episodes from the Epics, stories like Harischandra being especially popular, and many troupes also included adaptations of Tamil folk stories. Each troupe included at least one artist to prepare the backdrops and create the effects on which this kind of entertainment depends. The elaborate backdrops were part of what distinguished these "special dramas" from the more ancient Tamil street theater (*teru kuttu*) dramatic forms.[11]

The heritage of drama backdrop painting is evident in several ways in the style of contemporary popular art. First, the backgrounds of calendar and *pūjā* prints of deities often are elaborate architectural settings based on the drama backdrop style. The temple pillars, thick draperies, and graphically rendered decorative scrollwork of popular prints, often employing several contradictory ranges of perspective, are drawn directly from the large painted cloth backdrops of the dramas. Painting highlights onto backgrounds as if the scenes were dramatically lit is another feature that has survived from drama scenes into the printed image.

In the earliest Indian lithographed prints (those from the Varma presses at the turn of the century, for example) the artists had favored pastoral backgrounds, gods and goddesses in outdoor settings, the styles of which were heavily influenced by European-derived landscape painting. The next generation of painters for the popular market replaced this preference for nature with "fancy" (architectural or fantasy) backdrops, yet the pastoral backgrounds that survived in the work of artists of Kondiah's generation show a flattening and conventionalization that is more like drama scenery painting than the easel-painting realism attempted by artists in Varma's day.

A second way in which drama backdrop styles influenced the development of popular art is the relationship between the primary figure or figures and the background. The earlier attempts by painters for the popular market to integrate the key figures into the scenes (e.g., a startlingly human-looking Shiva walking casually in a forest) were modified by artists trained on backdrops to a presentation in which the key figures were conceptually separate from the paintings' backgrounds. Popular images since Kondiah's time look more like actors on a stage, more like the pervasive traditional Indian conventions of presenting the deity within a context or frame and yet separable from it, simultaneously a character in a story and an icon, and accessible in either way for the viewer/devotee. This apparent tension is evident in village drama itself. Actors have described to me how the narrative flow of dramas is occasionally interrupted by members of the audience worshipping main characters. Entertainment and worship in India often coexist (see Hiltebeitel 1988; Blackburn 1988).

PHOTOGRAPHY

The settlement of Kondiah and his followers in Kovilpatti introduces another influence on the evolving South Indian popular style — that of photography. In 1944, only two years after coming to the town, Kondiah established the Sri Devi Art Studio as a storefront for his work and that of his students, and before long each of his four original followers was involved in both photography and painting. T. S. Arunachalam, who took over Devi Arts, specialized in photo retouching (a skill that became essential to the recycling of popular designs in the printing industry). T. S. Meenakshi Sundaram, who had painted backdrops for the drama troupes, opened Lalitha Studio for general photo work. Saradha Studios, established by T. S. Subbiah, Arunachalam's brother, specialized in photo enlargement. Sankaiya, the fourth original disciple, also opened a studio.

The relationship between popular printed pictures and photography has been discussed by Gutman (1982) and Smith (1978), particularly in regard to photography's influence on portraiture and popular images of saints and political leaders. Gutman's collection includes examples of photos that have been inset into paintings, photographs that have been overpainted, and, of course, paintings derived from photographs. It is likely that Kondiah and his followers were involved in all these processes, resulting in their establishment of conventionalized portrait versions of important figures, probably derived from photos, and also well-known versions of important carved or cast temple images painted from photographs, for which the demand continues to grow at pilgrimage centers. In addition, the stylized backdrops, drawn from the drama scenes and used by the Kovilpatti studios for portraits, "frame" both the wedding couple and the deity in many early paintings mass-produced by the printing industry.

Yet there are other connections between the print and the photograph, perhaps less direct but more profound. Kondiah and his followers were vitally interested in the technology of image production and reproduction. Their status in Kovilpatti was bound up with photography, a medium still regarded with considerable awe by most people in Tamil Nadu in the middle of this century. They were anxious to improve their product and to experiment with any new equipment or technique that became available for either photography or painting.

PAINTING MATERIALS

The flowing graphic style that Kondiah and his group introduced to South Indian popular art changed printed images from reproductions of paintings to mature and flexible poster images in their own right. This transition was based on several key innovations. One was the nature of the painting materials themselves. When Kondiah and his followers first settled in Kovilpatti, they and most other painters for the print market were using oil paints on canvas and prepared surfaces. A major painting took a month or more to complete. They quickly changed to German powder tempera colors and more recently to Camlin watercolors, with which a painting can be finished in three or four days. The painting surface became standardized to 20″ × 30″

panels of artist's board. Another major innovation was the acquisition in the early 1960s of the airbrush, the key to subtle shading effects that previously could be achieved only by laborious overlays in oil or wash techniques in water. Airbrushing became a central part of popular aesthetics.

THE PRINTING INDUSTRY

Perhaps most important in the style set by the Kondiah group was their understanding of the printed image's potential as a communication medium. They simplified the image of the deity passed down to them from the first generation of painters who had their work reproduced and made it bolder, more colorful, and more visually compelling. They made their representations livelier and more harmonious with the increasing role of prints in public spaces. Being photographers as well as painters, they understood the changes taking place in the printing industry. Kondiah and his group had their paintings first printed just as photo-offset machines were beginning to replace the more laborious lithographic presses. In Sivakasi, where virtually all their paintings were printed, the first modern photo-offset press was installed in 1956, the same year a Kondiah design appeared in printed form.

If settling in Kovilpatti was pure chance, as Kondiah's life story and interviews indicate, then it was a miracle of good fortune. Kovilpatti is only a few kilometers from Sivakasi, the largest printing center in India. The extraordinary efforts of the Nāṭār industrialists' community transformed this desert village from a small matchbox and fireworks producer to a major industrial center, India's "Little Japan." By 1979, there were 350 photo-offset machines and more than 1,000 litho and letterpress units in operation. Beginning, as Ravi Varma had, with imported machines and technicians from Germany, Japan, and Czechoslovakia, the Sivakasi printers developed their own skills and helped develop the Indian printing-press manufacturing capacity. It was to Sivakasi that Kondiah's group took their work; their close contacts there enabled them to keep in touch with the publishers and through them with the public whose response was to become so important to the direction their work would take.

Students

The relationship between teacher (*guru*) and student (*celā*) is crucial for understanding popular Indian art. The relationships Kondiah had with his students followed a sequence of watching, then assisting, then copying, then developing new versions. This is the basis of traditional artistic training in India and the process through which one can trace the course of popular art from Kondiah's first print in the early 1950s to the present.

Of Kondiah's original followers in Kovilpatti, T. S. Subbiah (1920–) became the most widely published artist. During the first phase of his training, he simply signed his teacher's name to all his work. Now, as an established artist in his own right, his *guru* dead for more than a decade, he still signs Kondiah's name above his own on all his work. Another of Kondiah's illustrious students who joined the master in Kovilpatti in 1947, M. Ramalingkum (1933–), signed Kondiah's name to his work from 1956 to 1958, both names from 1958 to 1962, his own name from 1962 to the early 1970s, and now signs his name and the name of his studio, Chithiralayam. In this way, the "signing" of paintings, which was imported to Indian art with European painting and mechanization, has been adapted to the Indian notion of the artist as a link in an artistic chain. I have recorded the names of seventeen of Kondiah's students who "flocked to the master like birds to a fruit tree" (Mahadevan 1976:25). Several of them work in the popular art industry, and many have signed his name to their work during some phase of their career. One result of the devotion of Kondiah's students (and perhaps the allegiance he demanded) is that it seems impossible now to establish how many published pictures were the work of Kondiah's own hand.

This kind of genealogy of artistic training helps to account for the continuity of process and style in painting for the lithographic market in South India during this century and to identify the elements, both local and imported, that combined to create the prevailing images. The close "hereditary" relationships of the artists and their attitude toward copying, reproducing, and recycling one another's designs is one factor that has contributed to the evolution of strongly accepted popular images of deities. On one hand, copying or plagiarism is one main feature of the history of all "poster aesthetics" and "each important poster artist partly feeds on earlier schools of poster art" (Sontag 1970:4). On the other hand, few Indian popular artists have absorbed the ideology of the modern artist in Western society—the notion of the creative individual, isolated, spontaneous, and self-motivated. Most of the artists here referred to consider themselves an integral part of a tradition, responsible to their families, *guru*s, and god in the course of their work.[12]

Figure 3.3. *Pūjā* room of M. Ramalingkum, Kovilpatti, 1981. Photo by S. R. Inglis.

The central shrine in M. Ramalingkum's worship or *pūjā* room ex-emplifies the attitude of the artist as an integral part of the history of an artistic movement. In a central location high on the main wall is a painting by Ramalingkum himself of Sri Senbahavalli Amman, the major deity of Kovilpatti who offered refuge and ultimately brought abundance to Kondiah and his followers (see Figure 3.3). Below this is a painting by Kondiah of Ganapati, the inaugurator deity as portrayed by the man who opened the door to Ramalingkum's career. Flanking these are two prints of the pioneer Ravi Varma's most important paintings, the female deities Sarasvati and Lakshmi, one the artist's patron and the other symbolic of his financial success.

Despite the multitude of commercial applications to which their popular images have been put, Kondiah's followers have retained attitudes toward their work that show continuity with the artist's traditional role in Indian society. These include the notion of the creative process as a sacred act and the artist as temporary priest, subject to certain domestic purity restrictions and rituals associated with work, especially work on paintings of deities.[13] These artists are keenly aware of the uses to which their printed designs are put in worship and feel the artist's responsibility as priest and the consumer's as devotee. Not only Kondiah but most of his students were born into traditional communities of artists — a majority are of the artisan (Asari) castes — and so were hereditarily prepared to approach their work from a traditional set of beliefs.

Although the general public in India never knew his name, Kondiah's images and those of his students became the prevailing source of the South Indian popular style. Many painters in Madras and Madurai, as well as Kovilpatti, credit Kondiah Raja as the source of most religious designs throughout India.[14] The master and the style he inspired live on in Kovilpatti through the work of T. S. Subbiah and his son S. S. Rajoo, M. Ramalingkum, his brother M. Srinivasan, and Ramalingkum's son, R. Marimuttu. Another half-dozen of Kondiah's students continue painting in other places in Tamil Nadu. His influence also persists through hundreds of artists throughout India who have been influenced by this work and continue to recycle the designs or their elements in their own painting. Perhaps most importantly, Kondiah's work, his background, training, teaching, and his vision of the divine survive in hundreds of thousands of framed prints in every conceivable public and private space, from *pūjā* rooms to *pān* shops, temples to taxi cabs.

The Use of Images

Most Indian paintings originally were an integral part of the buildings for which they were designed. The "portable" painting traditions, such as the scrolls of Bengal and Gujarat displayed by itinerant bards or the pilgrimage paintings of Puri or Nathdwara, were both highly localized and specialized. In South India most traditional painters worked for temples. People viewed paintings in the course of their visits to temples or monasteries (*maṭh*). Printing technology and rapid reproduction have led to a situation in which the direction is often reversed: the painting comes to the viewer rather than the viewer to the painting. In its travels, its meaning changes, or rather "its meaning multiplies and fragments into many meanings" (Berger 1976:19). Some of these many meanings are discussed below.

DISTRIBUTION

Much has changed since "Ravi Varma's pictures" were included in a list with "bouquets, gaslights and other items of foreign decoration" as high-class furnishings to "make houses grand and glorious, even in the eyes of modernists" (Sarkar 1917:65). Today prints are confined neither to grand houses nor to those of "simpler Hindus" (Basham 1977:ix). At the beginning of the century, Ravi Varma and his brother struggled for days to produce a few hundred prints. The business, according to a contemporary account, "was not believed to be paying" (Nagam Aiya 1906:265). By the time Kondiah and his followers were painting for the popular market in the 1950s, several large printing firms were turning out 200,000–300,000 prints a year. S. S. Brijbasi and Sons printed more than 7.5 million pictures in 1985 (Anton-Warrior 1986), and the larger companies such as Sankareswari, Orient, National, and Coronation in Sivakasi probably now produce more than 10 million images a year each. This has made artists like M. Ramalingkum, who has had single designs printed in runs of 100,000 and has been producing up to a hundred designs a year for several decades, one of the most published painters in history. But it has also assured that prints of Hindu religious subjects now appear in places and in forms that never existed before.

Whereas Kondiah's paintings of "Ganjendira Motsam" and "Minakshi Kalyanam" became two of the most beloved images throughout South India four decades ago, his disciples' most popular images can be found from Kanyakumari to Kuala Lampur and from Calcutta to Cape Town. In the course of this process, the "recognition factor" of various deities has been increased dramatically. Kondiah's particular depictions of Minankshi and Murugan are the way South Indians have come to visualize these deities, and these core images continue to resonate through the work of his students and those he inspired. These standardized portrayals of particular deities have become far better known and more easily recognized than any historical or regional representation could have been in the past. The same, of course, applies to the most widely published artists' representations of film stars, politicians, and saints (see Smith 1978). So pervasive have the "standard" images become that in smaller shrines and temples in South India, one often sees a printed image of the deity mounted outside the sanctum of a temple and even pasted on the wall above the carved image itself. In an ironic way, the printed image adds "authenticity" to the three-dimensional image. In the temples where this happens, the printed image adds prestige to the local version by linking it to the deity's larger network, which obviously includes the cities, bigger temples, and "famous places." There is an element of "hyper-reality" in these prints. Their bright colors, shiny finish, and appealing designs complement rather than detract from the dark, carved images.

Visualizing the deities through popular depictions links not only virtually all markets, temples, and pilgrimage places in India, but also Hindu residences, workplaces, shops, and places of worship throughout the world. One is tempted to propose here a "national aesthetic" that goes beyond religious identity alone, in that the prints with their particular stylistic history are distinctively Indian and yet are far more pervasive than any of the folk, regional, or classical styles, those officially "chosen representatives of a national tradition" (Singer 1959:ix). The ubiquity, portability, and mobility of these images have drawn Hindus closer to one another in the ways they perceive the divine and have provided a more unified vision of the Hindu pantheon. Printed pictures are thus one key element in the "Pan-Hinduism" that develops as Indians become increasingly mobile within their own country and find themselves part of regionally diverse Hindu communities abroad. Each year salesmen from the giant printing companies in Sivakasi set out with fat catalogues and order books to sell religious designs for calendars, book covers, labels, and posters throughout India and abroad. The catalogues include pictures of all the gods and goddesses, an *utsava mūrti,* or processional icon, to be toured among the devotees. Through this process, the power concentrated in sacred centers is diffused to wherever devotees live, work, and worship.

Figure 3.4. "Murugan with Valli and Devni" by M. Ramalingkum, here seen as an advertisement for a clothing store. Photo by S. R. Inglis; by permission of M. Ramalingkum.

COMMERCE

Although we do not know to what commercial uses Kondiah's earliest prints were put, we do know that his student M. Ramalingkum's first print was used for a Sri Ambal Coffee calendar (1956) and that K. Madhavan's first was for Burmah-Shell (1940s). Printed paintings of Hindu deities were used as part of commercial advertising as early as the 1920s, and in South India the large textile mills and snuff-tobacco companies were among the most consistent clients. By the 1950s, businesses of every kind purchased printed pictures of deities as advertising posters and calender images. Since that time, the same images have been used in various sizes and applications of greeting cards, schoolbooks, fans, and flyers as well as on all kinds of packaging and labeling.

Part of modern media's character is that members of the public are treated as both spectators and customers, and, in India as in other industrializing countries, printed images grew along with increasing mass consumption. But as we have seen, it would be erroneous to assume that a commercial context is essential to the printed image in India or that the artist is simply a hired hack trying to please a client. The commercial element of the divine image has remained secondary to its creation and distribution as an aesthetic expression in the broadest sense, an expression that transcends any particular slogan or advertisement. The same image is regularly sold as a "framing picture" and as a calendar illustration. To most of the public, the calendar's sponsors are secondary and interchangeable. A print used initially as a calendar illustration is often clipped and framed when the year expires, thereby becoming a sacred icon. Thus although the image may be symbolically appropriated by a publishing company (see Figure 3.4) and then by a consumer, the relationship between artist and audience and between deity and devotee is maintained.

WORSHIP

Among a collection of older printed pictures, one may be surprised at how many have been daubed with sandalwood paste or vermilion powder and even scorched with incense. It has been possible to record dozens of ways in which printed pictures are used in worship and to document how they have become an important form of religious icon in modern India.

There are few shops in India in which prints are not the focus of some daily ritual, and prints serve similar purposes in public buildings, schools, offices, and private homes. Framed prints are taken out in procession, mounted on temple chariots, and used by mendicants and beggars as portable images. There are probably few travelers who have not said a silent ecumenical prayer to a garlanded print mounted on the dashboard of a careening scooter, taxi, or express bus. The acceptance of the printed picture as a suitable focus of worship has several implications for patterns of ritual and religious practice.

Because prints are widely available, cheap or occasionally even free, almost anyone can afford to own any print he or she wishes. This may facilitate more private worship in the home and less at the temple. It perhaps also has contributed to the growth of particular cults, whose momentum often relies on a shared talisman or other symbol (e.g., Santoshi Ma or Aiyappan). The accessibility of the images, their portability and flexibility (in that they lack three-dimensional representations' conventional associations with priests and other specialists), enable people more easily to claim devotion to a deity whose image they possess. In the case of the lower castes, this could be a deity with whom interaction in temple worship is socially prohibited.

Another aspect of worship is pilgrimage. An important part of the pilgrimage experience, especially for Hindus, has been *darśan,* the chance to stand in the presence of a particular deity (Babb 1981). In some ways the pilgrim can perpetuate the experience by acquiring and subsequently worshipping a memento from the holy place. Through the wide distribution of printed pictures, the chance to obtain such mementos — and, by extension, the chance to "stand before the deity" — is no longer limited to those who have made the journey. The image of Tirupati Balaji in print form is available in Madurai, Puri Jagganath in Calcutta, or Nathdwara Nathji in Bombay. Any of them can be had in Nairobi or Singapore. One of the most widely circulated prints in South India today is the image of Aiyappan. While growing numbers of people make the rigorous Aiyappan pilgrimage to Kerala, those unable or unwilling to do so can still participate in the cult to some degree through the availability of the image in print form. Of course a printed picture does not replace or duplicate a pilgrimage experience, but perhaps their wide availability facilitates the often noted process of "vicarious" pilgrimage (Bharati 1963:165; Diehl 1956:250) within the larger process of vicarious ritualization in general (Singer 1959:141–82).

MULTIPLE IMAGES

Many years ago, on a journey to find a family friend living in a village near Hoshiarpur, Punjab, I sat in the office of the Communist Party of India looking up at a line of framed prints. They were identical in size and frame,

each daubed with sandlewood paste and garlanded with desiccated mar-
igolds. The line included Marx, Ganesha, and Gandhi. This mundane experience, confusing at the time, alerted me to the flexibility that printed pictures have introduced into the construction of visual and symbolic sets; as
meaningful as the choice and use of a single print may be, the juxtaposition
of printed pictures also offers an extremely rich field for analysis.

On one hand, the image-covered facades of modern Indian towns and
cities represent a kind of random display that links India with countries
throughout the world, but on the other hand, there are particular arenas in
India where prints are juxtaposed in patterns that express religious ideology
and change. One of these is the private space devoted to worship in larger
Indian homes, the *pūjā* room, in which the imagery of the family's religious
heritage is accumulated, often in conjunction with photographs, three-
dimensional images, and other souvenirs. Another is the temple, monas-
tery, or community hall in which framed, printed pictures often line the
tops of the walls, documenting the religious "genealogy" of larger social
groups. A third arena are shops in which framed prints have become a
major part of the physical and social ambience, whether they amount to a
few calendars hanging limply in a tea stall or a splendid series of framed and
garlanded prints in a traditional jeweller's or confectioner's shop.

In all these collections, elements of juxtaposition, made possible by the
ubiquitous nature of the printed image, give evidence of the religious ideology of the accumulators and the users. First, we can detect personal attitudes and allegiances in the selections, hierarchies established, and priorities clearly identified through relative size, quality, and placement. The
range and variety of images available allow an individual, family, or group
to construct creatively a particular pantheon, independent of the traditional
limitations of caste allegiance or craft prerogative. There is both a great deal
more choice of images and a great deal more flexibility for change than ever
in the past. A second dimension is the historical development of collections.
Using these groups of prints, we can now document important additions
over time to divine assemblages. The prints from the early part of the
century already have an aura of time past, and more conservative, traditional businesses seem to find it appropriate to retain a set intact, although
newer prints often are added to the older series when a new member of the
firm becomes influential, a new kind of customer emerges, or a family or
community event so dictates. Collections of prints are often a diary or
album of experiences for those who assemble them. Despite its initial disposability, a print can take on an aura of great social or cultural value

through the passage of time and incorporation into a physical and spiritual space. Print groupings also have a geographic dimension and often document their owners' travels to pilgrimage places or important temples. Each assemblage is symbolically a confluence of deities or places and thus a personal or communal map of the sacred geography of a family or group.

In all these ways, groups of prints are more than the sums of individual pieces. They become a means of group identification, a visual code by which members of subgroups announce and recognize themselves and record and depict their attitudes and alliances. When prints of other religious themes, movie stars, politicians, saints, children, and landscapes are juxtaposed — as they often are — with the images of gods and goddesses, the possibilities for expression are extremely varied. In all this there seems to be no risk of "cultural indigestion," in Sontag's term (1970). Prints of the Bengali patriot Netaji, the American President John F. Kennedy, the former Tamil Chief Minister M. G. Ramachandran, and the Hindu deity Minakshi coexist in the image-rich world of South India. The seemingly indiscriminate juxtaposition of printed pictures has become a way of "anthologizing" the divine hierarchy and often placing it in a context of other significant images that compete for attention in the modern world.

Conclusion

In all the ways suggested here, Indian painting has not only retained but expanded its sacred meaning in printed form, and in fact this meaning has become richer, more complex, and diverse. It is clear that the large volume of reproduction does not necessarily challenge the potency of the sacred image. Hinduism has a deeply rooted capacity to accommodate multiple versions and manifestations. The dynamics of connections between sources and emanations are fluid and receptive to sacred images' wider circulation through new media. Nor are the ephemerality and disposability of printed pictures necessary indications of a reduction of sacred power. Although prints are often framed and preserved, they also may be discarded. The cyclical nature of artistic creation and consumption is a central theme in Hindu religious practice, one that is reproduced precisely in the annual calendar cycle (Inglis 1988).

For artists like Kondiah and his followers, the transition from making paintings for specific clients and purposes to making paintings for printing was a natural one, a part of their evolving sense of the expanding role of images in South Indian society. The flexibility that enabled them to work simultaneously in several media and to serve with equal effect religion, politics, and entertainment is characteristic of their artistic heritage rather than a departure from it. Their special contribution was to "humanize" the stylized and remotely superhuman representations of deities in the Pallava, Chola, and Pandya styles; to "nationalize" the regional craft skills to which they were heir; and to integrate these styles with the evolving aesthetics of their own and other popular media, particularly the cinema. The printed versions of their paintings are directly accessible to ordinary people in India because they "quote" both the traditional structure of divine depiction and a modern style of public communication.

Notes

1. An observation by Mukharji in 1888, referring to pictures printed in oil colors (Nagam Aiya 1906).

2. For example, Ravi Varma Fine Art Lithographic Press, Bombay, and Calcutta Art Studio, Calcutta.

3. I wish to thank Erica Claus and K. Muthusamy Velar for their assistance in assembling the collections and information on which this chapter is based, and also H. Daniel Smith for many collegial exchanges of material and enthusiasm. My research in India has been supported by the Shastri Indo-Canadian Institute and by the Social Sciences and Humanities Research Council of Canada.

4. This school, which still operates as the Government College of Arts and Crafts, had been set up by a British surgeon in the Madras Army in 1850. The school has been described in a recent account as the "Madras School of Drawing and Painting" (Mahadevan 1976). The J. J. School of Art in Bombay was founded in 1857, and the Calcutta School of Art in 1854 (H. D. Smith, personal communication).

5. The companies he worked for included the Meenaloshani Bala Sathgura Sabha of the well-known Sankaradas Swami and the Palaniah Pillai Company.

6. See Appasamy (1980) and Ramaswamy (1976). Rājus also participated in "company painting," typical scenes of people and places painted for foreigners, which were popular between the early eighteenth century and the second half of the nineteenth. This fad introduced European paper and watercolor paints to Indian art, whose paint medium until then had been gouache.

7. For details on his life, see Chaitanya (1960) and Venniyoor (1981).

8. Ravi Varma first sent his paintings to Germany for printing, as many Indian artists had done and continued to do well after he established his own press in India. The production of the Varma presses was dominated by printing Ravi Varma's own oil paintings. Rival presses turned out hundreds of unauthorized versions of these designs in thousands of copies around the turn of the century (Anton-Warrior 1987).

9. Subba Naidu's grandson N. S. R. Regunatha Naidu (1930–) is now the head of the family, which traces its heritage back through the origins of popular painting in South India. The family still lives on the same street in Madurai and still renovates temple paintings, produces Tanjore-style paintings, and works for the print market.

10. He went on to be the leading calendar and magazine cover painter in Madras and to become known as the "Norman Rockwell of India."

11. Drama troupes still travel to virtually every part of South India, although their work has been regionalized and severely diminished through competition with the cinema. I have interviewed the last families of drama scenery painters working in Madurai and actors and musicians from several communities who make a part-time living in this business.

12. Of course there have been "breaks" in the chain and inevitable rivalry and jealousy among artists. Ramalingkum's split from Kondiah in 1962 was painful and irrevocable, and apparently Subbiah has been known to cast aspersions on his master (H. D. Smith, personal communication), although both students continue to honor their teacher in other ways. Kondiah was himself called before the Madras High Court in the early 1960s to answer charges that he had "stolen" the design of another artist; the case was dismissed (Ramalingam 1976).

13. The eyes of the deity, for example, are still always painted last, as a completion of the creative act, one of the most ancient artist's rituals known in India (Inglis 1984:240).

14. This refers to the prevalent South Indian opinion that North Indian artists simply copy South Indian designs (and badly at that). Another leading center of artistic production for the popular market is Bombay; its most prominent artists are members of the Śarmā community, originally of Nathdwara, Rajasthan (Maduro 1976).

References

Anton-Warrior, Helga. 1986. *Indische Farbdrucke im Besitz des Hamburgischen Museums fur Volkerkunde.* Mitteilungen aus dem Museum fur Volkerkunde. Hamburg neue folge. 16. Hamburg: Museum fur Volkerkunde.

Appasamy, Jaya. 1980. *Tanjavur Painting of the Maratha Period.* New Delhi: Abhinav.

Babb, Lawrence A. 1981. "Glancing: Visual Interaction in Hinduism." *Journal of Anthropological Research* 37, no. 4:387–401.

Basham, Arthur L. 1977. "Introduction." In *Hindu Epics, Myths, and Legends in Popular Illustrations,* ed. V. Vitsaxis. Delhi: Oxford University Press.

Benjamin, Walter. 1968. "The Work of Art in the Age of Mechanical Reproduction." *Illuminations:*219–253. London: Fontana/Collins.

Berger, John. 1976. *Ways of Seeing.* London: Penguin Books.

Bharati, Agehananda. 1963. "Pilgrimage in the Indian Tradition." *History of Religions* 3:135–167.

Blackburn, Stuart H. 1988. *Singing of Birth and Death.* Philadelphia: University of Pennsylvania Press.

Suitable for Framing   75

Chaitanya, Krishna. 1960. *Ravi Varma*. Delhi: Lalit Kala Akademi.
Diehl, Carl Gustav. 1956. *Instrument and Purpose: Studies on Rites and Rituals in South India*. Lund (Sweden): Greerlup.
Geertz, Clifford. 1976. "Art as a Cultural System." *Modern Language Notes* 91:1473–1499.
Gombrich, Ernst Hans. 1950. *The Story of Art*. London: Phaidon.
Gutman, Judith. 1982. *Through Indian Eyes: 19th and 20th Century Photography from India*. New York: Oxford University Press.
Hiltebeitel, Alf. 1988. *The Cult of Draupadi*. Chicago: University of Chicago Press.
Inglis, Stephen. 1984. "Creators and Consecrators: A Potter Community of South India." Ph.D. dissertation, University of British Columbia, Vancouver.
———. 1988. "Making and Breaking: Craft Communities in South Asia." In *Making Things in South Asia: The Role of the Artist and Craftsman,* ed. M. Meister, pp. 153–164. Philadelphia: University of Pennsylvania, Department of South Asia Regional Studies.
Lannoy, Richard. 1971. *The Speaking Tree*. London: Oxford University Press.
Maduro, Renaldo. 1976. *Artistic Creativity in a Brahmin Painter Community*. Research Monograph Series, No. 14. Berkeley: University of California, Center for South and Southeast Asia Studies.
Mahadevan, K. M. 8.8. 1976. "The Great Artist Kondiah Raju." *Mālai Muraco,* Tinevelly (in Tamil).
Nagam Aiya, V. 1906. *The Travancore State Manual* 3:259–71.
Ramalingam, M. 5.9. 1976. "Cajendira Motsam to Minakshi Kalyanam." *Āṇanta Vikaṭan,* Madras (in Tamil).
Ramaswamy, N. 1976. *Tanjore Painting: A Chapter in Indian Art History*. Madras: Kora's Indigenous Arts and Crafts Centre.
Sarkar, B. K. 1917. *The Folk Element in Hindu Culture*. London: Longmans, Green and Co.
Singer, Milton. 1959. "The Great Tradition in a Metropolitan Centre: Madras." In *Traditional India: Structure and Change,* ed. Milton Singer, pp. 141–182. Philadelphia: American Folklore Society.
Smith, H. Daniel. 1978. "Hindu *Desika* Figures." *Religion* 8, no. 1:40–67.
Sontag, Susan. 1970. "Posters: Advertisement, Art, Political Artifact, Commodity." In *The Art of Revolution,* ed. D. Stermer, pp. 1–17. New York: McGraw-Hill.
———. 1977. *On Photography*. New York: Dell.
Venniyoor, E. 1981. *Ravi Varma*. Madras: Government of Kerala.

INTERVIEWS

T. S. Subbiah (Kovilpatti), 1981.
T. S. Meenakshi Sundaram (Kovilpatti), 1981.
M. Ramalingkum (Kovilpatti), 1980–81.
Mrs. K. Madhavan (Madras), 1981.
P. N. Subbaiyar (Madurai), 1981.
N. S. R. Regunatha Naidu (Madurai), 1980.

Frances W. Pritchett

4. The World of *Amar Chitra Katha*

The Indian comic book industry is large and growing, with comic books in English an especially popular product. Comics based on traditional Hindu mythological tales and historical figures seem to sell particularly well; they find markets not only in India, but in the West as well, among Indian immigrants. The purchasers tend to be adult, well-off, and educated — the kind of people who want their children to read in English and also want to assure them access to a cultural tradition that otherwise may seem increasingly remote. For the second-generation, Indian-American students I teach at Columbia University, such "Classics Illustrated" comics have replaced grandmothers as the primary source of stories about India. While these comics are normally bought and presented by adults, students remember reading them eagerly and with real enjoyment.

This flourishing genre has been dominated since the end of the 1960s by a single series, *Amar Chitra Katha* (*amar citra kathā*, "immortal illustrated story"), originally conceived and still edited by Anant Pai of India Book House (IBH) in Bombay. According to Anant Pai, however, the series had its real origin not in Bombay but in Delhi. There, in 1967, Pai had his first chance to watch television. As a government enterprise, television started in Delhi and only later came to the rest of the country. What fascinated Pai most was a quiz show for children. It fascinated him, that is, until a young boy was asked a question that turned his delight to consternation:

> They could answer every question about Greek mythology. . . . But in Delhi, mind you, where every year they enact the *rāmlīlā* — for ten long days they enact scenes from the *Rāmāyaṇa* — the youngster could not answer the question, "Who is the mother of Ram?"[1]

On Pai's return to Bombay, where he was on the editorial staff of IBH, other children commanded his attention. Since he and his wife have none of their own, these were nephews and nieces whom he encouraged, during their summer vacation, to try their hands at a monthly magazine. The children who produced *Family News* had never seen much of the world beyond Bombay; nonetheless they produced a story about a boy named Robert who lived in Warrington, a small English village near Birmingham. Robert wanted to be someone, and managed to get himself out of his village and off to London. Pai recalls thinking that something was wrong somewhere. "Their libraries were filled with books that came from England. I thought I must do something about it."

And so he did. The publisher at IBH, H. G. Mirchandani, had tried the year before to float Hindi translations of "Classics Illustrated" comics, but the effort had failed. Pai had predicted as much. He had once worked on the comic strip "The Phantom" at the *Times of India* and knew that the real sales for such a product were in the English-language market. Now Mirchandani was ready to let Pai try out his own suggestion: not Western classics in Indian languages, but Indian classics in English. Thus, in 1967, *Amar Chitra Katha* began publication.

IBH was a book publishing firm that showed little initiative in this new kind of marketing, so Pai remembers doing a good bit of stumping for *Amar Chitra Katha*. On one occasion he violated all manner of taboos by putting up a display rack in a restaurant with his own hands—an amazing action for a white-collar worker and a Kerala Brahman (Gangadhar 1988:139). Later on he demonstrated the value of *Amar Chitra Katha* as a learning tool by giving free copies to schools and arranging for students to be tested on what they read. The results were spectacular, and many school libraries became subscribers. The emphasis on annual subscriptions, so that the comics were received regularly through the mail like magazines, was another innovative part of *Amar Chitra Katha*'s vision.

Success came slowly. The first volume in the series, *Krishna,* which was ultimately to sell over half a million copies, was printed in an edition of only 10,000, and in the first two or three years even those took a long time to sell.[2] In its earliest days, the series endeavored to bring out one new comic a month.[3] The earliest titles were to be produced in "English, Hindi, Kannada, Gujarati, Telugu and Marathi,"[4] but so demanding a program was obviously hard to sustain. For the first few years the series lost money, but then its popularity began steadily increasing. Now sales are very satisfactory indeed, especially for the English versions. Moreover, sales of the English versions abroad are growing rapidly.[5] In 1986, IBH claimed to have sold a total of 50 million copies since the series began (India Book House 1986). In October 1988, the claim was raised to "over seventy-five million copies sold" (406:front cover); by 1993, "over 78 million copies sold" (563:inside cover). A cover in 1992 claimed that translations were made into "38 languages of the world." By the 1980s, the series was bringing out a new comic not once a month but once a fortnight, with much fanfare and extensive internal advertisement in other *Amar Chitra Katha* issues.

Every issue is first produced in English and is then translated into various regional languages as sales potential seems to warrant. Pai and his staff have claimed (to Hawley) that the languages regularly represented include Hindi, Marathi, Assamese, Kannada, Bengali, Malayalam, and Gujarati, with occasional translations into Tamil, Telugu, Panjabi, Urdu, and Sanskrit. This may be true, in principle. But K. T. Mirchandani told me that English is the primary language of distribution, with Hindi the only regular and numerically significant Indian language. Observation in the north tends to bear him out. Not only individual issues and annual subscriptions are available, but also various collections of issues, bound into books; most of these are in English, with Hindi running second. In the late 1980s, the emphasis was on pre-planned "miniseries" groupings; these will be considered at greater length below.

In part because of such innovative marketing techniques, *Amar Chitra Katha* was going strong by the mid-1970s. In 1975, notice was taken of it in a UNESCO publication. In 1976, it attracted for the first time a very different sort of attention. The issue *Valmiki* (46), published in that year, repeated the traditional story of the Brahman Valmiki's early career as a thief, before he composed his *Rāmāyaṇa*. This deeply offended the Valmiki Sabha, a group in the Punjab seeking to change their caste identity from sweeper to "Balmik": maintaining that Valmiki was neither a Brahman nor a thief, they actually attempted to sue Pai for libel. Though the legal case never got off the ground, Pai was burned in effigy in Jalandhar and Patiala. He showed a great desire for conciliation, and the controversy eventually died down. But Pai soon removed the issue on Valmiki from circulation — first the Hindi version, then the English. He waited quite some time before attempting another issue that raised the question of untouchability; when *Chokhamela* (292) came out in 1983, and *Ravidas* (350) in 1986, Pai and his staff took extreme care not to offend the sensibilities of lower-caste readers.

Since the mid-1970s, and in some cases even before, great caution has been shown in preparing issues about characters from other minority communities as well. Pai and his staff point out that whenever an issue involving Sikh characters is drafted, an expert consultant on beards is employed. To show respect for Sikh feelings, the issue *Guru Nanak* (47), for example, depicts the holy man with a halo around his head from infancy, a distinction not accorded to Kabir or even Krishna. The treatment of Muslim characters is discussed below. (The complex problems of trying to satisfy conflicting demands from different groups is studied in detail in Chapter 5.)

Many titles in the series display the following pledge: "Amar Chitra Katha are brought out by people — who care for children; — who screen each word and each picture as they have a lasting impact on impressionable minds; — for whom Chitra Katha is more a vehicle of education than a business" (140:32). Pai obviously takes his role as an educator seriously. No doubt inspired by the success of *Amar Chitra Katha,* he now also runs a wholesome fortnightly "all-comics" magazine for young children called *Tinkle* (apparently started in November 1980, with monthly digests from it now available in bookstalls), and a magazine for older children called *Partha* (apparently started in September 1986). Both are frequently advertised in *Amar Chitra Katha* issues. *Partha* in particular is designed "to awaken the winner in you" (369:inside back cover). It is touted as "the self development magazine," "devised and edited by your own Uncle Pai." Subscribers are promised a free copy of Pai's book *The PARTHA Way to Success,* and long-term subscribers receive a cassette to accompany the book (361:33). The book interprets the word *PARTHA* as an acronym for the real secrets of success: "Positive thinking; Aim; Restraints; Training; Hard work; Abiding interest" (Pai 1986:5).[6] *Amar Chitra Katha* issues also advertise the Partha Institute of Personality Development, in which "responsible parents" are urged to enroll their twelve-to-sixteen-year-old children (333:inside back cover). *Amar Chitra Katha* is thus part of a loosely integrated entertainment and self-improvement empire that has come to span a number of media: comics, children's books, audio cassettes, magazines, correspondence courses, and recently even a videotape.

Pai's sustained, much-imitated, twenty-five-year-long oeuvre now includes well over five hundred comic books, with no end in sight. No doubt because this immense body of work presents itself as a lastingly valuable "vehicle of education," the series maintains the firm official position that all its constantly expanding repertoire of titles are truly *amar,* "undying." K. T. Mirchandani told me that all the (English) titles are periodically reprinted, so that the whole series is (in principle) kept constantly in print.[7] This is also the assumption of catalogues for the series, which list issues going back to the earliest.

Yet in practice sales do matter. Pai has said that an issue must sustain annual sales of at least 8,000 to 10,000 copies to be kept in print. One hundred eight regular issues that meet this criterion are listed in his "Editor's Choice" catalogue. The catalogue claims that "the Editor has selected the following 108 as the best ones in the series" — not, it should be noted, the best selling — and the number 108, which Hindus consider auspicious, already suggests that something more elevated than sales figures is involved. (In the 1990s, ads often extol "Deluxe Editions with heavier cardboard covers" and thicker paper of the "best 50" titles.) With the three-title "Bumper Issues," a more conspicuous sleight of hand is practiced: when one such issue is allowed to go out of print because of poor sales, another with the same number replaces it, so that the impression of a continuous series is maintained.

But if sales matter, it is still possible for other considerations to outweigh them. Pai has often been urged to do an issue on the new and very popular goddess Santoshi Ma; such an issue would be a sure-fire winner, for much of her constituency is drawn from the urban literate middle-class world to which Pai has the best access. Yet he steadfastly refuses, for he does not approve of her. He considers the theology of Santoshi Ma retrograde and undesirable: she punishes her most faithful worshipper cruelly for a flaw in her food offerings (sour food substituted for sweet) — a flaw for which the devotee could hardly be blamed, since she was entirely unaware of it. This is not, in Pai's view, an edifying way for a deity to behave. As he put it, a "punitive god" such as this would "hurt the sentiments of any intelligent Hindu." The tension between financial and educational values is thus a powerful one; it amounts to a constant tug-of-war between competing goals. This tension was also reflected in the increasing presence of advertisements in the comic books in the late 1980s — a presence apparently acceptable to Pai himself, though some of his staff had serious reservations about it. The new Deluxe Editions published in the 1990s advertise only IBH publications.

Moreover, in the years since the incident with the Valmiki Sabha, Pai has become increasingly sensitive to the responsibilities imposed by *Amar Chitra Katha*'s emerging canonicity. When he reflects on the problem, he is apt to highlight its scholarly aspect, recalling especially a moment when on a trip to Delhi in 1975 he overheard a disagreement between two highly placed government officials about a point having to do with the *Rāmāyaṇa*. To settle the argument, they turned to an *Amar Chitra Katha* comic book. Pai was taken aback, and resolved thereafter to be as exact in his scholarship as possible. However, this goal often conflicts with one of Pai's general maxims, the Sanskrit phrase "satyam brūyāt priyam brūyāt mā brūyāt satyam apriyam," which he quotes with approval. His translation: "You must tell the truth; you must tell what is pleasant. And that which is unpleasant — just because it is true, you need not say it."

Pai and his staff thus create each issue in a field of tensions: sales versus educational values; scholarly accuracy versus the need to appease particular interest groups; a commitment to Indian history versus a commitment to national integration. And Pai addresses all these complexities in the comic book medium — a medium with its own potent qualities, its own effects, its own opportunities and constraints. The result is a fascinating phenomenon, the product of an extraordinarily complex series of choices.

A Taxonomy of the "Glorious Heritage of India"

Amar Chitra Katha prides itself especially on its completeness and scope. Parents are repeatedly urged to use the series to acquaint their children with "the cultural heritage of India." The series boasts of its power: "Amar Chitra Katha bring to life personages and events from the musty pages of Indian history" (171:back cover). The claim of universality, addressed not to children but to parents, is sweeping and explicit: "You want your children to know all about the culture of India. Amar Chitra Katha takes you on a trip right down to the roots of your heritage" (188:inside back cover). In December 1987, "Amar Chitra Katha — the Route to your Roots" was used on an advertising flyer inserted into at least one issue (395). A 1988 "Editor's Choice" catalogue offered "the quintessence of Indian culture and folklore." And in March 1988, the claim became even more ambitious: "Amar Chitra Katha . . . 5000 years of India's mythology, history, legend — the very soul of Indian culture — packed in volumes of 32 colourful pages" (399:inside back cover).

Such claims make it especially interesting to look at the ways in which the series organizes and presents itself. By now, after two decades of increasingly successful publication, *Amar Chitra Katha* consists of more than five hundred titles. Since many of the earlier issues are constantly being reprinted, the claims of the series to unity and universal scope are dinned into the reader's brain. Thirteen thousand pages are surely enough to define a universe. What does the series include — and, perhaps even more to the point, what does it exclude? How does *Amar Chitra Katha* define "the very soul of Indian culture"?

In its catalogues, *Amar Chitra Katha* analyzes itself into several seemingly arbitrary (and often overlapping) categories that nevertheless appear to remain stable over time. The most recent full catalogue that I have been able to obtain (India Book House 1986) uses the following taxonomy: "Mythology" (90 titles), "Sanskrit Classics" (12 titles), "Regional Classics"

(13 titles), "Teachers and Saints" (27 titles), "Poets and Musicians" (7 titles), "Folk Tales and Legends" (56 titles), "Buddhist Tales" (24 titles), "Jaina Tales" (6 titles), "Tales from Ancient Indian History" (14 titles), "Tales from Medieval Indian History" (5 titles), "The Mughals and their Adversaries" (10 titles), "The Rajputs" (7 titles), "The Marathas" (6 titles), "The Sikhs" (8 titles), "Heroes who Fought the British" (2 titles), "The Indian Revolutionaries" (5 titles), "Glimpses of 1857" (4 titles), "Monuments and Battles" (3 titles), "Great Women of India" (13 titles), "Makers of Modern India" (13 titles), "Scientists and Doctors" (4 titles).[8]

If the taxonomic divisions are worthy of attention, the issue numbers themselves are also suggestive. In a series like this, conceived from the beginning in ambitious and idealistic terms, the lowest-numbered titles must be at the heart of things. The first ten titles are: *Krishna* (11), *Shakuntala* (12), *The Pandava Princes*[9] (13), *Savitri* (14), *Rama* (15), *Nala Damayanti* (16), *Harishchandra* (17), *The Sons of Rama* (18), *Hanuman* (19), and *The Mahabharata*[10] (20). Some of these titles are apparently now being reissued under new numbers as well, starting with *Krishna* (501) and *Hanuman* (502) (563:back cover).

But readers need not buy according to catalogue headings or issue number alone, for the series practices much more concrete forms of self-classification. *Amar Chitra Katha* titles not only are sold individually and by annual subscription, but are also grouped by IBH into larger, more book-like units. One can order a series of deluxe hardbound volumes containing the whole series bound sequentially in sets of ten. Or one can choose from a group of forty "Bumper Issues." Or one can also buy any of ten hardbound, nicely produced "Navaratna Deluxe" volumes, numbered 1–10, each containing nine related titles.

An especially interesting example of such after-the-fact groupings is "Navaratna No. 2," "Stories from the Ramayana."

"Stories from the Ramayana"

Three of the first ten *Amar Chitra Katha* issues were stories from the *Rāmāyaṇa* tradition. In the course of time the number of such free-standing tales continued to increase, until the series included *Rama* (15), *The Sons of Rama* (18), *Hanuman* (19), *The Lord of Lanka* (67), *Vali* (101), *Dasharatha* (105), *Ancestors of Rama* (122), *Mahiravana* (207), *Kumbhakarna* (220), *Hanuman to the Rescue* (254), and *Ravana Humbled* (305). Nine of these stories have been amalgamated into "Navaratna No. 2," called "Stories from the Ramayana." Each of the ten Navaratna volumes costs Rs. 45 and is nicely bound in a handsome hardcover format: a bright red cover seemingly tied both front and back with a green ribbon and bow, suggesting the idea of a gift for a favorite child. The cover is further adorned with miniature reproductions of all the nine colorful covers of the titles bound inside. In short, the volume has the appearance of a real book and is probably as close as many children will come to the *Rāmāyaṇa*. For some of its readers, this book—an amalgam of Kalidasa, Valmiki, Tulsidas, Krittivasa, and Bhavabhuti, in proportions fixed by Anant Pai—may actually *be* the *Rāmāyaṇa*. It has joined the "many Ramayanas" read and told in South Asia (Richman 1991).

The nine stories inside are arranged in proper narrative order. First comes *Ancestors of Rama* (122). Its introductory note begins, "Tradition has it that Rama was the ideal king. Gandhiji was only reinforcing it when he named his ideal state 'Rama-Rajya.'" Rama's predecessors were "as valiant and as benign" as Rama himself, but not perfect. "The heroes of epics have their tragic flaws because epics always tell the whole truth. Like Rama, his ancestors also had flawed characters despite the glory of their personalities." But we are given no insight into Rama's "flawed character." Instead, the note goes on to identify the source of the story as Kalidasa's *Raghuvaṃśa*. The story itself recounts the lives of the three Ikshvaku kings: Dilipa, his son Raghu, and Raghu's son Aja, father of Dasharatha.

Next comes *Dasharatha* (105), described as "drawn mainly from Valmiki's famous epic poem." It is devoted to Dasharatha's whole adult life, from the time he incurs the well-known curse until his death.

The introduction to *Rama* (15) tells the story of the krauncha bird and emphasizes unity in diversity: "The Ramayanas of Kamban, Tulsidas or Tunchan, are all, but variations, on the same theme. This lofty theme, embodies in the characters of Rama and Sita, the highest ideals of 'man' and 'woman.'" The story is said to be derived from Tulsidas's medieval eastern Hindi version, the *Rāmcaritmānas*. Being a very early, stand-alone issue, *Rama* retells the entire story in compressed form, from the birth of Rama through the death of Ravana, ending with Rama and Sita enthroned in splendor.

Vali (101) is attributed to the Valmiki *Rāmāyaṇa* and describes the combat between Vali and Sugriva, Rama's intervention, Vali's repentance and death.

Hanuman (19) is also drawn from Valmiki. Its hero, we are told, "was born a monkey and yet attained a prominent place among the Hindu Gods, by his sterling character." He was "the greatest of the Bhaktas (Devotees) ever known" — never "narrow minded, or supercilious," but always "compassionate." And, the note concludes, "Whether Hanuman was a monkey or not is beside the point for those who can see the noble spirit in this apelike form." Actually, his form is not at all "apelike," but almost entirely human; this is a point to which we shall return. The issue itself, no doubt because it is so early in the *Amar Chitra Katha* cycle, once again recapitulates the whole story, from Hanuman's meeting with Rama to the death of Ravana and Rama's triumphant enthronement, emphasizing Hanuman's heroic role in these events.

The Lord of Lanka (67) is attributed to Valmiki's *Uttarakāṇḍa*. "Unlike the Mahabharata," the introductory note informs us, "the story of Rama has no historical foundation," yet it has become "an intrinsic part of Hindu life." The issue recounts Ravana's antecedents and earlier life, then in the final seven pages depicts his encounter, "disguised as a monk," with Sita, his abduction of her, leading rapidly to his fatal battle with Rama; the story ends as Vibhishana is crowned king of Lanka.

By contrast, *Kumbhakarna* (220) is retold from the Bengali version of the *Rāmāyaṇa* by Krittivasa, who is described in the introductory note as a "poet of the people" who used "simple language" and "metaphors that are easily understood." Kumbhakarna is frighteningly gigantic, but he is depicted as potbellied, clumsy, and a bit ludicrous; his whole life is narrated, right up to his death on the last page — a last page that also reports that Ravana was killed by Rama and ends with Vibhishana being crowned.

Hanuman to the Rescue (254) is also derived from Krittivasa's version. It records Hanuman's adventures as he fetches Mount Gandhamadana, with its herb that will restore the wounded Lakshmana to life. It ends as Lakshmana recovers and Hanuman releases the Sun God, whom he had imprisoned under his arm.

Finally, *The Sons of Rama* (18) is based on Bhavabhuti's *Uttararāmacarita*. It starts with the washerman's taunt to his wife and ends with Sita's return to the earth and Rama's reconciliation with Lav and Kush.

These nine originally separate comics indeed tell the story of Rama, after a fashion: they don't contradict one another, and the narrative does proceed from earlier to later stages. Yet it is clear even from this brief summary that the fit is not ideal. It could not be, for it was created after the fact. *Rama* (15) and *Hanuman* (19) in particular go over much of the same ground, with many additional repetitions in other volumes as well. The separate identity of the parts remains paramount. The volume they make up when bound together is only a loose and casual collection; it does not really become a coherent version of the *Rāmāyaṇa*.

In contrast to this after-the-fact approach, *Amar Chitra Katha* has begun in the last five years or so to develop pre-planned "miniseries" sets. By far the more ambitious of the two published so far is a miniseries that attempts to render the whole *Mahābhārata*.

"The Mahabharata in 60 Volumes"

It is clear that *Amar Chitra Katha* has had a strong commitment to the *Mahābhārata* from the start. Even a partial listing of titles is impressively long: *The Pandava Princes* (13), *Nala Damayanti* (16), *Mahabharata* (20), *Karna* (26), *Bheeshma* (34), *Abhimanyu* (35), *Drona* (57), *Ghatotkacha* (61), *Draupadi* (72), *Parikshit* (115), *The Gita* (127), *Krishna and Jarasandha* (147), *Tales of Yudhisthira* (174), *Tales of Arjuna* (198), *Gandhari* (209), *Bhima and Hanuman* (214), *Friends and Foes—Animal Tales from the Mahabharata* (238), and so forth. Four triple "Bumper Issues" (#11, #16, #20, #28) have been created out of such *Mahābhārata* stories, and one nine-issue "Navaratna Deluxe" (#3) as well.

All these titles are based on particular, independent episodes; even publishing them all in a single immense volume would not have created a *Mahābhārata* in any real sense. In March 1985, therefore, a new project began, "in response to a persistent demand from our readers for a comprehensive account of the epic." The whole "immortal epic of Vyasa as narrated by Vaishampayana" was to be told in sixty "volumes." This ambitious new miniseries was officially introduced in an advertisement in early 1985: "Amar Chitra Katha brings you THE MAHABHARATA in 60 Volumes" (Figure 4.1).[11] The ad was quite explicit, promising "60 volumes of 1920 illustrated pages in colour." These "volumes"—or issues—were to come out at a rapid pace: "One volume a month beginning from March 1, 1985." Every other *Amar Chitra Katha* issue would thus be from the "Mahabharata" series; readers were even offered the chance to subscribe only to the twelve "Mahabharata" issues a year (Rs. 48) rather than the whole *Amar Chitra Katha* set of twenty-four.

These pledges have since been modified. The pace has been sometimes a bit slower than an issue every fortnight; in 1988 *Amar Chitra Katha* issued only one issue a month, so that "Mahabharata" numbers came out only

Figure 4.1. *Amar Chitra Katha* issue number 101, back cover, as included in Bumper Issue #2, heralding the "Mahabharata" miniseries, early 1985. Courtesy of India Book House Pvt. Ltd.

every two months. But the most striking change has been in the number of issues. The most recent issue I have seen, *Yudhishthira's Coronation* (408), is identified within the miniseries as "Mahabharata — 40." And this issue, with characteristic self-referentiality, advertises "Amar Chitra Katha's Mahabharata," which is "[a]cknowledged as an authentic source," and which is "the complete Mahabharata in 42 lucid, highly readable issues" (408,32) (Figure 4.2). The ad ends with the exhortation "Read it to enjoy your Sunday viewing!"; it thus seems possible that the miniseries was hastened to a

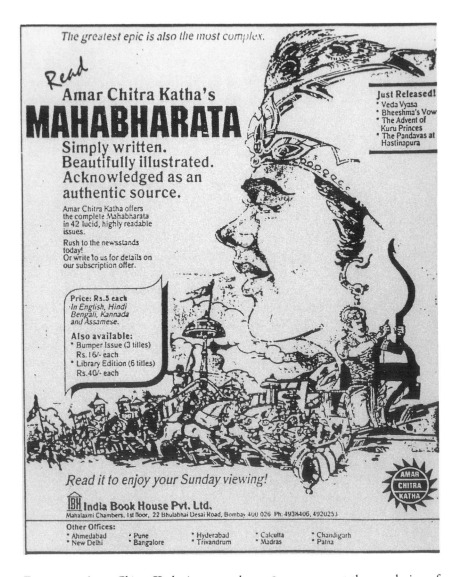

Figure 4.2. *Amar Chitra Katha* issue number 408, p. 32, run at the conclusion of the "Mahabharata" miniseries, December 1, 1988. Courtesy of India Book House Pvt. Ltd.

close to take advantage of the "Mahabharata" series then (1989) being shown on Indian television.

The first issue of the miniseries, "Veda Vyasa" (329), introduces the *Mahābhārata* as "shrouded in mystery": "Can the levels of Painted Grey Ware and Northern Black Polished Ware, or the names of present-day cities and plains, or the radiocarbon tests of excavated materials, vouch for its historicity?" Though there is no "conclusive answer," the core of the story, the war, "must have had its roots in some real event." This preface is followed by a bibliography naming four *Mahābhārata* versions said to have been used in preparing the series: a Sanskrit text with Hindi translation by Pt. Ramnarayandutt Shastri Pandey (Geeta Press, Gorakhpur); a Malayalam verse version by Kunjikuttan Tampuran (S.P.C.S., Kottayam); Pratap Chandra Roy's venerable English prose version (Munshiram Manoharlal, New Delhi); and the modern Pune critical edition published by the Bhandarkar Oriental Research Institute (329:inside front cover).

As a part of its efforts to achieve scholarly legitimacy, the miniseries attempts to preserve the layers of emboxed narration. The first issue begins with Vyasa acquiring Ganesha as his scribe and starting the dictation; it then soon moves on to Vaishampayana narrating to Janamejaya. (This latter pair persist throughout the miniseries, appearing from time to time in panels colored a uniform bright gold to remind us of their privileged status.) At the end of the last page appears, "And thus ends the first session of our rendering of Vaishampayana's recital (during the intervals in the rites of Janamejaya's sarpa satra) of Vyasa's immortal itihasa, The Mahabharata" (329:31). This elaborate closing statement is simplified a bit in later issues, but is never abandoned.

But how is the young reader to know, for example, what a "sarpa satra" is? In this case, "sarpa" is defined in a one-word footnote at the bottom of the page as "snake" and "satra" as a "12-year-long yagna" — which would leave many readers still bewildered. Page 32 of this first issue also consists of a "Pronunciation Guide and Glossary," with names and terms first given in Devanagari script, and then — in some but by no means all cases — explained. Such last-page glossaries are provided for the first six "Mahabharata" issues; after that, they disappear forever.

Amar Chitra Katha boasts that its miniseries "faithfully follows the original Sanskrit text even as it is condensed" (359:inside front cover), and while that somewhat paradoxical claim cannot be taken at face value, the resulting diction is certainly, for the most part, lofty and decorous. Yudhishthira says to Bhishma, "O Grandsire, this ocean of kings is agitated with ire"

(361:19). An ordinary bystander in Hastinapura observes to his friend, "This is the restoration of Yudhisthira who with unerring justice takes care of us as if we were his kin!" To which his friend replies, "It is as if Pandu himself has returned from the forest for our general weal!" (353:20). At one wonderful point, Sanjaya tells Dhritarashtra, "Cussedness on the part of you and your children will be the cause of the destruction of the Kauravas" (383:3).

Although many passages respond to modern didactic concerns, others emphatically do not. Though Anant Pai is normally acutely sensitive to caste politics, in this series the Ekalavya story is told with hardly a hint of disapproval at its aggressive casteism: Drona is described as "aware of the rules of right conduct" when he refuses to take the low-caste Ekalavya as his pupil, and even though Drona says "cruel words" to Ekalavya, the latter is apparently acting properly ("steadfast in the path of truth") when he obeys them and hacks off his thumb, while Drona's action evokes not a further word or hint of narrative criticism (337:17–22).[12] Later, Yudhishthira tells Sanjaya that every "varna" (defined in a footnote as "caste") "should strictly adhere to its own dharma." If a man "takes recourse to the dharma of another caste" without strong need, "his conduct is thoroughly reprehensible" (381:28). Nothing in the treatment of the episode calls this judgment even slightly into question.

Moreover, the graphically depicted burning of the huge Khandava forest, including the deliberate burning alive of all the creatures in it (357:9–14), calls forth not a quiver of humanitarian or environmental uneasiness. And as for women, Krishna advises Arjuna at some length: "In matters of marriage, abduction by a bold Kshatriya is also approved by the learned. Therefore, Arjuna, carry away my sister by force. Who knows what her choice will be at a swayamvara?" (355:15). In this miniseries *Amar Chitra Katha* seems to be claiming exemption from its usual concerns — including its oft-repeated promise to take seriously its "lasting impact on impressionable minds" — by digging in behind the carefully reinforced bulwark of textual fidelity.

"The Epic of New India"

Another miniseries was introduced even more recently (January 1986) than the "Mahabharata" one, and with at least as much fanfare: "Amar Chitra Katha Presents the Epic of New India: The March to Freedom in 6 Vol-

Figure 4.3. "The Epic of New India," *Amar Chitra Katha* issue number 348, January 1, 1986, p. 32. Courtesy of India Book House Pvt. Ltd.

umes" (348:32) (Figure 4.3). The titles of the six issues were announced in
advance, as a planned group, before they were published: *The Birth of the
Indian National Congress* (348), *A Nation Awakes* (356), *The Saga of Indian
Revolutionaries* (360), *The Call for Swaraj* (364), *The Salt Satyagraha* (368),
The Tryst with Destiny (372). Lacking a traditional source, this "March to
Freedom" miniseries is much more arbitrarily defined than the "Mahabha-
rata" one.

The first issue of the miniseries, *The Birth of the Indian National Congress* (348), introduces itself as bringing to life the "epic story of our freedom struggle," an epic that "cuts across barriers of caste, community, region, language, haves and have-nots." This epic is endangered; it is "fast
becoming but another chapter in textbooks." Epics, however, are "eternal,"
and we must preserve this new one as well as the old ones. "Yes. We must
know what our parents, grandparents and their grandparents suffered under the British rule. We must know why they fought and what they fought
for" (348:inside front cover).

The scholarly ambitions of this miniseries are even more conspicuous
than those of the "Mahabharata" one. The bibliography provided for the
first issue alone consists of seven academically oriented volumes; six of these
are by Indians and the seventh is Joseph Schwartzberg's *Historical Atlas of
South Asia*. The bibliography for the second issue, *A Nation Awakes* (356),
consists of eleven scholarly volumes, ten by Indians; for the third issue, *The
Saga of Indian Revolutionaries* (360), nine volumes, all by Indians, are cited.
The scholarly emphasis continues within the stories themselves. The ratio
of narrative prose and static panels to vivid pictures and action panels,
which is high in the "Mahabharata" miniseries, is even higher here. Excerpts from proclamations, letters, speeches, newspaper articles, and other
such historical source materials frequently appear.

Even more strikingly, whole pages of documentary-style abstract prose
are occasionally inserted into the midst of the stories. In the first issue, we
find four prose pages in a row: a centerfold called "India Under the British
Yoke," subdivided into "The Wealth Drain," "Torture to Exact Land Revenue," and "Famine Deaths"; it is immediately followed by "Lest We Forget," a compendium of anti-British remarks by eight Englishmen who were
"much ahead of their time" (348:16–19). A few pages later we encounter a
full-page map and chronology called "1857, The Great Revolt" (348:23).
The second issue in the miniseries offers three concluding pages of prose: a
two-page spread on "The Swadeshi Enterprise," followed by the one-page
"Vivekananda Taught Self-Esteem" (356:30–32).

The narrative voice in this miniseries has also changed radically: it now speaks at great length and chiefly in the first person plural. This nationalist narrative is consistent, passionately defended, and based on a clear sense of economic as well as political grievance. Such a nationalism is present not only in this miniseries but, less explicitly, in a great many other *Amar Chitra Katha* titles as well. It is a nationalism that generates a force field with two crucial poles: the rejection of the negative "them" and the close mutual bonding of the positive "us." This is a point worth examining at some length.

The British are, of course, "them," and they are depicted as negatively as possible. The cartoon drawing itself in these issues is often caricatural, with the British arrogant and ugly, the poor ordinary Indians abject and stereotypically oppressed-looking, the anti-British Indians resolute in battle and saintly on the gallows. Indians who are part of the British system are hardly even acknowledged, and if they are briefly depicted, they are unattractive — unless they are doing something with anti-British implications. This narrowed perspective naturally leads, despite all the trappings of historicity, to inadequate understandings of the past.

To take one important example, 1857 is portrayed in the miniseries as a united national struggle: "Our farmers, traders, professionals, rajas, nawabs all, all joined the struggle against the British" (348:24). But if anything like "all, all" the Indians had ever united in this way, the British would simply have been pushed into the sea. In fact in 1857 Indians were divided: some actively supported the rebels, some actively supported the British, and a great many simply lay low and waited for things to settle down again. Because the *Amar Chitra Katha* version does not acknowledge this situation, it ends up making the British sound like supermen, with vague but irresistible powers: "Though the British suffered heavy losses in the beginning, they were able to regroup, deploy forces and regain lost positions" (348:24). Later on, "The March to Freedom" gives brief but very favorable treatment to Subhas Chandra Bose, who did his best and "fought valiantly" with the Japanese-backed Azad Hind Fauz [sic]. "However, the Allies emerged victorious in the war" (360:29–30), the narrator says, without comment.

If "they," the British, are so clearly outside the pale, "we" must obviously be all inside it together. "We" emphatically includes the Scheduled Castes, to whom *Amar Chitra Katha* devotes several titles — *Babasahib Ambedkar* (188), *Guru Ravidas* (350), *Narayana Guru* (403), etc. — and whose interests are generally defended in other titles when the opportunity offers.

"We" must certainly also include all the religious groups of modern India, which means that Hindus and (above all) Muslims must be shown acting in mutual loyalty and solidarity. At the very least, they should not be shown as hostile to one another. Given the checkered course of modern Indian history, this result is not always easy to achieve.

Yet "The March to Freedom" makes quite a thoroughgoing job of it. The participation of both Hindus and Muslims in the rebellion of 1857 is made very clear (348:24). The cover design of *A Nation Awakes* shows a poor Hindu girl happily tying a *rākhī* on the wrist of a poor Muslim man. The role of Muslims in opening national schools is mentioned (356:11), communal harmony among ordinary Bengalis is repeatedly emphasized (356:1–2, 23–24), riots are attributed to economic rather than religious causes (356:24) and to British divide-and-rule tactics (354:3, 24–25). The heroic revolutionary Ashfaqulla is asked by the police superintendent Tasadruk [sic] Khan, "Why should Muslims fight for Hindu India?" He replies, "Khan Saheb, I am quite sure Hindu India will be much better than British India." To make sure we have taken the point correctly, the narrator hastens to reassure us, "Of course Ashfaqulla, Bismil and others were fighting for all our countrymen" (360:23).

"Us" versus "Them": Toward National Integration

Not only in "The March to Freedom," but in other related titles as well, all communal conflict has been airbrushed out of history. Bankim Chandra Chatterji's famous Bengali novel *Ānanda Math* is full of anti-Muslim sentiment. One hero delivers the solemn warning, "Unless we drive these tipsy long-beards away, a Hindu can no longer hope to save his religion." The revolutionaries look forward with longing to the day when they will be able "to break the mosque to raise the temple of Radha-Madhava in its place" (Chatterji 1929:35,146). Yet this novel is featured quite early in the *Amar Chitra Katha* series. In the *Amar Chitra Katha Ananda Math* (86), the heroic Bengali Hindu freedom fighters do battle with evil British officers who command highly stylized but Muslim-looking troops. In the first, full-page panel the narrator denounces British oppression, then adds, "The Muslim king, who ruled, was a puppet in British hands" (86:1). This glancing, exculpatory aside is the only reference to Muslims in the whole issue. No doubt this is the most tactful way to treat *Ānanda Math* — if it is necessary to treat it at all. The *Amar Chitra Katha* introduction praises the novel for promoting the nationalist movement in Bengal and for generating the famous song "Vande Mātaram" (86:inside front cover).

Even more conspicuously retouched is an issue on the life of Vinayak Damodar Savarkar, the patriarch of the Hindu Mahasabha, famous for his concept of *hindutva* as the basis of Indian nationality. According to Savarkar, "in Hindusthan the Hindus are a nation," while other groups are "communities" relegated to a marginal status (Purohit 1965:140). Here, one would think, is a personality who cannot fail to be divisive. But the *Amar Chitra Katha* version of his life, while it is called "Veer Savarkar" (309), is carefully subtitled "In the Andamans." As the introductory note explains, it depicts the lives of the exiled revolutionaries imprisoned in the Andaman Islands — the hardships and sacrifices they endured for their country. Savarkar is shown involved with his comrades in bomb-making and speech-making, then is arrested on page 9. He attempts to escape and is recaptured on page 11. By page 15 he is en route to the Andamans. Pages 16 and 17 are devoted to an illustrated factual insert called "Kala Pani (Andaman and Nicobar Islands)," page 18 to an advertisement for *Amar Chitra Katha*, pages 19 to 32 to his sufferings and heroic resistance in prison. The very last panel informs us that he was set free in 1937 and "took an active part in the struggle for freedom" (309:32). No doubt this is the most tactful way to treat V. D. Savarkar, if it is necessary to treat him at all. Since other, less communally tainted nationalist leaders are available for the series to depict, why make a point of depicting a communal one — and then trying to airbrush him into blandness?

But the *Amar Chitra Katha* vision of the freedom struggle, and indeed of modern Indian history in general, is far more invidiously selective than the above examples suggest. In the 1986 catalogue, "The Indian Revolutionaries" command excellent coverage, with five issues: *Bagha Jatin* (156), *Bhagat Singh* (234), *Chandra Shekhar Azad* (142), *Rash Behari Bose* (262), and *Veer Savarkar* (309). Netaji himself is not of their number, but figures in the "Makers of Modern India" series. According to *Amar Chitra Katha,* the "Makers of Modern India" are the persons enshrined in the following issues: *Babasaheb Ambedkar* (188), *C. R. Das* (344), *Dayananda* (120), *Jayaprakash Narayan* (206), *Lokamanya Tilak* (219), *Lal Bahadur Shastri* (271), *Rabindranath Tagore* (136), *Senapati Bapat* (303), *Subhas Chandra Bose* (77), *Subramania Bharati* (286), *Thanedar Hasan Askari* (286), *Vidyasagar* (108), and *Vivekananda* (146).

Netaji thus had his own issue as long ago as #77, followed by all the other important violent revolutionaries; V. D. Savarkar has his own is-

sue; the industrialist G. D. Birla (382) now has his own issue — how to-
tally inconceivable it is that Mahatma Gandhi does not have an issue! A delay of well over twenty years, in Gandhi's case, is inexplicable. Nor does
either Motilal or Jawaharlal Nehru, nor Sardar Patel, nor Rajagopalachari,
nor Krishna Menon, nor so many others who really were irrefutably among
the principal makers of modern India — while the list contains a couple
of names that would hardly appear on anyone's roster of major modern
figures.

Compared to these central and altogether glaring omissions, other
omissions appear almost unsurprising. There are as yet no women on the
"Makers of Modern India" list — no Sarojini Naidu (surely the obvious first
choice), no Kasturba Gandhi, no Kamala Nehru, no Durgabai Deshmukh,
no Anasuyabehn Sarabhai, no Vijayalakshmi Pandit. (And, it should be
noted, no Indira Gandhi.) Moreover, even outside the "Makers of Modern
India" category, there are no educated, urban, twentieth-century women in
the *Amar Chitra Katha* series at all — no women who lived in the kind of
world for which Pai is preparing his nephews and nieces. In fact, "Scientists
and Doctors" seems to be the only post-Independence category of honored
activity, the only one actually open to readers of *Amar Chitra Katha*. There
are four people in it: three male Hindus and Albert Einstein.

On the "Makers of Modern India" list there are no Muslims to speak of
either — no Dr. Zakir Husain, no Maulana Abul Kalam Azad, no Hakim
Ajmal Khan, no Asif Ali, no Khan Abdul Ghaffar Khan, no Sir Sayyid
Ahmad Khan. There is only *Thanedar Hasan Askari* (286), an issue devoted
to an idiosyncratic, apolitical police inspector in Uttar Pradesh in the 1930s.
This is the whole of what the introduction to the issue has to say about him:

> Sayyad Hasan Askari was born in an affluent and renowned family of Uttar
> Pradesh.
> After a brilliant record at the Police Training College, he became an instruc-
> tor at the same institute.
> Fourteen years later he was transferred to Kanpur as a police officer.
> Askari distinguished himself as a man of principle.
> This Amar Chitra Katha brings you a few episodes in the life of this extraor-
> dinary policeman. (286:inside front cover)

Thanedar Hasan Askari catches dacoits (the cover shows him leaping out at
them from a palanquin in which he has been posing as a woman) and
embarrasses his British superiors with his independence of mind. Once, to
make an obscure point, he rides a horse into a courtroom. Later, he suc-

cessfully practices homeopathy. He is loved by the people. Being too honest to curry favor, he retires as a lowly *thānedār.* Apart from his name, there is nothing Muslim about him.

The staff of *Amar Chitra Katha* claim that they are worried about Muslim "iconophobia" and have thus refrained from dealing with the Prophet and other Muslim religious figures. But this anxiety, though plausible in some contexts, cannot apply to modern and secular personalities. Yet Muslim readers are offered issues devoted only to a few early figures: they have *Shershah* (56) and *Sultana Razia* (110); they have the Mughals, who are portrayed on the whole rather favorably; and they have virtually no one since. There are no Sikh "Makers of Modern India" either. But the Sikhs get, in proportion to their numbers, far better coverage for their major historical and religious figures than the Muslims do. In fact, *Amar Chitra Katha*'s uniquely explicit ads for its coverage of "Sikh History and Legend" name a dozen titles, one of which is a Bumper Issue called *The Three Gurus* (96:inside back cover) (Figure 4.4). Interestingly, such communally focused advertising treatment is accorded only to the Sikhs — not to the Hindus, and certainly not to the Muslims, nor to any other religious group.

The Vision: Toward Cosmic Integration

Compared to other popular pamphlet genres like the traditional *kissā* (Pritchett 1985), *Amar Chitra Katha* is a remarkable feat of centralized control and consistency, over vast reaches of time and space. It has little in common with *kissā* and related genres. It is addressed to a different public: to Westernized children, rather than to traditional adults. It uses a different medium: comic book format, rather than plain, unillustrated prose. It is infinitely more highly organized, since it is deliberately designed by one editor, rather than haphazardly brought out by a large number of publishers. It has a different purpose: to educate and influence, rather than to delight and entertain. Invented, developed, and still controlled by one editor, *Amar Chitra Katha* has ultimately a single vision behind it: a vision of the cosmos, of the human place in it, of India as a certain kind of nation.

Religiously speaking, the chosen deity of *Amar Chitra Katha* is unquestionably Krishna — particularly in his cosmos-embodying form. National integration can thus become a special case of what might be called cosmic integration. The very first issue in the series was *Krishna* (11). The issue has been reprinted so often that it now has a flashy new cover (a

Figure 4.4. "Sikh History and Legend," *Amar Chitra Katha* issue number 96, March 1982, inside back cover, reprint edition. Courtesy of India Book House Pvt. Ltd.

"butter thief" one, like the original cover) and a (retrospectively added) introduction that begins with a flat statement: "Krishna is the most endearing and ennobling character in Indian mythology." All of the first twelve issues of the "Mahabharata" miniseries open with illustrations of the *Bhagavad Gītā* setting, with Arjuna kneeling before Krishna on the battlefield.

Figure 4.5. The cosmic Krishna breaking out of his full-page frame. *Amar Chitra Katha* issue number 127, p. 27. Courtesy of India Book House Pvt. Ltd.

Elsewhere in this miniseries too, the glorification of Krishna is emphasized (361:11–20), including his revenge on Shishupala (361:27–32).

A prominent feature of this glorification is an illustration of Krishna in his cosmic *puruṣa*-like form (361:17), with animals adhering to his legs, men and gods located higher on his gigantic body; this image is repeated on the front cover of the issue, and elsewhere at crucial points in the miniseries.[13] Most suggestively, in the early *The Geeta* (127), the awesome epiphany of Krishna as *kālānala,* the fire of time, with beings rushing into his gaping jaws and sticking between his teeth, is passed over entirely in favor of still another benevolent cosmic Krishna, a full-page rendering suffused with radiant beams of light (127:27) (Figure 4.5). This latter is, as far as I know, the only illustration anywhere in the whole *Amar Chitra Katha* series that breaks out of its frame: the crest of Krishna's headdress sweeps right on upward beyond the ruled border at the top of the page.

If the cosmos is assimilated into Krishna, all other living creatures are more or less assimilated into the human species. Hanuman, as we have seen, theoretically has an "apelike" form, yet not only he but the other chief monkeys as well are in fact, visually speaking, human beings with statuesque limbs, tall, fair Caucasian-flesh-colored hairless bodies, slightly convex faces, and tails that stick out at unobtrusive angles from the waistbands of their *dhotīs* (101:12); sometimes the tails themselves are omitted (101:25). Female monkeys look even more human, for they seem to wear their tails under their skirts (101:7–8). A particularly interesting example occurs in *Tales of Arjuna* (198), when Arjuna meets in the forest a small, brown, unclothed, furry, monkeylike monkey, who challenges him to a test of bridge-building skill. Later on, however, the monkey assumes a large and tall size, clothing, gold jewelry, hair on his head, and an upright stance, to reveal himself as Hanuman (198:1–8). Looking like a real monkey turned out to be Hanuman's disguise — and a very effective one.

It is not only monkeys who are basically human but the demonic Rakshasas as well: they tend to be large, stout, crude-looking, hairy, ugly humans, often potbellied, sometimes with small fangs, who wear fur loincloths (345:3). The Rakshasis are similar, except that they frequently transmute themselves into beautiful and entirely human-looking women. Even nature gods like "Ocean" are humanoid: Ocean turns out to have, protruding from the waves, the head of a white-haired gentleman with a curly mustache (101:1) (Figure 4.6). Ravana, by contrast, with his ten heads so firmly established in tradition, presents a special case — he is no gift to the

Figure 4.6. Humanoid monkeys, humanoid Dundubhi, humanoid Ocean. *Amar Chitra Katha* issue number 101, p. 1. Courtesy of India Book House Pvt. Ltd.

Figure 4.7. Ravana awake and asleep. *Amar Chitra Katha* issue number 254, p. 15, and issue number 19, p. 11. Courtesy of India Book House Pvt. Ltd.

cartoonist, and it turns out to be extremely difficult to portray him satisfactorily in action (254:15), or even asleep (19:11) (Figure 4.7).

When it comes to the Nagas, it seems visually that all the important ones are completely human, while some of the minor ones, such as those who attack Bhima, are completely snakelike small snakes (335:19–21). Yet the human ones (the only ones who speak) speak as snakes. "He woke up when we bit him," says a nice-looking, ornamented, fully human Naga about the attack on Bhima (335:21) (Figure 4.8). When the Nagas realize that the Pandavas are their blood relatives, they treat Bhima with generous hospitality and give him a lavish boon (335:22–23). A footnote observes:

Figure 4.8. Nagas: fully snake or fully human. *Amar Chitra Katha* issue number 335, p. 21. Courtesy of India Book House Pvt. Ltd.

"According to many scholars the Nagas were a race of people with whom the Aryans freely mixed" (335:19). A glossary entry in the same "Mahabharata" issue will surely complete the confusion of any young reader: "Literally the serpents—Also refers to the race of snake-worshippers or a race which has the snake for its totem. Perhaps the ancestors of the modern inhabitants of India's north-eastern state Nagaland" (335:32). Later Arjuna is seduced by the Naga princess Ulupi, who is portrayed as a beautiful, lovable, fully human girl, and who gives him a boon after their enjoyable night together (355:2–4). But then in the very next issue a whole clan of Nagas are among the inhabitants deliberately burned alive in the Khandava Forest by Agni—with the active, unquestioning, even enthusiastic help of Krishna and Arjuna (357:15). The rationalistic "humanization" practiced by *Amar Chitra Katha* on all other species thus creates new problems of its own.

Moreover, the human species itself is assimilated as much as possible into a uniform, idealized, muscular, fair-skinned, blank-faced physical type. With very few exceptions, men have a generic classically proportioned male body, and women a generic full-breasted, slim-waisted female one; they all have the same regular features and extremely fair skin color. They all live in the same nondescript kind of palaces and dress themselves in the same limited range of "classic" styles. They all speak the same lofty "Sanskritic" language. In issues set in the modern world, these pressures are sometimes resisted; but they are still often operative, especially for the depiction of heroes and heroines.

Amar Chitra Katha: An Evolving Tradition

Many of the changes in the series over the last twenty-five years are minor and unsurprising. Some involve an increase in publishing sophistication. Pages used to have nothing on them except picture panels. By now, however, they are equipped not only with page numbers but also with headers naming alternately the title and the series. Moreover, the inside front cover now offers the date of publication (which never used to be given) and full bibliographic information. Spellings of proper names are now somewhat more scholarly, though not perfectly so. Footnotes also now occur from time to time, usually defining problematical words or citing related stories.

One trend to which I have called attention, that of publishing *Amar Chitra Katha* issues in book form, seems likely to increase. The "Editor's

Choice" catalogue, published in 1988, contains only bound volumes. This trend too, like *Amar Chitra Katha* itself, is a considerable innovation. In traditional genres, many separate, related pamphlets may occasionally be bound and sold as a unit. For example, in the case of the *Ālha khaṇḍ,* the individual episodes — which usually center on a battle (*laṛāī*), or a wedding (*byāh*) — are most often sold separately; sometimes a few giant fat books are made by binding many pamphlets together to create some (never definitive) approximation of the whole cycle. But this is an uncommon practice, confined in any case largely to the assembling of various segments of preexisting long cycles. It is due chiefly to the demands of buyers who want large amounts of material in portable form.

In the case of *Amar Chitra Katha,* collecting the comics into book form makes sense for the sellers. By now, since well over five hundred titles are (at least theoretically) in print, not even the most zealous bookseller has the space to display them properly. If they are gathered into books — especially hardbound ones — they can be displayed much more conveniently, standing upright on shelves, with their binding revealing their titles. Yet entirely independent stories do not always harmonize well; it may not be possible to put them together into units attractive enough to induce customers to pay the higher prices involved. One result, naturally, is the pre-planned miniseries. This means that *Amar Chitra Katha* is gradually tending to produce, in effect, book-sized narratives of varying format (containing comics, prose, maps, advertisements, and even bibliographies) in serialized installments, rather than the thirty-two-page, free-standing comic books of tradition. It is not for nothing that both the originally planned length of the "Mahabharata" miniseries (sixty issues) and its actual length (forty-two issues) divide perfectly into six-issue volumes — as does the six-issue "March to Freedom" miniseries.

Amar Chitra Katha promises parents to "screen each word and each picture as they have a lasting impact on impressionable minds," to be "more a vehicle of education than a business." As the series has progressed, it has become obvious that this "vehicle of education" offers much better transport to some of its readers than to others. Readers who happen to be of the wrong gender, the wrong politics, or the wrong religion will find themselves only scantily represented in what is ultimately a vision of the future at least as much as of the past. *Amar Chitra* should be paid the compliment of being held to its own oft-professed standards: it can and should do much better.

Despite such serious reservations and criticisms, however, there is much to commend in *Amar Chitra Katha*. All things considered, the influence of the series is undoubtedly constructive. *Amar Chitra Katha* readers may indeed be led to hate the British, who are no longer there to object, but they will also be led to hate untouchability and to feel outrage at the plight of the poor and to admire the gallant deeds of at least some women and some non-Hindus. And they will never, in any issue that I've seen, be led to feel hostility toward one another. They will have a strong, positive sense of India as a multicultural nation in which they can all work together.

Notes

1. Anant Pai, interviewed by John S. Hawley in Bombay on January 9, 1989. All quotations, direct or indirect, attributed to Pai in the text that follows are drawn from this interview. Jack Hawley's work has contributed greatly to this paper, and I very much appreciate his assistance. In addition, I want to thank the editors, L. A. Babb and Susan Wadley, for the careful, thoughtful work they have done in helping this paper to attain its present form. Susan Wadley also provided more recent material from the 1990s to supplement my own work done in the late 1980s.

2. Anant Pai, interview by J. S. Hawley.

3. See, for example, the inside back cover of issue *Harischandra* (17). Parenthesized numbers after titles refer, throughout this chapter, to the issue's ordinal number within the series, a number assigned and used for reference by the series itself. Where relevant, the issue number is followed by a colon and the appropriate page number(s) within the issue.

4. At least, they were so advertised inside the front cover of *Rama* (15).

5. K. T. Mirchandani, head of the IBH branch in Delhi, interview by F. W. Pritchett, August 20, 1986.

6. The word is also more conventionally explained as referring to the Pandavas, sons of Prtha (Pai 1986:29).

7. K. T. Mirchandani, interview by F. W. P., August 10, 1986.

8. Only 327 titles are included in this taxonomic list, making it a bit out of date even for 1986, but the titles published since the catalogue came out are generally advertised within the same categories. As of mid-1989 this 1986 catalogue was still the one mailed out by the U.S. distributor, Admans Enterprises; I do not think a later one has been produced yet.

9. Their lives are described from childhood until the triumphant conclusion of Yudhishthira's *rājasūya yajña*.

10. Originally advertised as *The Battle of Kurukshetra* (17:inside back cover).

11. This advertisement appears on the back cover of the reprinted version of *Vali* (101) included in the Bumper Issue "Stories from the Ramayana" (#2).

12. The Ekalavya story, carefully stripped of its macabre conclusion, is actually used as an example in *The PARTHA Way to Success:* the statue of Drona, it seems, "helped Ekalavya to think positively"—which "does demonstrate the power of positive thinking" (Pai 1986:21).

13. For example, when Sanjaya describes Krishna's grandeur (383:25), and when Krishna seeks to overawe Duryodhana into seeking peace (385:17).

References

Gangadhar, V. 1988. "Anant Pai and his Amar Chitra Kathas." *Reader's Digest* [of India], August.

India Book House. 1986. *Catalogue: Amar Chitra Katha.* Bombay: India Book House.

Pai, Anant. 1986. *The PARTHA Way to Success.* Bombay: India Book House.

Pritchett, Frances W. 1985. *Marvelous Encounters: Folk Romance in Urdu and Hindi.* New Delhi: Manohar Publications; and Riverdale, Md.: The Riverdale Company.

Purohit, B. R. 1965. *Hindu Revivalism and Indian Nationalism.* Sagar, M.P.: Sathi Prakashan.

Richman, Paula, ed. 1991. *Many Ramayanas: The Diversity of a Narrative Tradition in South Asia.* Berkeley: University of California Press.

John Stratton Hawley

5. The Saints Subdued: Domestic Virtue and National Integration in *Amar Chitra Katha*

Amar Chitra Katha is an ungainly beast, including everything from stories of the Mughal jokester Birbal to portraits of great "scientists and doctors" and "the makers of modern India." Yet one theme unifies the series in the eyes of its founder and editor, Anant Pai, and that is its moral resolve: the commitment to preparing today's Indian children, especially the urban and English-speaking among them, for a modern world. Almost every story is in some way intended to show how India's shared and for the most part premodern past can provide these children with guidelines for right living.

One of the major vehicles for achieving this objective is hagiography, the full-color portrayal of consistently, unerringly, and overwhelmingly exemplary lives. A good deal of this hagiography is implicit, as various figures from the life of Humayun or the plot of *Ānanda Maṭh* are brought forward and bathed in the light of exemplitude. But there is explicit hagiography too: the special issue devoted to Jesus Christ, the comic concerned with the Jain *tīrthankara* Mahavira, the issue depicting Vivekananda and subtitled "The Patriot-Saint of Modern India," and, of course, the many volumes that deal with *sant*s, *bhakta*s, and *ācārya*s from the more distant Hindu past. In this chapter we will investigate a subset of these Hindu hagiographies that allows us to make comparisons between *Amar Chitra Katha*'s idea of what a sainted life was about and versions that were produced in earlier centuries. By studying the new against the background of the old, we hope to see more clearly the process of selection that makes an *Amar Chitra Katha* saint a saint.

At issue will be the six volumes of *Amar Chitra Katha* that deal with North Indian poet-saints of the so-called *bhakti* period, that is, the late fifteenth to early seventeenth centuries. We will begin with Mirabai, since Anant Pai and his staff did the same and since her life touches on several matters that Frances Pritchett has raised in speaking about attitudes toward gender in *Amar Chitra Katha* in Chapter 4. Mira, too, shows how an exemplar of religious ecstasy — her traditional role — could be transformed into a paragon of general female virtue, a good model for character-building for young middle-class Indians of the late twentieth century. Then we will turn to the five other saints in the group, devoting particular attention to the way in which they are made to serve the *Amar Chitra Katha* goal of encouraging "national integration." In all these lives, *Amar Chitra Katha* has developed its own perspective on Indian religion, and Pai's theological commitments, especially his vision of the inclusiveness of truth, have been worked out in a variety of ways. Finally, we will consider the extent to which this new understanding of Indian religion is forced on the comic-book series not just by the theology of its editor and his staff but by the distinctively new medium in which they work.

Mirabai Improved

The six poet-saints within our range are, in the order adopted by *Amar Chitra Katha,* Mirabai (36), Nanak (*Guru Nanak* [47]), Kabir (55), Tulsidas (62), Surdas (*Soordas* [137]), and Ravidas (*Guru Ravidas* [350]).[1] The order and spacing of this list may reflect the values of Pai and his associates, but they undoubtedly also provide a rough indication of their guess as to the relative importance of these saints in the national imagination. Unquestionably Mirabai comes first, a judgment that would be confirmed by the number of commercial films made about her since the inception of Indian sound cinematography.[2] In explaining Mira's widespread popularity not only in the north but in the south, the *Amar Chitra Katha* staff specifically cited the influence of these films, especially the one in which M. S. Subbalaxmi, a Tamil, played and sang the leading role (Sadashivam 1947).[3]

I have elsewhere described primary elements in the traditional hagiography of Mirabai, for which our earliest sources are the brief paean offered by Nabhadas in his *Bhaktamāl* of about 1600 C.E. and the more extended treatment of Priyadas, who in 1712 prepared a commentary on that work called the *Bhaktirasabodhinī* (Hawley and Juergensmeyer 1988:122–27). Numerous other versions of Mira's life have appeared in print during the three-and-a-half-century span since the composition of the *Bhaktirasabodhinī,* and in them important departures from Priyadas's understanding of Mira are recorded. The most obvious of these concerns Mira's placement in history.

Judging by what Colonel James Tod was told near the beginning of the nineteenth century, it was conventional at least in western Rajasthan at that time to conceive of Mira as the wife of Rana Kumbha, the great Marwari king who was the outstanding builder of its first capital, Chittor. When it was observed, however, that this would ill accord with the dates ascribed to Mira's father in Merta, a husband later in the line of Mewari princes and kings was selected to fill the role of the unnamed *rāṇā* in Mira's poetry and early hagiography. This was Bhojraj, whose sixteenth-century dates fit nicely with those of Mira's supposed father. Bhojraj had a further advantage—he died young, which meant that his own good name could remain unchallenged while the role of "bad *rāṇā*," so important in the legend and poetry of Mirabai, passed from him to his younger brother Vikramajit. The latter became the one who tried to poison Mira and could be held largely responsible for driving her from her in-laws' house. This solution to the puzzle of accommodating the legend of Mira to Rājpūt history has remained intact even to the present. The national media, especially radio, have undoubtedly played a role in standardizing this version of the story, but whatever the cause, Rājpūt women living in Udaipur today accept it as truth and apparently know no other (Harlan 1987:ch. 7).

Amar Chitra Katha also accepts this version of the story, but prefers to tell it without naming the evil prince as Vikramajit. This obviates the need to insult any member of the heroic Mewari line directly and thereby damage the cause of "national integration"—or, incidentally, the size of *Amar Chitra Katha*'s readership. It illustrates one of Pai's general principles of operation, the Sanskrit maxim "satyam bruyāt priyam bruyāt mā bruyāt satyam apriyam." As mentioned in Chapter 4, his translation is: "You must tell the truth; you must tell what is pleasant. And that which is unpleasant—just because it is true, you need not say it."

If *Amar Chitra Katha* leaves something out, it also puts something in, and that too in the apparent cause of domesticating Mira. Nabhadas placed great emphasis on Mira's fearlessness, and the object to be feared—though she does not—was the *rāṇā* into whose family she had married. (Whether this *rāṇā* was her husband or her father-in-law is unspecified; context makes the latter seem more likely than the former.) Similarly for Priyadas, the linchpin in the entire tale of Mira's life was her defiance of codes of obedience and loyalty that govern the behavior of any Hindu wife, certainly a Rājpūt. Her rebelliousness was the measure of her conviction that she was married to a higher Lord, Krishna.

In the Mirabai comic book all this is changed: Mira's *bhakti* is made

Figure 5.1. Mira in her household. *Amar Chitra Katha* issue number 36, p. 4. Courtesy of India Book House Pvt. Ltd.

consonant with her fulfillment of a woman's *dharma*.[4] The text asserts forthrightly that "Mira was an ideal Hindu wife" and that she "was loved by her husband" (36:4), claiming that she would perform her "household duties" fully before turning her attention to "her divine husband—her Gopala—whom she had brought with her [to Chittor]" (36:4). The illustration makes the point even more emphatic by giving primary attention to a scene in which Mira bows at Bhojraj's feet. That vignette, representing what the text describes as Mira's priorities, is rendered in color and is allotted the greater part of the band in which it appears. The remainder, a scene showing Mira seated in devotion before her icon of Krishna, is smaller and done in silhouette (36:4; see Figure 5.1).

In the pages that follow, the plot line further buttresses the reader's sense of Mira's fidelity to her *rāṇā*. The moment at which Mira crosses the threshold in Chittor and defiantly refuses her mother-in-law's command that she should embrace the tutelary goddess of the royal household (*kula-devī*) is transposed from the place it held in Priyadas's account to the scene that follows the one we have just seen. This means that Mira defies her mother-in-law (with tearful apologies) only after her devotion to her husband has been established; and lest this conflict between mother-in-law and daughter-in-law be too brilliantly apparent, the plot at this point turns quickly away from Bhojraj's mother. Priyadas goes on to tell how the older woman complained bitterly to her husband, the senior *rāṇā*, who determined at that point to kill Mira, but *Amar Chitra Katha* attributes no responsibility to the mother-in-law. It transfers the onus to Bhojraj's sister Uda, whom Priyadas depicts in a more favorable light and does not mention by name (Priyadas in Nabhadas 1969:716–18). As in many a popular movie and pulp novel, this sister-in-law, now an evil force, connives to turn her brother against his new bride, and ultimately succeeds.

Two incidents are involved, and both involve further alterations in the order given by Priyadas. The first vignette is the one in which the *rāṇā* hears Mira whispering sweet nothings to a lover behind closed doors. In Priyadas's version this episode follows the one involving poison, but here it precedes. The "punch line" of the story is, of course, that the *rāṇā* discovers his would-be rival to be none other than Krishna himself, present to Mira in image form. That outcome persists here, too, but the evil Uda is made responsible for the fact that the king's suspicions are aroused in the first place. Since the *rāṇā* does no actual harm to Mira in this incident—the only cost is to himself, for he comes across as a fool—it is an appropriate one to associate with good prince Bhojraj. Hence it is moved forward. The at-

Figure 5.2. Mira with her companions. *Amar Chitra Katha* issue number 36, p. 11. Courtesy of India Book House Pvt. Ltd.

tempt to poison Mira is quite a different matter and must be reserved for his wicked brother.

The second incident inserted at this point is the story that Akbar once joined the throngs who gathered to hear Mira sing. This tale, too, is related in Priyadas's *Bhaktirasabodhinī*, but, again, later. When given its new position earlier in the story, it can be put to a clever use, for Akbar, after he hears Mira sing, asks permission to lay a garland at the feet of her lord. In a motif that echoes the traditional story of Mira's accepting the poison the *rāṇā* offered to her image of Krishna, Mira says she cannot refuse. Akbar makes the offering, but it is reported to Bhojraj, presumably by Uda and her ilk, as if Akbar had touched not Krishna's feet but Mira's own. "For the disgrace you have brought to the fair name of Rajputana" — by allowing "a Muslim cur" to touch her feet — the angry Bhojraj commands her to leave and go drown herself. This provides an occasion to convert Mira's courage, the guiding leitmotif in older tellings of her story, into a display of wifely decorum. She remains silent through the entire tirade. As the final caption in this scene puts it, "Mira, the true Hindu wife, did not protest" (36:11; see Figure 5.2).

At this point Mira goes off to Brindavan, where she is perceived as "Radha reborn," an artful adaptation of an evaluation made long ago by Nabhadas, that "like a latter-day *gopī*, she showed the meaning of devotion to our devastated age" (Priyadas in Nabhadas 1969:712–13). The old story of her confrontation with Jiv Gosvami in Brindavan there is omitted, an encounter in which she implicitly accuses him of theological stupidity. He refuses to see her because he is observing a vow that prevents him from having any contact with women so that he can avoid any temptation to compromise his total devotion to Krishna. Mira points out to him, through a messenger, that if one sees things aright there is really only one male in the world, Krishna himself, so the question of any other attraction between the sexes disappears.

In the story as Priyadas tells it, Jiv relents and all is well, but evidently the element of contest seemed out of character for the Sita-like Mira depicted by *Amar Chitra Katha*. Instead her presence in Brindavan is used as an occasion for Bhojraj — a good-hearted man, after all — to see the error of his ways. He is delighted to learn that Mira is still alive and hastens off to beg her forgiveness and urge her to return to Chittor. She accepts and they depart together, quite over and above anything Nabhadas or Priyadas ever suspected; it is on that note of conjugal amity that Bhojraj expires.

His death provides the occasion for another new twist: Bhojraj's father orders Mira to prepare herself to become a *sati*. Mira resists on the grounds that she is not yet a widow — her true husband, Krishna, is still alive — and her refusal explains the animosity that is directed against her in the palace at Chittor ever after. The famous incident of ineffectual poisoning follows — not once but twice, for by the nineteenth century one story had been cloned into two. Even so, it is only a letter from Tulsidas, her brother in the family of *bhakta*s, that persuades Mirabai to leave Bhojraj's family behind. The existence of such a letter is reported in the *Mūl Gosāī Carit,* in all likelihood another nineteenth-century document (Lutgendorf 1993), and its receipt is very convenient at this point in Mira's biography: she leaves for her natal family in Merta.

Then she is finally at peace, and though she leaves Chittor with the black hair of a woman no older than middle age it is only "a few more years" before her hair is shown as white. The text says "Mira was growing old. She knew that her end was near" (36:29). At that point she sets out again for her old haunts in Mathura and Brindavan, and then moves on to Dvaraka, where she "fell into a trance and fainted on her Lord" (36:31). In the final scene she is shown as an inset in Krishna's heart. The text says she "became one with the Lord she had worshipped and yearned for, ever since she had taken him for her bridegroom, at the tender age of five!!" (36:32).

Several elements are worth noting about the way the *Amar Chitra Katha* version of Mira's story ends. First, it happens in old age, a matter about which Priyadas has nothing to say. Old age is convenient because it adds further justification to Mira's decision to leave her husband's family behind, as a female ascetic, a *sanyāsinī* or *vairāginī,* might do. Though certain of the poems attributed to her do suggest that she yearned for such a life (Hawley, in press), this desire squares ill with the image of "a perfect Hindu wife." In old age, however, the offense is blunted, since that is the proper time for a person to choose a life of wandering — particularly a man, of course, but if at all the case arises, a woman as well.

Second, something like a *digvijaya* — the "world victory tour" that is a frequent feature in the lives of philosophically minded saints — is introduced. While Priyadas knows only of a pilgrimage to Dvaraka, it is here amplified to include the Braj region. This serves also to underscore the romantic relation between Mira and Krishna that is so evident to any reader of the series.

Finally, a significant alteration has occurred in the image of how it was that Mira ultimately died. The traditional story states that she was absorbed into the image of Krishna at Dvaraka, but here we have not a word about such an event. Instead, Mira falls into a swoon and Krishna — the image, as it were — is shown bending over to receive her (see Figure 5.3). This does not exactly contradict the traditional story, but it also does not exactly repeat it: the element of miracle has been omitted. The text says that Mira "becomes one with the Lord" (36:32), and the drawing represents this event by showing her as a medallion in the heart of the living Krishna (see Figure 5.4).

Despite the comic book idiom, in which it would be both possible and effective to show that miracles do happen, it is a general feature of *Amar Chitra Katha* policy to play down this element in volumes that are not explicitly mythological in nature. There are exceptions, particularly early in the series — several of the miracles of Jesus figure in "Jesus Christ" and the cover of the issue on Kabir shows him walking on water — but when one compares the *Amar Chitra Katha* versions of these lives to traditional accounts, as in the case of Mirabai, the element of moderation becomes clear.[5] An introductory disclaimer has appeared on the inside cover of reprints of the Mirabai comic at least since 1980, to the effect that "the story of Mira, as narrated in this book, is based on legends about her and not on historical facts." But even so, a restraining, rationalizing hand seems to have been at work bringing the saint within the purview of what modern children and their parents might construe as the realm of the possible. Here one sees shadows of the Protestant Reformation and the Enlightenment, as conveyed in the English language education that has shaped India's middle and upper classes since the nineteenth century.[6]

A somewhat parallel matter, one that intrudes into secular lives as well as religious ones, is the problem of what to do with violence. Here too the restraining hand prevails, and the staff at *Amar Chitra Katha* has a clear sense of its "satyam bruyāt priyam bruyāt" policy. They wish to keep too much blood and gore from the eyes of children, but are at pains to serve this "pleasant" (*priyam*) desideratum while they stay as close to the truth (*satyam*) as they can.

For them, the famous case concerns Akbar's cruelty as a young king. The writer of the volume on Akbar had wanted to show how Akbar's increasing maturity meant that he put aside this aspect of his character, but to make the point some episode from his early years had to be told. His beheading of Hemu was chosen, but it was reported only in the text. The accompanying illustration shows not the beheading itself but the gallows where it occurred, and that, like Mira's late-in-the-day devotion to Krishna, only in silhouette. It is the illustration that makes the lasting impression, the

Figure 5.3. Mira in a trance. *Amar Chitra Katha* issue number 36, p. 31. Courtesy of India Book House Pvt. Ltd.

Figure 5.4. Mira as one with her Lord. *Amar Chitra Katha* issue number 36, p. 32. Courtesy of India Book House Pvt. Ltd.

staff observed, not the text. But lest children be aghast at what Akbar did, the text mitigates the blame: "Poor Hemu's headless body was displayed on a gibbet. This was a cruel practice in those days" (200:7).

Violence and the emotion it engenders, fear, are downplayed in the religious realm, too. Pai rejected a proposal to do an issue on the snake goddess Manasa because it might have stimulated too much fear in children, and for the same reason he several times fended off an *Amar Chitra Katha* entry on Santoshi Ma.[7] The culminating episode in the story, in which this goddess goes on a rampage of destruction because someone had tampered with food offered to and blessed by her (*prasād*), was dismissed by Pai as being not only fearsome but unworthy and superstitious, a "degradation of Hinduism." Another version of the same motif would have had to figure in a proposed issue on Satyanarayanan of Tirupati — another reject, despite the publisher's enthusiasm for the fact that it would have had guaranteed sales. There again, as Pai explained, a "punitive god" demands restitution when a devotee forgets to eat *prasād,* and this he would not print. After all, "there is no point in fostering faith in God for the wrong reasons."[8]

A final area in which restraint is thought to be called for is that of sex. Priyadas's account of Mirabai's life tells with relish of an incident in which a lecher makes his way into the company of Mira's devotees, then manages to force his attentions on her when she is alone. He tells her that her Giridhar — that is, Krishna — has commanded her to submit, and she is never one to challenge Krishna's word. All she requires is that whatever they do be done in the proper *bhakti* setting — before the eyes of all the other devotees. This amazes the evil man and brings him to his senses; her unquestioning submission to even a lecher's invoking of Krishna brings about his conversion.

This episode, which appears as well in the lives of other female saints memorialized by Priyadas and must have been a major motif in the Vaiṣṇava hagiography of his time, is omitted in the *Amar Chitra Katha* retelling of Mira's life. And no wonder: Kamala Chandrakant, who was associate editor of the series for fifteen years, quipped that Pai often seemed to think it would strain the bonds of propriety to show a man and a woman sitting together on a couch having a normal conversation (Chandrakant interview). But if sex is out, romance of a certain sort is definitely in. The scenes of amorous devotion in which Mira encounters Krishna are lavishly, delicately depicted (Figure 5.5) (36:13). The Krishna to whom Mira referred in her poems may have been Giridhar Nagar, the heroic "clever Mountain-

Figure 5.5. Mira with her Lord. *Amar Chitra Katha* issue number 36, p. 13. Courtesy of India Book House Pvt. Ltd.

Lifter," but the Krishna we see here is definitely the erotic Krishna, the one who bears the flute, not the mountain.[9]

The *Amar Chitra Katha* staff took a nonsectarian pride in the fact that the illustrator for this issue was Yusuf Lien (nowadays Yusuf Bangalore-wala), a Muslim. Pai recalled the special care that Bangalorewala lavished on this volume by telling how he once visited him at his house to urge him toward completion, only to find the artist in tears as he drew. Bangalore-wala's explanation of how he could accomplish what for a Muslim ought to have been a feat of interreligious imagination was that he had the Muslim "saint" Rabia in the back of his mind much of the time. Here is a man who happily fulfills the hope enunciated by V. Raghavan over All-India Radio in 1966, that the *bhakti* saints ought to serve and in fact do serve as "The Great Integrators" of Indian culture: "Emotional integration which helps to sustain territorial integration is an achievement on a different plane and is a matter of culture, personal, social and national" (Raghavan 1966:15).

Pieces in a Puzzle of National Integration

The motif of national integration is sounded at various levels in the comic book lives of the saints of North India—sometimes explicitly, sometimes not. Little could be more direct than what is said about Kabir on the cover of the English-language version of the volume describing him: he is billed as "the mystic who tried to bring the Hindus and the Muslims together."[10] The text reinforces the theme. One caption says "It pained the good man to see religion, caste and creed keeping people apart" (Figure 5.6) (55:14), and in the scene that follows we see Kabir addressing the multitudes with these words: "Let people worship God according to their convictions" (55:14). This live-and-let-live attitude is not without exception. In the following frame Kabir is shown challenging what is called, in the biblical phrase, "idol-worship" (55:14), but this is used to introduce the enmity that Hindus felt in response, and the last scene in the sequence returns us to the integrationist perspective. Kabir prays, "God, give me the strength to break the barriers of hate between men" (55:14). This message is reinforced on the inside front cover of the English-language version. As in the Hindi counterpart, five epigrams attributed to Kabir are quoted (in translation). Four of the five are the same, but the fifth—the clincher, as it were—appears to be an *Amar Chitra Katha* invention in English that puts together

Figure 5.6. Kabir. *Amar Chitra Katha* issue number 55, p. 14. Courtesy of India Book House Pvt. Ltd.

elements from various poems in Hindi: "In the beginning, there was no Turk, nor Hindu — no race, nor caste."

In fairness, it is well to observe that this synthetic ideology of saint-hood is less clearly articulated in the case of Nanak than in the case of Kabir, perhaps in response to Sikhs' own sensitivity to a depiction of their faith as a simple amalgam of Hinduism and Islam. Nanak is shown as Kabir should be: a critic of malpractice on the part of both Hindus and Muslims, and a member of neither camp (47:19–20, 24–25). In other saints' lives, how-ever, the theme reasserts itself. Tulsidas, for example, is portrayed as a peace-maker between two Hindu rulers, Rana Pratap of Mewar and Raja Man-singh of Jaipur, as he persuades Mansingh to abandon an aggressive course of action pursued on behalf of Akbar. Remarkably, Akbar is pleased (62:27–30).

In the volume on Surdas, which lays particular emphasis on Sur's childhood, this irenic motif is seemingly translated into the idiom of chil-dren themselves. In the hagiography presented in Hariray's commentary on the *Caurāsī Vaiṣṇavan kī Vārtā,* probably composed in the late seventeenth century, Sur's father despairs at the impact a blind child will have on the family's already meager finances, and in the *Amar Chitra Katha* version this motif is expanded into cruelty on the part of both Sur's parents. Again, there is some precedent in the *Vārtā* (Hariray in Parikh 1970:401–3). What is new is that Sur's brothers, who are nowhere mentioned in the *Vārtā,* are brought into the act. In a true-to-life motif, these children are depicted as having been even crueler than the adults.[11] They torment poor Sur mer-cilessly (137:2–5). The enmity between Sur and his brother does not, however, go unmended. Years later — and again, in an episode I have not encountered elsewhere — two of Sur's brothers hear him sing, see him ac-claimed, and are moved to beg forgiveness for the sins of their youth. The happy scene that ensues is a model of reconciliation. Sur says, "Dear, dear brothers! Don't put me to shame by uttering such words. I have nothing but love for you" (137:22).

This story of reconciliation is a recent one, if not actually invented for *Amar Chitra Katha.* Another motif that buttresses the spirit of national integration is a genuinely traditional one, however, and is made to play a prominent role in the comic book classics. I refer to the notion that the saints of North India were in communication with one another or were related in other ways, either because they were approached with reverence by the same rulers or because they took initiation from one another or a common guru. *Amar Chitra Katha* seems eager to establish the existence of this far-reaching network of saints. As in seventeenth-century hagiography (Parikh 1970:415; Nabhadas 1969:721), both Sur and Mira are made to receive visits from Akbar (36:7–9, 137:24–28), and — a more recent addition to legend — Akbar dispatches a message to Tulsidas as well (62:29–30). Other stories, apparently first attested in the nineteenth century,[12] tell of direct contacts between Tulsidas and the other two saints, and these are happily repeated as well (36:27, 137:29).

In instances where legend reports contacts between the various saints for the purpose of showing that one is superior to another, *Amar Chitra Katha* remains not unexpectedly silent. We hear nothing of the Sikh legend in which Kabir acknowledges the primacy of Nanak, for example,[13] and there is nothing to suggest that a rivalry exists between Kabīrpanthīs and Ravidāsīs, as one deduces from accounts of debates between the supposed founders of these two communities (Hawley and Juergensmeyer 1988:45– 46). Caution is also observed in dealing with the numerous stories intended to show that most of these saints have a Brahman connection; only Mira and Nanak escape. Sur and Tulsi are commonly assumed to have been Brahmans, but Kabir and Ravidas were not. So certain among Kabir's hagiographers tell a version of "Moses in the bullrushes" to show how he, though brought up in a low-caste Muslim family, was really a Brahman, and Priyadas portrays Ravidas as a Brahman in the life immediately preceding his birth as an Untouchable.[14] Then when Priyadas tells how, in a confrontation with some Brahman foes, Ravidas peeled back the layers of his chest to reveal a sacred thread inside, this inner Brahmanhood already has its physical antetype.

To repeat such stories in the form in which they have been received would scarcely serve the cause of national integration, so they are either omitted or foreshortened. We see Kabir being discovered by his Muslim foster parents at the riverbank (not in the river, which might have seemed needlessly miraculous), but nothing is said of his true parentage (55:1–3). As for Ravidas, his comic book life makes no mention of his being a Brahman at all, interior or otherwise. This is one of the best known episodes in traditional accounts of Ravidas's life, even as told by many Ravidāsīs,[15] so the omission is striking. Certain recent interpreters of Ravidas from among the Camār community have wished to disown the story altogether, especially the influential Lucknow writer Candrikaprasad Jijnasu, who desired so intensely to separate Ravidas from the Brahman and even the larger Hindu tradition that he made him out to be a Buddhist (Jijnasu 1969).[16] *Amar Chitra Katha* did not go so far as to embrace that point of view, which is accepted by most Camārs in any event, but especially after the Valmiki incident it wanted to be prudent about the whole affair. The result was silence.

On another matter, however, silence was not possible. Just as the Ravidāsī community preferred that the incident of the thread be omitted, so did they insist that another incident be included. This was the episode in which it is asserted that Mirabai traveled to Benares to be initiated by Ravidas. This story has a complicated history; if it is accepted as true by the public at large, that phenomenon is only recent.[17] The roots of the tradition are probably to be traced to a similar-sounding episode involving a Rajasthani queen named Jhali, who is said by Priyadas to have come to Benares in search of initiation and to have chosen Ravidas as her *guru* (Priyadas in Nabhadas 1969:477–78). At some point the increasingly well-known Mira seems to have superseded this Jhali, and the story itself changed in response. Gone now is the story of how the initiation was vindicated at a banquet from which Ravidas had been excluded by the Brahmans in Queen Jhali's entourage: miraculously he took his place between each pair of them as they began to eat. Instead we have the simple story of Mirabai being initiated by Ravidas, and no one to challenge.

The staff of *Amar Chitra Katha* was faced with a delicate situation when urged by low-caste leaders to include Mira in its account of Ravidas. On the one hand, it wished to be as conciliatory as possible, but on the other hand it did not wish to raise the hackles of others in Mirabai's much broader and more loosely defined community of devotees. The result was a careful compromise. Mira would be included, but there would be no mention of initiation as such. Instead, she comes to Ravidas to be cured. She says, "My love for my husband [Krishna, that is] has driven me mad" (350:30).

Even with this alteration, however, the tilt is toward the Ravidāsīs, who after all would figure largely in the readership of this particular issue. In the title itself Ravidas is called "Guru Ravidas," a fact that not only sets him parallel with the Sikh *guru*s, as Punjabi Ravidāsīs have for some time wished, but describes his relation to Mira. Moreover, he is shown with a halo, while Mira is not; and he is shown lecturing to her while she says nothing in response. Most pointedly, she is made to set down her image of Krishna at the conclusion of this one-sided colloquy. She faces Ravidas as he lifts his hand in what might be a gesture of blessing (350:31; Figure 5.7).

If one has closely followed the text, one would certainly interpret this as a response in which Mira subordinates her erstwhile *saguṇa* religiosity to

Figure 5.7. Guru Ravidas. *Amar Chitra Katha* issue number 350, p. 31. Courtesy of India Book House Pvt. Ltd.

the message of *nirguṇa* faith, for Ravidas has told her that with her and Krishna "God and devotee have become one" (350:31). She needs her image no longer. But if one has been less than fully attentive to the text, things might look different, for there is an element of compromise. As Mira puts down her icon, she picks up her *tambūrā*, and, though the text makes no mention of the fact, readers would quickly assume that she is singing to Ravidas. This puts the shoe on the other foot — Mira gives, Ravidas receives — and it is well to recall in this connection what Pai's staff have to say about the relative impact of word and illustration: the latter, unquestionably, registers the stronger impression.

Amar Chitra Katha's handling of Mira seems an adroit way of telling truth in an inclusive fashion and making the saints serve the cause of "national integration": a relation is established and, one hopes, neither party to the meeting is offended. And if this inspires admiration, one may also be impressed by the comic book treatment of the Ravidas story line as a whole. He is by no means made a Brahman — the old indigenous vessel for "national integration," at least in its cultural mode — but he is made to enunciate a theology that sounds very much like the Vedantin position held in esteem by many of India's new elites. These are still in large proportion Brahman, but the Brahmans are joined by merchant-caste groups such as the Birlas, whose charitable trust underwrites the publication of the script for Pai's videotape "Ekam Sat" and one of whose family members is featured in a recent volume of *Amar Chitra Katha*.[18]

The Ravidas comic begins with a long section showing how as a boy Ravidas became aware of the discrimination directed against his caste and refused to accept it. None of this is reported as such in the traditional hagiographies, which do not concern his childhood; the fact of prejudice is simply assumed. Because *Amar Chitra Katha* is aimed in large part at children, however, this is a logical place to amplify received tradition, and the Ravidas comic does so by describing a process of enlightenment in which Ravidas depends on the words of his *guru*, Sandan Svami. According to Priyadas this is incorrect — Ramanand, a Vaiṣṇava and a Brahman, was Ravidas's guru — but because of the caste dimension this is one of the points that modern-day Ravidāsīs sternly disavow. They are not in total agreement as to who Ravidas's *guru* actually was, but the preponderance of opinion favors Sandan Svami.

Little is usually said among Ravidāsīs about the explicit content of Sandan's teaching, so *Amar Chitra Katha* had room to invent. On the inner cover the staff claims to have done so on the basis mainly of Ravidas's own poems, and the canon consulted is named as many Ravidāsīs would like to see it named: *Ādi Prakāś*, "The Primal Illumination" (350:32).[19] The essence that emerges has a distinctly Vedantin ring. Ravidas appeals to Sandan, "I want to know about myself and about the God who created me" (350:9). He receives the answer that "It is the same thing, Ravidas. When you know yourself, you will know God" (350:9). The solution Sandan offers to the problem of caste discrimination is: "See yourself as you are. Do not see yourself by the label" (350:10). And this is what causes a transformation in the young Camār and ultimately enables others to see themselves in a new light too — as Ravidāsīs (350:27).

The comic book bears a definite social message. It shows that Brahmans — Brahmans who perform brahmanical rituals, that is — can be cruel to lower-caste people (350:28–29), and it shows that Ravidāsīs, armed with their new sense of self, can "walk like a lion" and ignore them (350:27). But it does not preach overt resistance to social oppression. The emphasis is on transcendence instead (350:26, 29). In this respect, *Amar Chitra Katha* stops a good bit short of the Ambedkarite position Jijnasu would tease out of the poetry of Ravidas and is therefore closer at least to the Ravidas whose poems are collected in the *Gurū Granth Sāhib* than is Jijnasu. But it contravenes important elements in Ravidas's poetry and hagiography — the saint's suggestion, for instance, that *bhakti* made it hard for him to do a good day's work (Hawley and Juergensmeyer 1988:24), or his emphasis on the value of his inferior position as a privileged point of access for *bhakti:* it attracts the attention of a merciful God (Hawley and Juergensmeyer 1988:10–11). *Amar Chitra Katha*'s Ravidas — along with its Ramanand (55:12) and its Tulsidas (62:26) — imbibes and preaches the doctrine, if not of caste equality, at least of the common origin of all human beings (350:10).

All this amounts to the vision of *bhakti* propounded by that great modern Brahman, V. Raghavan: *bhakti* is the "democratic doctrine which consolidates all people without distinction of caste, community, nationality, or sex" (Raghavan 1966:32). Its result is envisioned as a social integration that follows from a common sense of relatedness to God or the One. Its behavioral manifestations are even-handedness in the social sphere, devoted labor in the economic, and a sense of individual dignity in the personal realm. This gentle amalgam contrasts markedly with the biting criticism and ecstatic extravagance one can find in the saints' own compositions.

The Message and the Medium

And now we must ask: to what extent are these saints of *Amar Chitra Katha* products of the medium in which they are presented?

Undoubtedly, the medium plays a role. First of all, these are comics. Although the staff is well aware that a portion of the *Amar Chitra Katha* readership is made up of adults, the adults concerned are primarily those who have children. Children define the ambience. On the whole they are middle-class children, with parents not in their twenties but, among women, in their mid-thirties and among men even somewhat older (Pai interview). The vast majority are Indian, although some readers are expatriate, and the most heavily subscribed languages are English — the language in which all issues of *Amar Chitra Katha* are first composed — and, interestingly, Malayalam. For in Kerala more than in any other state, literacy reaches well beyond the English-speaking classes.[20]

In the view of Anant Pai, at least, this readership places certain constraints on the series that are felt in the realm of religion. Children should not be exposed to violence, prejudice, sexual license, or superstition. And other constraints are imposed not just by the audience but by the medium itself. Except for comic books belonging to the increasingly florid miniseries genre, each story must be short, direct, and complete. Because it is illustrated — and because it must appeal to children — each must involve action. The plot must therefore be simple, coherent, and devoted to developing the "core personality" of the lead personage (Chandrakant interview). Anything that would dilute that purpose must be omitted, so the medium creates its own justification for Pai's grandly articulated policy of selective omission in the service of truth.

While the comic book medium requires a fair amount of simplification, however, it does not entirely eliminate the possibility of subtlety. Because it combines text and illustration, and because it permits the existence of certain words outside the confines of the pictures, it affords the *Amar Chitra Katha* editors a margin of flexibility. We have seen several occasions on which they made use of the distance between print and picture to accommodate the expectations of more than one group of readers. The possibility of using black and white in addition to color creates another opportunity for nuance. Motifs that need to be included in the plot but seem best relegated to the background can be dealt with in just that way: they can be rendered in silhouette.

The Indian comic book medium does not exist in a vacuum. It owes an obvious debt to European cartooning, a genre that played an explicit role early in Pai's career—he worked on "The Phantom"—and in the upbringing of Kamala Chandrakant, who for so long was his associate editor. As a child raised in an urban, English-speaking family, she devoured practically the whole of "Classics Illustrated." For other members of the staff, indigenous media have played a stronger role. Some of these genres are also influenced by contacts with Europe, as is the case with the poster-art industry that has defined so much of the aesthetic canon one sees in *Amar Chitra Katha*. But it is well to remember that the tradition of manuscript illustration is a venerable one in India, and there too one often sees that the verbal element does not strictly determine the visual (Hawley 1994). In *bhakti* poetry, in fact, an implied icon can determine the shape of a poem (Bryant 1978:72–112). Hence this series of "illustrated classics," as they are sometimes called when marketed in sets, has a right to be seen not just as an Indian adaptation of "Classics Illustrated" but as an expression of an indigenous concept of what makes a classic—typically something at least as much visual as verbal.

Some Indian classics bear the unmistakable mark of individual inspiration—the plays of Kalidasa, the *Rāmcaritmānas* of Tulsidas, certain of the poems attributed to Kabir or Sur—but others, particularly the epics and large collections of poetry, owe their existence to a more complicated process, often one that took place over the course of several centuries and registered the contributions of groups with varying interests. The work of producing a composite classic—a canon—at *Amar Chitra Katha* involves a similar process of creation by committee. While Pai's individual imprint is still strong, it has increasingly been registered in an editorial rather than an authorial capacity. *Amar Chitra Katha* comic books are group efforts. Although Pai is responsible for charting the new "Mahabharata" miniseries, individual issues apart from that tend to come to him as the ideas of others, and often these are proposed not just by individuals but by representatives of whole communities. In such circumstances the term "classic" comes to imply more a judgment about what ought to be included within a canon than a determination about what has intrinsic artistic worth. This reading of "classic" is strengthened by market considerations, for each *Amar Chitra Katha* comic must be judged capable of selling a minimum number of copies before its printing can be justified.

So *Amar Chitra Katha* is a business, but it is also, increasingly, a quasi-public institution. Because of Pai's marketing efforts, schools have become important subscribers, and in part because so many copies must be sold to make production cost-effective, it has until recent years been hard for competitors to enter the market and challenge *Amar Chitra Katha*'s effective monopoly. This has meant that Indians from the prime minister on down — particularly English-educated Indians — are aware of what *Amar Chitra Katha* does, and has meant that Pai himself has become a public figure, the subject of magazine articles and the recipient of public awards. It has also meant, as we have seen, that *Amar Chitra Katha* is exposed to pressure from various groups, political and otherwise. The Congress Party, for instance, urged Pai to create an issue commemorating its centennial in 1985; Pai had to find a means to accommodate that desire while not falling into the trap of taking political sides. The result is the miniseries called, with seeming neutrality, "The March to Freedom" — but the first issue in the set concerns *The Birth of the Indian National Congress* (348).

Then too, there is the elaborate process of negotiation that has related *Amar Chitra Katha* to communities of low-caste people. As has been mentioned, Anant Pai's sensitivity to the subject was first stimulated by the reaction of Untouchables in the Punjab to the way *Amar Chitra Katha* depicted Valmiki. Pai made a substantial effort to meet their charges, traveling personally to Jalandar and Patiala, and later attempting to enlist Jagjivan Ram, the Untouchable who had risen to the office of deputy prime minister under Indira Gandhi, as a mediator in his relations with lower-caste groups. As for the comic book on Ravidas, it was issued only at the end of a five-year process that also involved the careful editing of the issue on Chokhamela. At the time it emerged, there were again severe tensions between lower-caste and upper-caste communities: the city of Aurangabad was torn by riots. So Pai was careful to orchestrate an inaugural event at which Buta Singh, an Untouchable leader who was the home minister in the national government, appeared as the guest of honor.

The members of the editorial staff at *Amar Chitra Katha* insist that they are creating a library of comic book classics on a body of history and mythology that is Indian, not Hindu. Looking back, they even hold this up as a way to justify their instinct for preferring to represent Mira's Krishna as Muralīdhar, a flute-playing lover accessible to all, rather than as Giridhar, a miraculously endowed lifter of a definitely Hindu mountain. But one cannot escape the fact that Pai's own Neovedantin, Hindu, or (as he would have it) Vedic theology helps greatly in guiding the emergence of such a canon. The line between "Indian" and "Hindu" has always been blurred: it can be argued that "Hinduism," as a distinct, internally consistent system running parallel with other "religions," is an invention of the nineteenth century (Hawley 1991). For better or worse, readers of *Amar Chitra Katha* are not likely to be able to disentangle Hinduness from Indianness with any ease. And at least in one view, a view that is now being vocally espoused by such groups as the Vishva Hindu Parishad, the cause of "national integration" forbids that they should.

Notes

1. Numbers in parentheses after titles refer to the issue's ordinal number within the series, a number assigned and used for reference by the series itself. Where relevant the issue number is followed by a colon and the appropriate page number(s) within the issue. *Amar Chitra Katha* has also produced studies of Tukaram (68), Narasinh Mehta (94), Eknath (123), Jnanesvar (155), Tiruppan and Kanakadasa (186), Ramanuja (243), Tyagaraja (245), Ramana Maharsi (290), and Chokhamela (292). Many other figures also qualify as exemplary but would not normally be described as saints.

2. According to a study prepared for the National Film Archive (Gokarn 1984), ten films have been devoted to portraying Mira's life, four each for Tulsidas and Surdas (whose life story has been conflated for this purpose with that of Bilvamangal), and smaller numbers for Nanak, Kabir, and Ravidas.

3. The original dialogue of Sadashivam's *Meera* is in Tamil, but it has been dubbed in various Indian languages; the songs are in Hindi in all versions.

4. Madhu Kishwar and Ruth Vanita (1989:100–101) have discussed several features relating to this topic in an article that was printed after I had drafted this chapter. Their emphasis on the highlighting of Mira's otherworldliness in *Amar Chitra Katha* is somewhat different from mine, but other points — even specific passages — drew our common attention. Further background on similar themes may be found in Kumkum Sangari (1990), but the reader is cautioned against Sangari's acceptance of a "vulgate" Mirabai, in regard to both hagiography and poetry. Sangari fails to separate out this twentieth-century Mirabai from earlier conceptions, and one must read her conclusions with that in mind.

5. The story of Nanak falling asleep in Mecca with his feet toward the *ka'ba* is a striking example. The Sikh *janam sākhīs* represent this episode in a variety of ways; in the earlier ones, Nanak is said to sleep in a mosque outside Mecca, with his feet toward the *mehrab*. In either case, Nanak is set upon by a *qāzī* who berates him for his irreverence, but the *ka'ba* itself (or the *mehrab*, depending on the story) provides the response by rotating in Nanak's direction as a gesture of submission to his holy feet. Only one *janam sākhī*, the *Miharbān* (a document that represents the work of rationalizing commentators in the nineteenth century), reports the story differently, and it is this account that *Amar Chitra Katha* follows. Here neither *ka'ba* nor *mehrab* does anything, and Nanak provides his own response. As reported by the *Miharbān Janam Sākhī*, "Turn my shoes in that direction where the House of the Lord will not go. Place my shoes in the direction where the Ka'bah is not." *Amar Chitra Katha* makes the message even plainer and more generic: "To me the whole world is the

house of God. Now turn my feet to where God is not" (47:26). See McLeod 1980a:34, 135–144; the translation from *Miharbān* is p. 143n.

6. Hence nineteenth-century reformers such as Rammohan Roy and Svami Dayananda were at pains to cleanse Hinduism of its miraculous element, and Sir Syed Ahmed Khan projected a similar view of Islam.

7. Other comic book publishers have not been so particular. An issue on Santoshi Ma has been produced in a series called *Adarsh Chitra Katha* (Sukhatankar n.d.). I am grateful to H. Daniel Smith for supplying me with a copy.

8. Interestingly, Pai recalled an incident from his own childhood concerning the issue of unwanted *prasād*. The reluctant consumer was himself, and his grandmother warned him of the consequences if he cast the food aside. Pai remembers having thrown it in the gutter in disgust — not only at the *prasād* but at the idea of God that it represented.

9. Even so, the staff maintained that they often fought off romantic excesses from their contributing writers. Gayatri Madan Dutt, in particular, was famous for wanting full-page illustrations in which the handsome hero chucks the heroine under the chin.

10. Of course this vision of Kabir is not confined to *Amar Chitra Katha*. One sees it, for example, in the title of a recent study by Muhammad Hedayetullah (1977) called *Kabir: The Apostle of Hindu-Muslim Unity.*

11. On the other hand, children within the lineage of Vallabhacarya are spared the opprobrium of having once tried to play a trick on poor blind Surdas, as the *Vārtā* reports. The ruse is attributed instead to unnamed adults (cf. Bharati 1977:30 and Parikh 1970:421–422).

12. The source is the *Mūl Gosāī Carit* attributed to Beni Madhavdas, *dohās* 29–32 and the accompanying *caupāīs* (Gupta 1964:285). For further information, see Hawley and Juergensmeyer (1988: 158, 211) and, on the dating of the *Mūl Gosāī Carit,* Lutgendorf (1993:82–85).

13. For this dialogue in its earliest known form, see McLeod (1980b:151–155).

14. On Ravidas, see Priyadas (in Nabhadas 1969:471). The Brahmanizing of Kabir apparently comes later, for both Priyadas and Anantdas accept him as Muslim by birth. As to who might have been responsible for the change, see Vaudeville (1974:32).

15. In the temple to Ravidas in the Camār community at Sri Govardhanpur near Benares, for example, a large picture of Ravidas displaying his inner sacred thread is framed and preserved under glass.

16. This work's subtitle is "A Discriminating Biography, Written from a Buddhist Point of View." James G. Lochtefeld (1988:6) has noted that the original publication date, 1956, was the year in which Ambedkar repudiated Hinduism.

17. Parita Mukta (interview; cf. 1989:97) reports discovering in the course of fieldwork recently undertaken among artisans and peasants of Mewar and Marwar that the connection between Mira and Ravidas is taken as fact. And the tradition of their association may indeed, even if disputed, be old. It would be tempting to explain the inclusion of a poem of Mirabai in some manuscripts of the *Gurū Granth Sāhib* as natural enough if she was understood to be an initiate of Ravidas, whose position in that collection is firm.

18. "G. D. Birla, Who Revolutionized Indian Industry" (382).

19. On the association of "primalist" (*ādi*) language with low-caste movements, see Juergensmeyer (1982).

20. Economics also may play a role in the success of the Malayalam version: these comic books cost less than other editions of *Amar Chitra Katha*. IBH leases the rights to an independent publisher and distributor, who sells at lower rates than IBH.

References

Bharati, Pushpa. 1977. *Soordas*. Bombay: India Book House Educational Trust.

Bryant, Kenneth E. 1978. *Poems to the Child-God*. Berkeley: University of California Press.

Gokarn, Kusam. 1984. "Popularity of Devotional Films (Hindi)." Pune: National Film Archive Research Project 689/5/84.

Gupta, Kisorilal. 1964. *Gosāī Carit*. Varanasi: Vāṇī-Vitān Prakāśan.

Harlan, Lindsey. 1987. "The Ethic of Protection Among Rajput Women: Religious Mediations of Caste and Gender Duties." Ph.D. diss., Harvard University.

Hawley, John Stratton. 1991. "Naming Hinduism." *The Wilson Quarterly* 15, no. 3:20–34.

——. 1994. "The Bharat Kala Bhavan *Sūrsāgar*." In *Studies in South Asian Devotional Literature*, ed. Alan W. Entwistle and Françoise Mallison, pp. 480–51. Delhi: Manohar.

——. in press. "Mirabai as Wife and Yogi." In *Asceticism*, ed. Vincent L. Wimbush and Richard Valantasis. New York: Oxford University Press.

Hawley, John Stratton, and Mark Juergensmeyer. 1988. *Songs of the Saints of India*. New York: Oxford University Press.

Hedayetullah, Muhammed. 1977. *Kabir: The Apostle of Hindu-Muslim Unity*. Delhi: Motilal Banarsidass.

Jijnasu, Candrikaprasad. 1969. *Sant Pravar Raidās Sāhab*. Lucknow: Bahujan Kalyāṇ Prakāśan.

Juergensmeyer, Mark. 1982. *Religion as Social Vision*. Berkeley: University of California Press.

Kishwar, Madhu, and Ruth Vanita. 1989. "Modern Versions of Mira." *Manushi* 50–52:100–101.

Lochtefeld, James G. 1988. "Clutching at the Elephant: Four Perspectives on the Life of Ravidas." Unpublished paper, Columbia University.

Lutgendorf, Philip. 1993. "The Quest for the Legendary Tulsidas." *Journal of Vaiṣṇava Studies* 1, no. 2: 79–101.

McLeod, W. H. 1980a. *Early Sikh Tradition*. Oxford: Clarendon Press.

——. 1980b. *The B40 Janam-Sākhī*. Amritsar: Guru Nanak Dev University.

Mukta, Parita. 1989. "Mirabai in Rajasthan." *Manushi* 50–52:94–99.

Nabhadas. 1969. *Śrī Bhaktamāl*, with the *Bhaktirasabodhinī* commentary of Priyadas and an exposition in modern Hindi by Sitaramsaran Bhagavanprasad Rupkala. Lucknow: Tejkumar Press.

Parikh, Dvarkadas, ed. 1970. *Caurāsī Vaiṣṇavan kī Vārtā,* with the *bhāvprakāś* of
    Hariray. Mathura: Śrī Bajarang Pustakālay.
Raghavan, V. 1966. *The Great Integrators: The Saint-Singers of India.* New Delhi:
    Publications Division (of the Government of India).
Sangari, Kumkum. 1990. "Mirabai and the Spiritual Economy of Bhakti." *Economic
    and Political Weekly,* Special Articles (July 7) 1464–1475 and (July 14) 1537–
    1552.
Sukhatankar, Bharati. n.d. *Santoshi Mata.* New Delhi: Argus Central Enterprises.
Vaudeville, Charlotte. 1974. *Kabīr.* Oxford: Clarendon Press.

INTERVIEWS

Kamala Chandrakant (Bombay), 1989.
Parita Mukta, private communication, 1989.
Anant Pai (Bombay) 1989.

Section 2

Audio Recordings

Susan S. Wadley

Introduction

The two essays in this section deal with some implications of audio recording technology for South Asian religious life. In moving to the realm of audio recording, we find ourselves in a technological milieu substantially different from that of Section 1. It must be remembered that although the kinds of printed images discussed in Section 1 belong to the twentieth century, they represent extensions of a printing technology that is hundreds of years old. Audio recording is much newer. It was invented in the nineteenth century, and its full potential was not realized until electronic amplification techniques evolved in the twentieth century (initially vacuum-tube–based and later utilizing solid-state devices). The world of recorded sound is, technologically, very much a twentieth-century world. It is a twentieth-century world in the experiential sense as well; the pervasiveness of recorded and electronically amplified sound would surely be among the most noticeable features of our world to a visitor from another time.

Recording technology, such as it then was, became available in South Asia around 1900. From 1908 until the advent of cassette technology, audio recording was dominated by the British Gramophone Company (HMV, also called EMI). Further, until recently Hindi film music has been the primary product of recording companies in India, with Bombay film music producers developing a uniform aesthetic, "film music," for millions of listeners. Only recently have regional styles become more readily available, although commercial producers never ignored popular regional styles.

The early 1980s saw the growth of the cassette industry in India, with the monopoly of the Gramophone Company challenged by the simpler technology and lower costs of cassette production. As the music industry was restructured, some three hundred cassette companies began production. Sales also increased dramatically, from some $1.2 million in 1980 to over $12 million in 1986 (Manuel 1991:191). The surge in production and producers has led to important innovations in what kinds of music are available, with local renditions and genres being produced by firms in small towns throughout India. Here local variation plays a key role, as producers respond to the demands of an increasingly affluent rural population not necessarily attuned to the film music standards of Bombay. The demand has increased also for religious recordings of many kinds: *mantras,* epics, or rituals proclaimed by Hindu priests; sermons by Muslim leaders; musical recordings from well-known devotees at particular shrines.

In this section, in her chapter on *qawwālī,* Regula Qureshi examines the enormous impact modern recording technology has had on relationships between performer and listener, and on religious context in which performance is received. Scott Marcus's chapter traces some of the religious and cultural implications of the remarkable audio-cassette revolution currently transforming India's recording industry.

Reference

Manuel, Peter. 1991. "The Cassette Industry and Popular Music in North India." *Popular Music* 10:189–204.

Regula Burckhardt Qureshi

6. Recorded Sound and Religious Music: The Case of *Qawwālī*

South Asian religious life is permeated with musical sound. Scriptural chanting or recitation[1] is foundational to the practice of Hinduism as well as to Islam and Sikhism; it remains an important domain of religious specialists who set and maintain appropriate standards of execution as well as transmission. For lay members of all these religions, reciting from their scriptures is part of their religious practice, but the predominant medium for both individual and collective religious expression is the singing of devotional poetry in vernacular languages.[2] At least since the spread of the *bhakti* movement around the sixteenth century, such hymns have become the central focus for devotional assemblies. Whether Hindu *bhajan* and *kīrtan*, Sikh *shabd kīrtan*, or Muslim *majlis* and *qawwālī*, words set to music become a compelling medium for articulating an emotional religious message. And in extending their sound acoustically, these songs are able to attract and bind those who hear them into a community of devotees through the shared experience of listening and responding to their message.

Devotional song performers range from amateur to professional, but there are also traditions of competence that continue to exist within families and lineages (e.g., Hindu *kīrtankār*, Sikh *rāgī*, Muslim *qawwāl*), supported by traditional relations of service and patronage. At the same time, recording technology has become an integral and pervasive facet of religious music. Loudspeakers bring devotional hymns to the street; radio broadcasts guide private devotions; records replace living performers. Most of all, India's thriving record industry includes close to a century of devotional song recordings. Yet technology has been kept at arm's length in the study of music no less than of religion in South Asia. A curious cultural conservatism has sanctioned the use of recording technology for documentation but continues to treat it as a transparent medium, supported by a traditional scholarly reluctance to engage with the "popular" musical results of recorded production. The following case study reflects both the rudimentary state and the multiple dimensions that characterize the impact of recording technology on religious musical expression, but first and foremost it reflects the need to begin by focusing on the musical result of this impact: religious music on record.

Probably the most popular genre of recorded religious music in South Asia is not Hindu but Muslim. *Qawwālī,* the group song emanating from the ritual practice of Islamic mysticism, is rich in textual resources, flexible in structure, rhythmically dynamic, acoustically intense. Above all, *qawwālī* is, by definition, highly adaptable to the needs of its audience. When Fred Gaisberg, touring agent for the Gramophone Company, made the first documented set of Indian sound recordings in Calcutta in 1902, he included *qawwālī* songs by at least three artists (Joshi 1988:147). Since then *qawwālī* has evolved and flourished as a recorded genre of religious music, also extending into an entirely secular genre of popular music. Discussions of Indian popular and film music refer to *qawwālī* as an entertainment genre divorced from its religious roots (e.g., Manuel 1988) while little attention has been paid to the primary, religious genre on record. Participants in the Sufi tradition, on the other hand, consider recordings of little direct relevance to Sufi practice, perhaps because of the decontextualized quality of recorded sound.

The fact is that recording technology has a pervasive presence, generated by the dissemination through record sales and — more important in South Asia — through broadcasting, with further expansion and diffusion resulting from the introduction of cassette technology. As a result, religious *qawwālī* records, like all recorded music, have acquired their own audience. The use of recorded music implies a shift from a religious community sharing the music of a ritual to a generalized anonymous community of listeners separated from those who create the performance, with only a label identifying performer and producer or patron.

Sound recording freezes a musical performance into a reproducible object physically separable from those who produce it, thereby removing it from its original context and making its communicative potential universally accessible through playback and broadcasting technology. As such, the entire process of music production is subject to industrial relations of production in which a producer with capital and technology converts music into a marketable product to be sold for profit. A song is fragmented through the production process, removing its original creator from its user, the consumer, and thus depersonalizing it. Mass manufacture results in a loss, or at least a control of diversity and an adaptation of the physical characteristics of the music to the parameters of the manufacturing process, along with a standardization of demand in response to a standardized offering. Ultimately, the market becomes the locus of patronage, which makes the consumer the ultimate determinant of production.

The impact of recording technology on the religious musical genre *qawwālī* can be located primarily in the body of recorded *qawwālī* music. To assess its significance, however, requires situating this impact beyond the recorded object to the community of its users, by asking not only how sound recording affects the idiom itself but also what results from it, both in the sphere of religious practice and in the larger Muslim sociocultural realm. The goal is to understand the pattern of interaction between the production of recorded *qawwālī* music and its reception in the wider sense. To this end, I propose here to examine in its broad features the musical-textual content of recorded *qawwālī* in the context of the conditions and process of its production and with reference to the audience it serves. This includes a consideration of the impact of recorded *qawwālī* on the Sufi community and its ritual practice. A sense of this dynamic is best conveyed through a broadly historical account featuring a set of representative examples.

The Live *Qawwālī* Tradition

The origin and continuous reference base for the development of the idiom of recorded *qawwālī* and its functional-connotational content is Sufi religious tradition, which is embedded in the Indo-Muslim conception of religious music. Emanating from the Islamic norms that govern music (Roychaudhry 1957) and influenced by the cultural performance norms of South Asia (Singer 1972a), this conception accounts for a highly functional and contextualized musical tradition, unique in its conceptual separation from secular musical genres into a category of "recitation" or "chant."[3]

Given the total exclusion of music from the religious sphere in the ideology of Islam, the term "music" is really a misnomer for what is a set of four interrelated sound communication idioms employed in the ritual and devotional practice of Muslims throughout South Asia. *Qir'at*, the chanting of the Quran, is linked to its Arabic textual and musical roots and spans many contexts. The other three idioms consist of hymns of vernacular poetry, each linked to a distinct context of performance: the Sunni *mīlād* assembly to praise the Prophet Muhammad through *na't*, the Shi'a *majlis* assembly to commemorate the martyrdom of Husain, grandson of Muhammad, through *marsiyā* and other related hymns, and the Sufi *sama'* assembly to achieve states of mystical arousal through *qawwālī*. Their predominant language is Urdu, enriched by phrases and metaphors from both classical Farsi and Hindi in addition to Arabic expressions drawn from the Quran. *Qawwālī* in particular uses entire verses and poems in Farsi, the classical language of Sufism, and Hindi, the language of Hindu devotional poetry, thereby addressing itself to both the Muslim elite and the unlettered devotee. A strict ideology of textual primacy governs all chant idioms, which results in the subordination of musical to textual features and in the exclusion of musical instruments and indeed of any musical features not dependent on the poetic text.

The significant exception to this is *qawwālī* with its traditional complement of rhythmic and melodic instrumental accompaniment on *ḍholak* and harmonium, which Sufis justify by their impact on emotional arousal. *Qawwālī* is thus the closest to "real" music; its performers, *qawwāls*, are essentially hereditary professional musicians who are related but considered musically inferior to their secular counterparts. At the same time *qawwālī,* like the other religious musical idioms, is subject to a specific religious function, which it serves in a specific context of performance with its own setting and procedure. In summary form the function of *qawwālī* music is: to present mystical poetry—addressing the Prophet or Sufi saints, or expressing spiritual emotion—in a musical setting, so as to arouse mystical love, culminating in ecstasy, in listeners with diverse spiritual needs. The music is placed entirely in the service of this spiritual aim, mainly acoustically (arousing drum beat and clapping; group alternation, volume and enunciation for text emphasis), durationally (musical rhythm represents poetic meter, frequent stress repeats for arousal), and structurally (musical form represents text units, flexible structuring for text repetition and insertion to serve diverse listeners).

Qawwālī assemblies are covered and presided over by a Sufi sheikh who is responsible for the spiritual goal of the event. The performers are charged with choosing and shaping the songs, but control is in the hands of the sheikh, so that the performer is only a mediator, lacking religious (or social) status. Clearly, the absence of anything sacred residing in either performer or item performed renders *qawwālī* and *qawwāl* uniquely adaptable to nonreligious contexts. Indeed, because of its musical character and made possible by the fundamentally unorthodox ideology of Sufism, *qawwālī*—and *qawwāls*—are documented as open to secular music making and musical entertainment at least from the early eighteenth century onward (Dargah Quli Khan 1949, Dhond n.d.). The record of both textual and circumstantial evidence[4] indicates that *qawwālī* has always served as a medium to extend communication to all potential followers of the Sufi path, which in effect means all societal groups, including the non-Muslim majority and ranging from the highly literate to the unlettered. In the light of this background it is hardly surprising that *qawwālī* became the first and most-recorded religious genre in South Asia.

Recording Technology Comes to South Asia

Recorded Muslim religious music in South Asia has a history longer than living memory. What that music sounded like before sound recording eludes us, since historical documentation of the domain is both scant and problematic. Sources do, however, indicate an ongoing performance tradition, at least since the eighteenth century, of Muslim religious music, including *qawwālī* (Meer Hasan 1973, Dargah Quli Khan 1949, Imam 1959–60, Ruswa 1963, Ja'far Sharif 1972). Strictly speaking, then, we are limited to tracing the evolving impact of sound recording without being able to establish precisely what recording technology was having an impact on.

South Asia's history of recorded sound is characterized by the hegemony of the British Gramophone Company (later EMI), one of the "Big Five" in the world, which established record production in India in 1908 (Gronow 1981:257). Its monopoly started to erode only in the late 1970s, when a few competing companies were finally able to enter the market (Kinnear 1985:xiv). The salutary diversification resulting from this was quickly superseded by the shift to cassette technology in the 1980s. EMI's hegemony fell and so did the production of records, clearly because of the absence of any copyright protection. This trend appeared earlier in Pakistan, where an open market permitted the free influx of cassette recording and playback equipment, unlike in India, where this is a more recent development. Pakistan, in fact, now produces only cassettes and in both countries the offering of every kind of commercial recordings is in a process of flux.

Ultimately a concomitant of the centralized nature of the colonial state, the initial monopoly of the Gramophone Company extended to the manufacture of gramophones and to all distribution; it was further reinforced by the equally centralized broadcast media (Lelyveld 1986). Indeed, the continued state monopoly over radio and television in both successor states is largely responsible for the as-yet relatively minor impact of recent diversification in the sound production industry. Both media have always played a central role in disseminating recorded music, given the fact that in a society where the ability to buy and maintain recorded sound and its playback equipment remains confined to a relatively small elite.

The normative impact of the media thus continues to have a powerful effect on preferences. This is ultimately a function of sociopolitical organization, for both India and Pakistan continue to be highly stratified societies dominated by, and thus oriented to, powerful central elites and their local counterparts. Sufism, too, is hierarchically constituted, with its focus on the highest saint (Mu'inuddin Chishti of Ajmer, Nizamuddin Auliya of Delhi) and their shrines. This is musically manifested in the regionwide emulation of their ritual core repertoire (Qureshi 1986). Another important factor contributing to the highly conservative character of the Indian recording market is the central role of oral tradition throughout all levels of society, which reinforces the power of memory, and of things — or recordings — remembered. All these forces have continued to exercise their impact, even though record manufacture, like all mass production, did entail a shift of orientation from the feudal to the commercial segment of society, from the resource holder to the cash holder.

The Gramophone Company pursued a clear policy of exploiting separate religious communities as markets, as is evidenced by the release of the same film music on two different records aimed at Hindus and at non-Hindus by means of communally differentiated advertising (Joshi 1977:8). But the company also developed a certain uniform musical character for its products: a solo voice accompanied by harmonium and *tablā* became the standard ensemble for all recorded song, including *qawwālī*. With the development of autonomous music for silent movies, and with "talkies" in the 1930s, this basic studio instrumentarium was expanded to include clarinet and other Western instruments, including also the *bulbultarang*, a simple board zither with typewriter keys introduced from Meiji Japan as *teshokoto* (Qureshi 1980a:108) which became a favorite with performers of popular *qawwālī*. These Westernized innovations are hardly surprising given that record and film production as well as broadcasting were Western imports and initially in the hands of Western producers (Lelyveld 1986). Even after the gradual indigenization of the industry, the long years of exclusive dissemination and the glamour of its studio identity has given this instrumentarium great staying power up to the present.

In order to reach all possible audience groups, the general policy was to target religious and language communities and then to identify genres within them. By far the most widely recorded category, "Urdu Muslim Islamic," encompassed the *qawwālī* repertoire under consideration here. Initially, Urdu was the predominant language category for all gramophone recordings, given its primary status under British rule. In addition, the label "Urdu" represented the Muslim cultural identity and subsumed even songs in Hindi. The Gramophone Company's eclectic search for markets also led to some early recordings of unaccompanied chant, including a recorded segment of Quranic recitation (from *Surā Rahmān,* Lutfullah interview), although these appear to have been discontinued soon thereafter.

Recorded *Qawwālī* in India

The first *qawwālī* recordings made in 1902 by the Gramophone Company featured three artists who were to gain lasting fame: Pearu Qawwal, Kaloo Qawwal, and Fakhr-e-Alam (Joshi 1988:147). But it took until the 1930s for sound recording to become well established with a major local production facility and with wide dissemination through locally assembled Japanese phonographs and through the newly established All-India Radio.

From the outset, the Gramophone Company focused on recording urban professional performers and on music essentially of two types: One was the semi-classical courtesan song aimed at an elite audience, the other the popular religious song (Joshi 1977:19). Preferred by linguistically and musically less sophisticated Muslim audiences, popular religious song also held an appeal for the Muslim religious community at large. The prime market for this category of "Muslim Devotional" was located in urban business communities, located mainly in Bombay; these groups had diverse sectarian and language backgrounds but shared Islamic tenets as well as basic Urdu, both as a lingua franca and as a language of religious devotion.

Two excerpts from famous songs by Kaloo and Pearu Qawwal exemplify this style; both are hymns addressing the Prophet recorded in the 1930s and reissued on LP in 1968. The first is one of the best-known songs of early recorded music; this simple poem with a simple idea is set to a simple folk tune in a plain duple meter, which rather resembles *chārbait,* an urban Muslim folk song tradition of the Rampur region. Example 1 illustrates the recitative-like introductory verse, which leads into the song's central statement and refrain line very effectively, as is characteristic for *qawwālī*.

Example 1: Pearu Qawwal, "Madīne kā musāfir hūn"
        "I am a traveler in search of Medina" (Angel 3AEX-5191)

Introductory
verse: Whenever you bow before God in prayer, ask Him to help me
              I am a traveler in search of Medina, pray for me
              I do not know the way, nor do I know Medina
              God knows on which shore this boat will leave me
              As much as possible keep faith with me:
Refrain: I am a traveler in search of Medina, pray for me

Example 2 by Kaloo Qawwal is a song in *ghazal* form with complete couplets each leading appropriately into the refrain line. The melody is a standard Muslim hymn tune for this particular poetic meter (*mutadārik:* -u-/-u-/-u-/-u-).

Example 2: Kaloo Qawwal, "Ham mazar-e-Muhammad pe mar jāenge"
        "O let me die by the tomb of Muhammad" (Angel 3AEX-5191)

Verse: I offer my all in Ahmad's (Muhammad's) name
              He turns my life into a dream
Refrain: O let me die at the tomb of Muhammad

The early *qawwālī* recordings are solo songs with little evidence of the authentic sound character of Sufi music, a rhythmically emphatic group song. Of course, the three-minute duration of these recordings could hardly permit the freedom to repeat and amplify musical portions, so essential to that idiom. In fact, the early recordings share stylistic traits with contemporary urban entertainment music like *chārbait* and *nauṭankī,* as well as the music that accompanied silent films and was later incorporated into film songs (Joshi 1984:74ff.).

But ultimately the record industry did not invent this idiom; it only promoted and projected it, thereby giving preference to what were essentially freelance urban entertainers over the tradition-bearing hereditary *qawwālī* performers who were — and still are — affiliated with Sufi shrines in a quasi-feudal arrangement. Through this preference Pearu, Kalu, and Fakhr-e-Alam became "stars" who also performed widely before huge live audiences, both Muslim and non-Muslim (Enayatullah 1976) and in settings ranging from open-air grounds to recital hall (Lutfullah interview).

They were often dressed in Western clothes and sitting on chairs; Kaloo is remembered for always appearing in an impressively neat Western suit (Enayatullah interview).

The recorded solo style of *qawwālī* singing had a limited impact also on the religious *qawwālī* performed in shrines. By the 1940s two recording artists emerged, Azim Prem Ragi and Waiz Qawwal, who also widely impressed Sufi audiences at *'urs* (saint's death anniversary) celebrations, especially in Ajmer and Hyderabad. There both of them performed solo, rather than in the group-style traditional to *qawwālī*. While in proper Sufi settings they did not use studio instruments as was done for recordings; Waiz Qawwal intoned a simple melodic accompaniment on the *sitār*. The recognition of these performers in Sufi circles is reflected in the special titles—Waiz ("Religious Commentator"), Prem Ragi ("Minstrel of [divine] Love") — which were bestowed upon them by a great Sufi of the time, Khwaja Hasan Nizami. This fame in turn influenced the diversification of *qawwālī* recordings toward including some genuine Sufi items, like the famous Amir Khusrau poem (in Farsi) *Namī Dānam,* also performed by Azim Prem Ragi.

Out of this first interfacing between religious and recorded *qawwālī* styles there appears to have emerged a highly significant shift in structure, both textual and musical, toward what I term narrative *qawwālī*. The underlying principle is that of the *girah,* verse material inserted between reiterations of the same line of song text for the purpose of elaborating upon it or expanding its meaning, thus rendering its repetition doubly meaningful. Based on a literary precedent, the *tāzmīn,*[5] and on a respectable Sufi poetic repertoire dating from at least the nineteenth century, the *girah* was introduced into Sufi *qawwālī* around the turn of this century, according to the memory of senior *qawwāl*s (Gore Khan interview, Meraj Ahmad interview). The purpose was to explicate difficult Sufi texts and thereby enhance their meaning to the audience, especially that of classical Farsi poetry.

The growing popularity of this stylistic practice among Sufis coincides with the increasingly important patronage of the urban business communities who lacked the classical education of the traditional Muslim elite. Its most classical poetic form was the *xamsā,* a song of five-line verses, each consisting of four simple explicatory lines that culminate in the salient final line, often one of successive lines from a classical Sufi poem. Thus charged with meaning the final line would, in live *qawwālī*, be repeated extensively; in recording, too, the form introduced climax as well as a coherence of content not found in the two-line verse structure of standard Sufi *ghazal* poetry.

In popular *qawwālī* the *girah* technique of verse insertion was easily expanded into a form of storytelling where each episode is followed by a punch line that is repeated several times, clamorously.[6] Here the *qawwāl* controls what is a potentially arbitrary text sequence so that he can readily turn his song into a purely audience-oriented entertainment. For this reason, Sufis also call this style of *qawwālī* by the derogatory term *tukbandī* — arbitrarily stringing verse pieces together — or, even worse, *khicṛī*, after the traditional dish of lentils and rice mixed together. Recordings could present only a highly compressed version of this technique, but thanks to the *qawwāls'* proverbial ability to respond appropriately to any performance context, satisfactory versions abound even on three-minute records.

Example 3 illustrates the chainlike process of *girah*-making by the first famous Bombay *qawwāl*, Ismail Azad. A star of the 1940s and 1950s, he is associated with the Muslim trading area of Bombay, Bhindi Bazar, and he set the trend for Muslim *qawwālī* performers in early independent India to adopt the name *Azad*, ("free"), no doubt implying a patriotic reference.[7]

Example 3: Ismail Azad, "Muhammad hamāre baṛī shānvāle"
 "Our Muhammad is full of splendor" (EMI 4 TC 04B 3962)

Refrain: Our Muhammad is full of splendor!
girah: Muhammad gave his community the Faith
            In giving the Faith, he gave the Quran
            Through Him, the weak became strong
            Becoming strong, they became courageous too
            When Muhammad came, then blessing came too
            When blessing came, the good fortune came too
            When good fortune came, then abundance came too
            When abundance came, then benefaction came too
            And the splendor of Muhammad's prophecy came too
            On his brow the stamp of prophethood came too
            How great it is that Divine Law came too
            Sovereignty came and miracles came too
            Instantly the mantle of Faith came to all
            Muhammad came, and through him came the Quran:
Refrain: Our Muhammad is full of splendor!

The increasing use of the *girah* style in recorded *qawwālī* reflects a shift in preference toward narrative content as a self-contained reference base as against the evocative texts proper to Sufism, which are linked to the symbolic meaning system of mysticism. This narrative focus quite naturally led to a topical expansion in textual content, reflecting on conditions of the time, including changing political realities. Even a cursory review of sound recordings and also broadcasting show that they were profoundly affected by both the freedom movement and subsequent independence from Britain. The effect on *qawwālī* records is notable in a thematic shift toward a heterodox Sufism addressing Indian saints and embracing a general humanism that extols all religions. This accords with the spirit of independent India's commitment to secularism, a term that in the Indian context means less to eliminate religion from consideration than to give consideration to all religions.

Example 4 is a famous song extolling this ideal; it is quoted years later in an equally famous *qawwālī* by Ghulam Farid Sabri (see Example 12 below).

Example 4: Habib Painter, "Bhagvān isī men milte hain"
"This is where you find God" (EMI 7EPE 1440)

Verse: This man, this image made of clay is where you find God
           But when he forgets himself, this is where you find the devil
           This is the where you find God and this is where you find the devil
Refrain: This is where you find God
girah: See the observances of these Sheikhs and Brahmans
           As if God were confined to temple and Ka'ba
           To give you benefits. Never be deceived by the zealots!
           The same stone is in Kashi (Benares) as in Mecca
           True, they are separate offspring, but their essence is one and the same
           Whether Allah or Bhagvan, it is one and the same
           Their paths are separate, but the destination is one and the same
           Their thrones are separate, but the assembly is one and the same
           The way our body is built tells that we are one and the same
           The color of blood shows that we are one and the same
           Our Allah or Bhagvan, they are one and the same
           His kind is humankind, and all His religions are humane
           Yet the Muslim says: come to the mosque
           As well, the Hindu says: the temple is best

Christians too say: come to the church
And the Sikhs claim: the gurdwara is best
But we received our lesson from the mystics, both sheikh or
    guru
The Ka'ba, the church, the gurdwara, the river Ganges,
Why be concerned with the differences among them?
Your purpose is to worship, do it wherever you please, you fool!
Refrain: You find God everywhere!

Essentially, the "storytelling" *qawwālī* represented an expanded influence of popular entertainment on record production; it was an ideally flexible vehicle for reiterating traditional devotional stories of saints and their miraculous powers (*karāmat*) as well as for making modern common sense socioreligious commentary, both taken over from existing oral practice. But its lower-class character evoked disapproval from the Muslim elite, beginning with elite performers themselves. G. N. Joshi reports a telling incident from 1952, when the great singer Begum Akhtar was almost irreparably lost to the Gramophone Company because an unlettered (Punjabi) producer made the offensive suggestion that she model her *na't* recording on Ismail Azad's *qawwālī* (Joshi 1984:71).

The fact is that the narrative *qawwālī* had, by the 1950s, turned into a highly successful secular performing genre, especially in the form of the *muqābilā* — a contest between two *qawwāl*s — and recordings by its star performers were excellent sellers. This turned Bombay performers like Ismail Azad and later Yusuf Azad into prime recording artists and in turn enhanced the impact of their "Bombay style" on recorded religious *qawwālī*.

A further factor in this complex feedback process is the film industry and its music, concentrated in Bombay after an initial phase in Calcutta. By the 1950s a distinct "*filmī*" vocal sound had become established, adapted to the microphone and reflective of the essentially romantic stereotype for the male hero. This somewhat crooning sound (*klās kī awāz*, actually *klāssikī*, from "classical") stands in distinct opposition to the vocal ideal of religious *qawwālī* but it has clearly influenced recorded *qawwālī*, and through it live *qawwālī* as well. Another facet of film music is its focus on melodic structure, composed or arranged to create a memorable tune at least for the main song line, as well as an attractive instrumental frame introducing the song and separating its verses. Both these features began to appear in *qawwālī* gramophone recordings, culminating, by the 1960s, in several "composed" sets of religious *qawwālī*, with music directors, some of them *qawwāl*s themselves. These include a set of *qawwālī* recordings from the one "Muslim Social" film made around India's greatest saint: *Hind ke Walī.*

Example 5 is probably the best-known of these songs, enhanced by the stunningly melodious voice of Shankar Shambhu.

Example 5: Shankar Shambhu, "Dīdār tumhārā hojāe"
       "O might I come face to face with You" (EMI EMOE 2378)

Introductory
Verse: My desirous eyes are longing to behold You
             Waiting to put my heart at ease, waiting for the lovers' 'Id
             [Festival of Joy]
Verse: May peace come to my restless heart, support to my troubled life
             My eyes thirst to see You, O might I come face to face with You
Refrain: O might I come face to face with You
girah: The world calls you messiah of our time
             A single glance from you can heal the lovesick soul
             (. . .)

But the most important impact of the film industry on *qawwālī* is its successful adaptation of the idiom to entirely secular purposes, invariably in films of the category "Muslim Social," where a colorful *qawwālī*-type group song, preferably sung by men and women, served to invoke a typical Muslim atmosphere while introducing musical and visual variety. To serve this purpose it follows logically that such songs should emulate the typical sound character of *qawwālī* — group song, hand clapping, rhythmic accentuation, and crisp articulation.

Example 6, the 1948 song from the film *Zeenat* that pioneered women's *qawwālī*, illustrates these features; set to a serious *ghazal,* it is one of the great hits of *filmī qawwālī.*

Example 6: Nur Jahan, Zohra, "Ahen nā bharīn shikwe nā kiye"
       "Never once did I sigh or complain" (Angel 3 AEX 5021)

Refrain: Never once did I sigh or complain, never once did I utter a
             sound
Verse: Still, I could not keep my love a secret whenever anyone spoke
             your name
             All I could do was to clutch my heart and quell my emotions

The sum total of all these developments was a diversification and dilution of the genre's religious character in its recorded form.

After Independence in 1947 and the initial years of consolidation, two distinct sound-recording histories began to evolve in India and Pakistan, although the Gramophone Company continued to hold a virtual monopoly in both countries and reissued as well as cross-released many *qawwālī* recordings. Their different religious-political foundations found expression both in record production and in the disseminating media of radio and later television. This in turn affected patronage and therefore the well-being and reproduction of recording artists themselves.

India made major changes to its broadcast policy that had an important effect on *qawwālī*. In contrast to the regular and generous appearances of Muslim religious music at least on every Friday during the first decade of All-India Radio,[8] they appear to have virtually disappeared from programming for some years after Independence. Under B. V. Keskar's policy of cultural nationalism, mainstream AIR programming focused mainly on the patronage of classical music and for five years even banned airplay of all popular or *filmī* records.

Beginning in the late 1950s, *qawwālī* reappeared in sharply reduced form on two "special audience" programs, which in an interesting way also reflect the two-tier "class structure" of *qawwālī*. One is the Urdu Programme, which serves to articulate Muslim culture in its cosmopolitan form; the other, the Rural Programme, addressed to a regional popular audience. At the same time, Bombay-style secular *qawwālī* could be heard on "filmī" broadcasts of Radio Ceylon and later AIR's Vividh Bharati.

Recordings made during the 1950s and 1960s reflect in their texts an increasing emphasis on Hindi vocabulary, on Indian saints — rather than the Prophet and Arabia — and on the religious tolerance of Sufism. Hindu performers gained more prominence in the recording field — though not in the Sufi centers of India. A contributing factor in this development was the loss of many talented Muslim *qawwāl*s to Pakistan (Henry 1988:214).

Recorded *Qawwālī* in Pakistan

In Pakistan, after an initial vacuum, both national radio and the recording industry were established in Karachi in the early 1950s. This newly constituted state's search for a musically expressed identity apart from India led to emphasis on distinctive elements in *qawwālī,* as the one musical genre with a clear Muslim identity. Radio Pakistan created and strongly propagated a *qawwālī*-like national genre based on the poetry of Iqbal, labeled *Iqbāliāt*. But despite massive dissemination on the radio this genre never gained popular acceptance. Example 7 is a recording by a Radio Pakistan ensemble of one of Iqbal's great Farsi *ghazal*s dating from about 1960.

Example 7: Iqbāliāt, "Bar tar az andesha" (Farsi)
          "Life's meaning"

Verse: Life's meaning is far above concerns for gain and loss
          Life's meaning comprises both living and dying
Refrain: Life's meaning is far above concerns for gain and loss
Verse: If you are truly alive, create your own world
          From his beginning, man has known the secret of creation
Refrain: Life's meaning is far above concerns for gain and loss

At the same time religious *qawwālī* was broadcast regularly on Thursdays and Fridays. The Pakistan Gramophone Company soon found the market supporting an increasing production of *qawwālī* while the limited demand for classical music could largely be satisfied with re-releases from India.

A fortuitous constellation of factors contributed to the creative expansion of the *qawwālī* idiom during the 1950s and 1960s. There was much elite patronage for *qawwālī*, especially among migrants (*muhājir*) from India with Sufi affiliation. Along with this came the convergence of numerous *qawwāl*s who brought different local styles from Sufi centers in India, with resulting competition, imitation, and mutual inspiration among them. All this was taking place during the years of *muhājir* hegemony in what was then the center of Pakistan, Karachi. The expansion was characterized by a mixture of traditional styles and by musical innovation, especially in the direction of art music, a development that had been pioneered earlier in Punjabi *qawwālī* by Mubarak Ali Fateh Ali (Enayatullah 1976).

Recordings became the effective vehicle for standardizing and disseminating these musical innovations, predictably within the parameters of the established "Bombay" model of popular *qawwālī*. What made this possible and really pushed recorded *qawwālī* into a place of musical prominence in Pakistan was the belated advent of long-play technology in the 1960s (Joshi 1977:25). By 1972 numerous 45 rpm and several LP records of religious *qawwālī* had appeared — including reissues from India — and more LPs followed throughout the 1970s.

These recordings contain "composed" studio performances with the conventional studio instrumentation and instrumental interludes, and with emphasis on a memorable tune at least for the major melodic segment of the song. At the same time, they are essentially replications of religious *qawwālī* and therefore contain not only religious texts but also the musical features that are meaningful to *qawwālī* as a religious idiom. These include the special powerful drum beat of *qawwālī* along with forceful handclapping on rhythmic accents, intense *takrār* repetition of salient phrases, appropriate *girah*s, and a performance style focused on consonant text enunciation and a strong, open-throated singing voice. The instrumental introduction is strongly rhythmic and is often followed — or replaced — by the traditional *rubaʿi,* an introductory verse sung in recitative. But in between verses instrumental interludes are absent or reduced to minuscule cadential formulas, so that the continuous verbal communication is not interrupted. In effect, the recording articulates the essentially open-ended sequencing of the verse structure, but presents it in a purposefully composed performance, for ultimately it aims at creating memorable entertainment even while invoking a religious experience.

Urdu is the standard language of the Pakistani *qawwālī* record; this also includes Urduized versions of Hindi devotional song texts. A "higher," Persianized and "lower" Hindi-ized version of Urdu have actually been pulled together into a single flexible idiom in the works of contemporary Sufi poets, often in the form of a precomposed set of Hindi-ized *girah*s appended to Persianized refrain verses. That the work of a few such poets dominates the new recorded *qawwālī* repertoire suggests an integrative perspective on an idiom targeted for a general audience.

Three leading performers from Karachi have led these forays into musical transformation and composition. All three hailed originally from Muslim elite centers in India; between them, their recorded repertoire embodies a wide range of recorded *qawwālī,* including songs specific to their Sufi lineages. All three first produced a number of 45 rpm records followed by several LPs, which have now been converted into cassettes. Manzur Nyazi and Bahauddin are *qawwāl bachche,* the highest pedigree among hereditary *qawwāl*s (Qureshi 1986:13f, 99f). But it is Ghulam Farid Sabri, from a *mīrāsī* lineage of Meerut, who came to dominate the entire development as an innovator and performer and within a decade went on to become the very embodiment of modern *qawwālī* in the Indian subcontinent and even abroad. Focusing on his music and its impact since the late 1960s illustrates the transformation of Pakistani *qawwālī* into a national idiom and the role of recording in the process.

In Ghulam Farid Sabri a number of qualities converge that have gained his recordings the widest distribution and recognition, turning them into models imitated and emulated in Sufi assemblies throughout the subcontinent. First and foremost are his well-composed and arranged tunes, appropriately fitted to the text in both style and structure, but also shaped to the need for tunefulness and memorability. Even where he uses traditional Sufi melodies, as in Example 8, they become part of a composed whole with carefully crafted tune components.

Example 8: Ghulam Farid Sabri, "Balaghul-ulā bā kamālehī"
"This Prophet of wondrous beauty" (Arabic and Urdu, EMI LKCA-20000)

Opening line:	At the Invitation of the Omnipresent
	the Prophet ascended to the infinite heights
girah:	So miraculous was his beauty
	that God could not endure to be separated from him
Opening line:	At the Invitation of the Omnipresent
	the Prophet ascended to the infinite heights
girah:	On the night of his ascension the Prophet
	was called to the Throne on high
	So displeasing to God had the Prophet's absence been
Opening verse:	At the invitation of the Omnipresent
	the Prophet ascended to the infinite heights
	Is there any limit to his exaltation?
	(A) Balagal-ula bā-kamālehī (This Prophet of wondrous beauty)
Opening verse:	At the invitation of the Omnipresent
	the Prophet ascended to the infinite heights
	Is there any limit to his exaltation?
	(A) Balagal-ula bā-kamālehī (This Prophet of wondrous beauty)

A second quality of Ghulam Farid Sabri's recordings is melodic and rhythmic variety, starting with the introductory verses and extending to melodic inserts as well as final invocational formulas, first introduced in *Tājdār-e-Haram*. Known and imitated by *qawwāls* all over South Asia, this is musically the most remarkable and certainly the most famous of all Ghulam Farid Sabri recordings. The text, too, features for the first time in recorded *qawwālī* the full linguistic and connotational range of Hindi and Farsi verse inserts, in addition to the main text in Urdu.

Example 9: Ghulam Farid Sabri, "Tājdār-e-Haram"
             "O Lord of the Kaʻba" (Muhammad)" (Urdu, with Farsi and
             Hindi, EMI LKCA-20000)

Refrain (Urdu):	O Lord of the Kaʻba, bestow your benign glance on us
	so that we, the deprived, may have a better life
girah (Farsi):	There is no sinner like me among all your followers
	Have mercy on my condition, you who are the blessing of the world
Refrain (Urdu):	O Lord of the Kaʻaba, bestow your benign glance on us
girah (Hindi/Farsi):	(H) What can I tell you, Prince of Arabia you already know what troubles my heart
	(F) O you who are entitled "unlettered," when I am apart from you
	(H) my nights just will not pass
	(H) Your love makes me forget all sense, how long must I wait for news of you
	(F) Won't you cast a secret glance toward me,
	(H) Won't you listen to my voice
Refrain (Urdu):	O Lord of the Kaʻba

Within the confines of this word-dominated genre, the Sabri recordings expand the role of instruments beyond the traditional *nagmā* or prelude, which prefaces the *qawwālī* item proper. Two contrasting instrumental introductions add both internal variety and stylistic profile. The first one, slow and unmeasured, prefaces the *rubāʻī* or introductory recitative, then a smartly paced, rhythmically emphatic prelude in the style of the *nagmā* introduces the main song. The instrumentation adds variety within and also between songs, underscoring their individual character. Thus they range from the traditional harmonium and *dholak* for items of orthodox religiosity to a full complement of studio instruments, with a touch of *sitār* to invoke classical music for sophisticated texts or, conversely, the "banjo" and disc-adorned tambourine of popular *qawwālī* for simple devotional texts.

Perhaps the most important of these trends was the emulation of Middle Eastern drum beats to enhance the increasingly popular Arabic text inserts or refrains by imparting an Arab flavor that acoustically suggests the abode of the Prophet. Example 10 has such an Arabized drumming pattern throughout, along with its highly effective refrain phrase.

Example 10: Ghulam Farid Sabri, "Mustafā"
          "O Mustafā (Muhammad)" (EMI LKDA 20050)

Refrain:	O Mustafā, Mustafā, Mustafā
	Mustafā, Mustafā, Mustafā salleʿala
Inserted verse:	The fiery heat of the day of judgment cannot harm anyone
	Who enjoys the protective shade of Mustafā's glance
Refrain:	O Mustafā, Mustafā, Mustafā

Finally, Ghulam Farid Sabri judiciously expands the element of art music, in his recorded idiom, just like Manzur Nyazi and Bahauddin, and earlier Mubarak Ali Fateh Ali. He does so through *rāga* melody and melodic virtuosity; both are self-consciously featured in the form of short improvisatory passages but timed so as not to break the flow of the text message. Favorites are salient phrases of popularly known *rāga*s like *darbārī*, a *rāga* associated with the court of Akbar, which serve to evoke Muslim high culture without demanding a sophisticated ear. This dimension also serves well in nonreligious live performance settings — like the Karachi Club — where social rather than spiritual status dominates the occasion.

In addition to the qualities of his music — many of which the two other important *qawwāl*s also share — what adds to Ghulam Farid Sabri's success is his own mastery as a performer supported by a consistently high standard of delivery from his entire group. His own forceful and open-throated voice is complemented by the more crooning or *"filmī"* voice of his brother Maqbool Sabri. He provides the *surīlā* (melodious) element with his responses and is featured prominently in lighter *qawwālī* selections with Bombay-style narrative *girah*s. The group has several other good solo voices and maintains a clean choral ensemble with good diction. As for building an international career, Ghulam Farid Sabri has the personal ability to project himself and respond successfully to changing trends in patronage and audience preference, taking his rich musical-religious heritage out of an essentially feudal dependence on a Sufi establishment into a freelance world of largely secular, though not necessarily private patronage.

This process received an important impetus when television and its cheap dissemination was introduced in 1967 and began to promote *qawwālī* performance as media entertainment. Its weekly *qawwālī* programs gave performers the opportunity to develop a national visual identity as media stage performers; furthermore the high status of television reinforced the image of *qawwālī* as classy and serious public entertainment. Hand in hand went the introduction of *qawwālī* "concerts" in clubs and government functions, culminating in outright government patronage in the form of cultural representation, delegations abroad, and finally international tours and record contracts.

Example 11 is a famous television performance song with a refrain theme popularized in the 1940–50s, first by Abdurrahman Kanchwala, who excelled in popular Bombay-style *qawwālī*, and also by Azim Prem Ragi (Enayatullah interview). Following the *bhakti* model, which is standard for Hindi *qawwālī,* the devotee is a woman, the great Hindu poetess Mirabai, who is here a devotee of Khwaja Mu'inuddin Chishti of Ajmer.[9] The song remains within the confines of the religious range of *qawwālī* but is presented as a narrative in an entertaining popular style, including spoken comments, which are common in secular entertainment *qawwālī*. An international audience of South Asian listeners is addressed here, invoking Hindu-Muslim unity through topic and language.

Example 11: Ghulam Farid Sabri, "Main to Xwājā kī dīwānī"
     "I am immersed in love for the Khwaja" (Urdu and Hindi)

girah (spoken):	Where He is, my heart is too, where my heart is, everything else is too Only one must first understand the condition of the heart
Inserted comment (spoken):	However, no one understands the condition of the heart Why?
girah (spoken):	Muslims always say: come to the mosque Hindus always say: come to the temple What do these disputes have to do with me?
Refrain:	I am immersed in love, immersed in love with the Khwaja
Inserted comment (spoken):	Three hundred miles from Ajmer Sharif there used to be a kingdom called Mer Taror. The Maharani Mirabai was a Hindu, but listen how much faith and love she had for Khwaja Gharib Nawaz [the Sustainer of the Poor]
girah:	Mira Bai who belonged to Mer Taror Was married to Rana Sanga Outwardly she was his wife

But in secret she was madly in love with Khwaja
She would travel three hundred miles
To get a glimpse of her Beloved in Ajmer
For twenty years she had been coming
But never has she been close to the tomb
Because she was wearing a Maharani's dress
And on her feet anklets of real pearls
The sound of her anklets would create a commotion
And the Khwaja would say: Mira you are disrespectful
But in the twenty-first year she could not contain herself
And standing on the first step of the shrine she cried out—
What was her cry? Here it is before you:
(H) My Khwaja's boundary wall[10] is so high, I can
    neither climb across nor get back down
Tell my Khwaja that he should grasp my arm and take
    me to him

Refrain: I am immersed in love, immersed in love for the Khwaja

Many more *qawwālī* records by additional performers were produced in Pakistan during the same decade of 1969–79, most of a more popular, narrative type and by *qawwāl*s of mainly Punjabi origin, including even a woman. Example 12 features Kausar Jabin Taji, accompanied by a male vocal group who has to strain to sing at the same pitch; it also illustrates the common practice of using the tune of a well-known *qawwālī* with a different poem composed on the same theme and pattern. The original *Xwājā Hind-ul-Walī ho nigāh-e-Karam* was famous in the recording by the Indian *qaw-wāl* Aziz Nazan, popular in the 1960s and 1970s.

Example 12: Kausar Jabin Taji, "Xwājā-e-Xwājagān"
           "Saint of Saints (Muinuddin Cishti of Ajmer)" (Angel EKDA
           20042)

Opening verse: Saint of Saints, protector of the destitute,
              give support to those who need you
         Keep our honor, Spiritual Master of India,
              for the sake of the one who carries the blanket
              (Muhammad)

Long-playing records, however, were accorded mainly to one Pakistani performer, Aziz Mian, who emerged in the mid-1970s with a vigorous didactic narrative style reminiscent of the earlier Waiz Qawwal, but reinforced by a strong backup group for intense *takrār* repetition. Significantly, his popularity for "fighting with God" in song arose directly from the impact of his flamboyant delivery on the by then well-established platform of "television *qawwālī*." Showmanship and golden *shervānī* coat notwithstanding, what is remarkable is his strict adherence to serious moralizing, if not strictly religious topics, by means of respectable Urdu poetry. This socioculturally adapted version of the popular narrative *qawwālī* style testifies to the middle-class market targeted by recorded *qawwālī* in Pakistan.

The most recent development in Pakistani recorded *qawwālī* is the rise to prominence of a once again more classically oriented performing team, Nusrat Ali Fateh Ali (now Nusrat Fateh Ali alone). Sons of Mubarak Ali Fateh Ali, they are heir to a special tradition of musical elaboration, both melodic and rhythmic; they are also heir to the classical Punjabi/Siraiki repertoire, which makes them nationally attractive, given the Punjabi majority and its cultural assertion in recent years (Nayyar 1988). This suggests that by the mid-1980s, there was a continuing demand for an elite version of *qawwālī* in Pakistan that could function as a representative sound idiom both nationally and internationally—an idiom or icon of incipient Pakistani "public culture" (Appadurai 1988).

The recent spread of cassette technology, with its universal and cheap copyability, is having a diffusing effect on the commercial recording in both countries; it has also increased the dissemination of recordings across the border between them (see Manual 1993). In India, record companies have more or less ceased recording religious *qawwālī,* given its very limited market, although they sell reissues, including Pakistani releases. Pakistan, on the other hand, is seeing a great diversification of religious recordings generally. In addition to reissues of current LPs on cassette, EMI is doing the same for recordings of the past, making "oldies" like Pearu and Kalu or Ismail Azad accessible again. This trend toward releasing archival recordings, mainly from radio collections, has an obvious economic motivation. The spread of unrestricted cassette reproduction, in India as well as Pakistan, has drastically reduced the recording industry's incentive to invest in recording new artists.

Two new forces can be identified in Pakistan during the 1980s. The first is Lok Virsa, the government-funded Centre for Folk Culture Studies, whose mandate includes the production of heritage recordings. Lok Virsa has produced an impressive cassette catalogue of archival and new recordings, which since 1985 have been distributed commercially and cheaply, but its emphasis is on Pakistani regional music. This means that Urdu songs and urban forms of *qawwālī* are of lesser importance, although the series contains an archival radio recording of the great Punjabi *qawwālī* team Mubarak Ali Fateh Ali. The second force is the Islamic movement, which finds expression in recordings produced by private companies. Tablīgh, the most prolific label among them, publishes only in Urdu and focuses on unaccompanied hymns—mainly *naʿt*. *Qawwālī* appears to be neglected, for it does not fit the orthodox conception of Islamic musical expression.

To review, the recorded product *qawwālī* emerged by the 1920s and 1930s from an unlettered version of the Sufi genre of *qawwālī*. Invested with facets of popular or film music as it develops, recorded *qawwālī* acquired qualities of entertainment and memorability, but as a solo genre. In the second phase (1940s to 1960s), the genre acquired a more characteristic profile through its group singing and the popular narrative *girah* style; this profile has also been introduced into popular film music to convey a "Muslim" atmosphere. By the 1960s Indian *qawwālī* recordings emphasized Hindi and multireligious themes while Pakistan created a resurgence of serious religious *qawwālī*, articulating Sufi elite traditions brought from India. The new idiom became a focus of musical creativity, drawing from popular as well as classical music while also paraphrasing the salient features of authentic religious *qawwālī*, although context specificity of text and structure were absent. Experiments with Arabic musical traits reinforced the quest for investing the idiom with a distinctly Islamic musical identity. The cassette era beginning in the 1980s has introduced a diversified offering including recordings of the past, but the weight of new religious musical production has shifted to the more orthodox genres of unaccompanied hymns.

The Impact of Recordings on Live *Qawwālī*

Where does all this leave the original context and function of *qawwālī*? Traditionally, spiritual leaders must pursue the purpose of the *qawwālī* ritual, which means encouraging traditional standards and a conservative repertoire and, above all, controlling the event in both setting and procedure. Performers must conform to these aims, but they also wish to please the audience whence their reward originates, and audiences are familiar with and partial to recordings. Indeed, many, especially young men, attend to be entertained by popular tunes: even sheikhs may ask for such a song, perhaps under the guise of a secluded lady's request (Meraj Ahmad interview).

The *qawwālī* performer is well aware of the opposition between the spiritual and entertainment purposes of music. It largely reinforces the ubiquitous dichotomy in Sufi assemblies between *xās* (special, spiritually elevated) and *ām* (common, spiritually inferior), which is often equal to the difference between catering musically to the spiritual elite or to the generality of untutored listeners in the assembly. It is to please the latter that *qawwāl*s include popular recorded *qawwālī* items in their repertoire; they also use well-known tunes as settings for more serious texts.

But most composed recorded tunes are frozen into a shape inseparably associated with the recording artist and reinforced at each hearing. Performing such a song is thus an obvious act of *urānā* (snatching), something below the dignity of a self-respecting hereditary performer. Adapting only the tune of such a song as a setting for a new poem is more acceptable. Typically, then, more recorded *qawwālī* is heard from untrained "common" *qawwāl*s, along with other trappings of popular music like extra instrumentation, a crooning vocal style and a preference for *tukbandī*. Indeed, the exposure to recordings has enabled nonhereditary or *atai* performers to swell the ranks of *qawwāl*s with a repertoire built of recorded songs.[11]

In their own way these performers and spiritual leaders are engaged in what amounts to a constant process of mediating between the established expressive tradition of Sufism, which is vested in the oral tradition of its affiliated performers, and the highly persuasive current idiom of "Sufi entertainment," which is enshrined in recording. The degree of compromise between the two varies nationally and regionally; its most significant correlates are spiritual status and cultural literacy among Sufi patrons and, to a lesser degree, among performers.

The locus operandi for this mediating process is the Sufi assembly, the clearly bounded context for *qawwālī* performance. The crux is that this context is functionally defined, and its functional priority is subject to enforcement by the Sufi spiritual leadership. Reinforced by the conceptual hierarchy of Sufism, a quasi-feudal arrangement obtains in which the sheikh controls the music by controlling the musician. This he does by preventing the musician from catering to the assembled listeners without reference to the spiritual leader who embodies the devotee's spiritual goal. In effect, the musical idiom is controlled by powerful consensus of its highly unequal participants. The impact of the recorded/*filmī* idiom is staved off or neutralized, not only by rejection but also by adaptation and even incorporation, as long as the ritual continues as a living, spiritually functional practice within a circle of Sufis.

A glance at the historical antecedents of recording suggests that the process of accommodating a new idiom is perhaps not a new one for Sufi music. Early Sufi history suggests that the Farsi elite accommodated the Hindi devotional idiom in order to address a wider local audience, thereby reflecting a dual identification, which appears to be characteristic of early South Asian Sufism: with the Muslim feudal elite—"Sufi and Sultan" (Ahmed 1963)—and with the Hindu commoner—"Sufi and populace" (Eaton 1974). In a parallel, later development, the idiom of Urdu was increasingly accepted to address the largely non-elite urban Muslims; once it was brought into the live ritual setting it acquired spiritual functionality. In this process, each successive language repertoire also introduced the symbols and flavor of its idiom along with a distinctive musical setting; what has integrated them into the Sufi system of signification can be summed up in one word: *nisbat,* the Sufi term to denote a spiritual link of mystical meaning. The core currency of *nisbat* is a rich, composite, and basically open-ended Sufi vocabulary, linguistic as well as musical, of symbols and metaphors, which is constantly validated by its ritual use. Extensions or new meanings are negotiated essentially through the test of their efficacy in the assembly. Thus there is no prescribed repertoire in the assembly; instead, *qawwāl*s freely choose what to perform and how, and visiting performers are invited in. The verdict rests with the listeners through what is the core activity of the *qawwālī* ritual: *sama'* (listening). Depending on its reception and the sheikh's response, a new poem or song will be either accepted or rejected, according to the procedural norms of the ritual that ideally suit this flexible process. If the effect on the listeners is deemed spiritually beneficial, even a purist sheikh will accept the performance of a recorded song, although the same sheikh may reject such a song when it is not appropriately presented.

Recorded *qawwālī* has certainly presented *qawwāl*s with a rich source of new repertoire. Already in the public domain, recorded items, textual or musical, are bound to have audience appeal at some level, but their spiritual acceptability is subject to factors that vary both situationally and regionally. The result is a shifting boundary between the generalized matrix of recorded *qawwālī* and those items among them that serve the proper religious function of Sufi music. The fact is that the perceived articulation of *nisbat* arises from a composite of overt semantic and subtle stylistic meanings. Like everything in the Sufi experience, *nisbat* can also be inspirationally perceived, given its religious-functional premise. Uniquely, even the sound of a *qawwālī* record, even a film song, can by analogy take the place of ritual *qawwālī,* as is evidenced from the special experiences of some Sufi adepts.[12]

The evidence overwhelmingly points to the strongly functional context of *qawwālī* as the basis for its continuing vigor as a living musical idiom with spiritual potency. This stands in contrast to the much-lamented destructive effect of recording on traditional secular idioms (Wallis and Malm 1984), a process that is encroaching even on some South Asian musical traditions (e.g., weddings songs; see also Manuel 1988). In the case of *qawwālī*, it is the recorded genre that continues to derive meaningful religious reference from the live ritual, resulting in a musical idiom that conveys to its listeners a functionally composite and portable experience of entertainment, Muslim identity, and devotional Islam all in one: a musical style package created by and for the now politically emancipated culture of Indic Islam.

However, once they are part of the political process, cultures are more directly subject to change. Given the changing socioreligious constellation on the Pakistani horizon, the success and proliferation of this *qawwālī*-style package may have reached its peak. For one, the first, dominant generation of elite immigrants, with their affinity for the literary religious culture of Sufism and its Indian local roots, are being succeeded by a more Westernized younger generation with a more local Pakistani orientation. This may well shift elite patronage away from Urdu toward regional language genres, and away from devotional toward secular musical expression. Second, the recent Islamization movement promotes an orthodox ideology that is reflected in the proliferation of recordings of properly religious "music": Quran recitation and unaccompanied hymns. This formidable new repertoire is remarkable for its faithful adherence to religious constraints on the music.

Qawwālī, however, may well hold its own. It is too early to be certain, but my impression is that precisely their exclusively religious association makes it impossible for even the most attractive *na't* recordings to take the place of *qawwālī*. Long before present-day "fundamentalism," a *na't* chanted by a courtesan singer in the early film *Talāsh-e-Haq* (1930s) evoked such protests from Bombay Muslims that the theater had to be shut down (Lutfullah interview).

Precisely because recorded *qawwālī* does not qualify as religious music in the orthodox sense, it has attained over its considerable life span an iconicity embodying a uniquely South Asian Muslim constellation of religious and national cultural identification.

Notes

1. In most Indian languages there is no separate gloss for chanting. Hindi and Urdu use the term *parhnā*, which covers both reading and reciting (see also the following section of this chapter, "The Live *Qawwālī* Tradition").

2. For a pioneering discussion of *bhajan* assemblies, see Singer (1972b); for discussions with a musical focus see Simon (1980), Qureshi (1980b).

3. Interestingly, this category lacks a collective term, nor is the Arabic *ta'bīr* (Farmer 1965) used in South Asia. Complete Urdu texts of the examples used here were included in the original seminar presentation of this paper. Due to the exigencies of publication, however, it was impossible to include them in the present volume. Complete Urdu texts are available from the author (Regula Qureshi, Dept. of Music, University of Alberta, Edmonton, Canada T60 2C9).

4. Musical evidence is not available until the introduction of sound recording.

5. A poetic composition elucidating a classical poem, usually in Farsi. Each Farsi verse line is preceded by a verse of three to five matching and explanatory lines in Urdu.

6. Multiple repetition refers to the practice, in *qawwālī*, of repeating a short text unit many times over in order to intensify its meaning. (For a discussion of this technique in live *qawwālī*, see Qureshi 1986.)

7. The name continued to be used by Muslim performers, most famous among them Yusuf Azad, who excelled in popular and secular *qawwālī*.

8. Friday broadcasts of group *qawwālī* were first pioneered by Kallan Qawwal.

9. Notwithstanding the historical fact that the two lived three centuries apart.

10. The word *menṛī*, a Hindi agricultural term for the mud dikes that separate irrigated fields, is here highly suggestive of nonurban Hindi culture.

11. For an example, see references to Song 7 and its singer, Iftekhar Amrohvi in Qureshi (1986:36, 102).

12. A senior *qawwāl* tells of an elderly Sufi who went into a trance in a theater on hearing the opening line of a devotional film song and had to be driven home in a *ṭongā* to the *qawwāl's* continuous singing of the same verse line (Meraj Ahmad interview).

References

Ahmed, Aziz. 1963. "The Sufi and the Sultan in Pre-Mughal Muslim India." *Der Islam* 38:142–53.

Appadurai, Arjun, and Carol Breckenridge. 1990. "*Public Culture in Late 20th Century India.*" *Items* (SSRC) 44, no. 4:77–80.

Dargah Quli Khan, Nawab. 1949. *Purani Dehli ke Halat* (original Farsi manuscript in Urdu dated ca. 1735), trans. Khwaja Hasan Nizami. Delhi: Mahbub Press.

Dhond, M. V. n.d. *The Evolution of Khyal*. New Delhi: Sangeet Natak.

Eaton, Richard S. 1974. "Sufi Folk Literature and the Expansion of Indian Islam." *History of Religions* 14:117–127.

Enayatullah, Anwar. 1976. "How Good Are the New Trends in Qawwali?" *Karachi Morning News* (February 15):6.

Farmer, Henry. 1965. "Ghina (Song)." *Encyclopedia of Islam* 2:1072–75. Leiden: Brill.

Gronow, Pekka. 1981. "The Record Industry Comes to the Orient." *Ethnomusicology* 25, no. 2:251–284.

Henry, Edward O. 1988. *Chant the Names of God: Musical Culture in Bhojpuri-Speaking India*. San Diego: San Diego State University Press.

Imam, Hakim Mohammad Karam. 1959–60. "Ma'danu'l-Musiqi" ("Melody Through the Centuries"). Partial trans. by Govind Vidyarthia. *Sangeet Natak Akademi Bulletin* 11–12:6–14, 13–26, 30, 49.

Ja'far Sharif. 1972. *Islam in India or the Qanum-i-Islam.* G. A. Herklots, trans. New Delhi: Oriental Book Reprint Corporation.

Joshi, G. N. 1977. "The Phonograph in India." *NCPA Journal* 6, no. 3:5–27.

——. 1984. *Down Melody Lane.* Hyderabad: Orient Longman.

——. 1988. "A Concise History of the Phonograph Industry in India." *Popular Music* (May):147–156.

Kinnear, Michael S. 1985. *A Discography of Hindustani and Karnatic Music.* Discographies, no. 17. Westport, Conn.: Greenwood Press.

Lelyveld, David. 1986. "Upon the Subdominant: Administering Music on All-India Radio." Unpublished manuscript.

Manuel, Peter. 1988. *Popular Musics of the Non-Western World: An Introductory Survey.* New York: Oxford University Press.

——. 1993. *Cassette Culture: Popular Music and Technology in North India.* Chicago: University of Chicago Press.

Meer Hassan, Ali. 1973. *Observations on the Mussulmauns of India.* 2 vols. Reprint of 1832 edition. Delhi: Idarah-i-Adabiyat-i-Delhi.

Nayyar, Adam. 1988. *Qawwali.* Islamabad: Lok Virsa Research Centre.

Qureshi, Regula Burckhardt. 1980a. "Pakistan." *The New Grove Dictionary of Music and Musicians.* London: Macmillan.

——. 1980b. "India, Subcontinent of; V. Popular Religious Music; Muslim." *The New Grove Dictionary of Music and Musicians.* London: Macmillan.

——. 1986. *Sufi Music of India and Pakistan.* Cambridge: Cambridge University Press.

Roychaudhry, M. L. 1957. "Music in Islam." *Journal of the Asiatic Society of Bengal* 13:43–102.

Ruswa, Mirza Muhammad Hadi. 1963. *Umrao Jan Ada.* Lahore: Majlis-e-Taraqqi-e-Adab.

Simon, Robert. 1980. "India, Subcontinent of; V. Popular Religious Music; Hindu." *The New Grove Dictionary of Music and Musicians.* London: Macmillan.

Singer, Milton. 1972a. *When a Great Tradition Modernizes.* New York: Praeger.

——. 1972b. "The Radha-Krishna Bhajanas of Madras City." In *When a Great Tradition Modernizes,* pp. 199–241. New York: Praeger.

Wallis, Roger, and Kirster Malm. 1984. *Big Sounds from Small Peoples: The Music Industry in Small Countries.* New York: Pendragon Press.

INTERVIEWS

Anwar Enayatullah (Edmonton, Alberta), 1990.
Qawwal Gore Khan (New Delhi, Nizamuddin Auliya), 1976.
M. Lutfullah (Edmonton, Alberta), 1989.
Qawwal Meraj Ahmad (New Delhi, Nizamuddin Auliya), 1975.

Scott L. Marcus

7. On Cassette Rather Than Live: Religious Music in India Today

Religious music has always played an important role in Indian society, whether as part of life-cycle rituals, annual festivals, monthly, weekly, and daily rituals of devotion, or the result of chance encounters with wandering singer-devotees. When the recording industry developed in the early twentieth century, industry officials realized the importance of religious music and decided to feature it prominently in their early releases. (See Chapter 6 by Qureshi in this volume.) After it became available on records and radio, the music reached new and larger audiences. However, many aspects of traditional live performances were changed or sacrificed. More recently, audio cassettes have replaced records as the dominant technology for commercial distribution of recorded music, which again helped increase audience size and affected aspects of the music. This chapter is concerned with the impact of the recording industries on religious music in India today, with special attention given to the cassette industry.

The audio cassette represents one of the newer forms of mass-media technologies, its presence becoming prominent in India only as of the mid-1970s. In India today, audio cassettes and cassette players are ubiquitous, in stores, buses, trucks, temples, and homes. There are hundreds of cassette companies, of which the biggest have huge factories in or near large cities, while the smallest occupy only a single room in a back alley of a minor city or town.[1]

In many ways, the audio cassette must be viewed as an extension of the media technologies that preceded it, notably radio broadcasting and disc recording. As such, analysis of the effect of the cassette industry on Indian music — and Indian religious music in particular — is not different from an analysis of the effect of music recording, in any form, on this body of music. However, the audio cassette has unique qualities that separate it from previously existing media technologies, most notably, an unprecedented ease and low cost of production. Thus, analysis of the effect of the cassette industry presents many new issues.

Before proceeding with a two-part investigation, focusing first on the effect of music recording in general and then on consequences resulting from the rise of the cassette industry, I would like to introduce three examples of traditional live performances of religious music.

Traditional Music Performance

These examples represent three different types of religious music, three of the many contexts in which religious music occurs in India, and three different types of performer-audience interaction. They offer an important frame of reference for much of what follows because they represent aspects of the Indian music world before the advent of recording.

The first example is a recording of a wandering *bābā*, a musician who travels from village to village singing *nirguṇ bhajan*s (devotional songs featuring a god without attributes), seeking handfuls of grain or old clothing in return for his singing. Throughout the ages, such wandering musicians have been important transmitters of much of Hindu philosophy to the villages of rural India. In eastern Uttar Pradesh, these wandering musicians commonly accompany themselves on the *sārangī* (a bowed string instrument) and often refer to themselves as *gorakh bābā*s, after the saint Gorakhnath.[2] I recorded this example in 1975, completely by chance. I was recording a group of musicians in a village some fifteen miles north of Banaras, when a *bābā* walked across the fields into the village and up to our gathering. This is a Kabir *bhajan;* that is, the text is said to be by the fifteenth-century saint Kabir.

Refrain: No one takes anything with him [when he dies].
Verse: Yam Raj [the god of death] will come and sit at the feet [of the
           dying one].
           The *prāṇ* [life force] will try to hide [in the body] but there is
           no place to hide.
Refrain: No one takes anything with him [when he dies].
Verse: Four men together pick up the bier,
           take it to the bank of the Jamuna [river].
           Five men perform the *panckarm* [the last rites],
           while the pyre, of wood, burns.

Refrain: No one takes anything with him [when he dies].
Verse: So says Kabir: Listen, my fellow beings,
            After today, my dear ones,
            I won't return to my home town.

In this type of devotional music, a wandering musician appears offering a chance encounter that is both personal and auspicious. The listener receives a powerful message and is given a chance to accrue religious merit by giving the *bābā* alms.

This example raises two points of vital importance for commercial recording. One concerns payment, the other recording per se. When we requested a second song, the *bābā* refused, saying initially that he still had a long distance to travel that day. When we persisted, he commented that this was not a prearranged engagement; he had not taken — and does not take — "advance" money that would have obliged him to keep singing for us. Traditionally, many people believed that one should not receive money for devotional singing. It is a form of worship, not an income-oriented profession.

A second, related issue was raised when the *bābā* amplified his refusal by remarking that he was aware that we were recording his music. (We had not tried to hide this fact. Quite to the contrary, we had asked him to position himself close to the microphone.) Many in India have believed that their music should not be recorded on philosophical and possibly religious grounds. This belief has been so common that it has undoubtedly been an issue for musicians of every traditional genre ever recorded, with many musicians simply refusing to have their music recorded. But there were others who were eager to record, often acquiring significant amounts of money and fame in the process. In time, those who refused came to see themselves as "falling behind"; soon they too were ready to record.

Many musicians in eastern Uttar Pradesh related stories about these two ideas to me. One of the most famous *birahā* musicians said, "My guru said, 'No, music is something which should not be sold [*nahī̃ gānā becā nahī̃ jātā*]. If you have your songs recorded by someone, he'll sell them.' People then thought that knowledge should not be sold [*vidyā ko becā nahī̃ jātā*]." "Singing" (*gānā*) is equated with "knowledge" (*vidyā*). Neither should be sold, nor should singing be recorded. Another folk singer who enjoyed major fame in the Banaras region in the 1940s and 1950s told me proudly that he "never sang for money, never!"

My second example of traditional live performance was recorded in a residential neighborhood in the city of Banaras. In Banaras, on Tuesdays and Saturdays (days considered especially holy for Vaiṣṇava worship), people frequently gather to sing devotional songs (*bhajan*s) as part of ongoing devotional music circles (*kīrtan maṇḍalī*s). Men of all castes come and share communal singing.[3] Each group generally has an acknowledged convener, and people take turns leading individual songs. The leader sings a line, and the others repeat it. The leader then might sing the same line again or proceed to the next line, the others continuing to repeat each chosen line. The group accompanies itself with one or more *ḍholak*s (double-headed cylindrical drums) and numerous pairs of *manjīrā*s (metallic hand cymbals). Individual songs are characterized by surges of energy and by an overall slow-to-fast progression. Song texts range from short calls praising various gods to longer poems extolling the gods' many deeds and attributes. An example of the former is:

Hail to Sita and Ram.
Hail to Radha and Shyam.
Hail to Hanuman.

Such events seem like group participation par excellence. Everyone in attendance sings along. However, a common, and many would say essential, ingredient of such singing sessions these days are loudspeakers, which broadcast the music to thousands who live in the surrounding streets and alleys.[4] What seems to be a participatory genre is, for many, nonparticipatory. However, for these passive participants, the music's context is clear. It is Tuesday night again, and this is their neighborhood's *kīrtan maṇḍalī*.

These two examples are types of music that have not generally been recorded, and so are not available on record or cassette.

The third example of live performance is a *nirguṇ bhajan* sung by a professional entertainment group. The genre is *birahā*, a folk genre of eastern Uttar Pradesh and western Bihar. A five-member ensemble is often hired to play at weddings and at temple festivals called *śṛingār*s. The ensemble consists of a lead singer, a *ḍholak* player, a harmonium player, and two chorus members who play two types of hand cymbals (the *kartāl* and the *jhānjh*). Loudspeakers as well as prior publicity and personal invitations usually attract audiences of hundreds of people. Attendance is free to all except the immediate patrons, either the groom's family or the contributors to the temple's *śṛingār* fund. Those in the audience who especially appreciate the music can walk up to the stage during the performance and present the singer with *inām,* a tip or reward.[5]

This example, performed by Hira Lal Yadav and Party at a Banaras temple *śṛingār* festival, takes us into the world of commercial recordings in two ways. It borrows its melody from an earlier commercial hit, and, with its new text, this song became so popular that it too was commercially recorded.

Many musicians across North India do not compose new melodies when they create new songs; rather, they pick a preexisting melody and write new words to fit the old melody. Traditionally, this has resulted in a situation where boatwomen sing boatwomen songs (*mallāh gīt*) using only one melody. Similarly, washermen (*dhobīs*) sing washermen songs (*dhobī gīt*) using only one or two melodies, and cowherders (*Ahīrs*) would sing their *birahā,* again, using only one or two melodies. When the commercial music industry started broadcasting newly composed melodies into North Indian cities and villages (on Radio Ceylon and All-India Radio), musicians found what has been an endless source of new melodies. Initially, musicians picked film songs for their new melodies. More recently, a wide variety of nonfilm melodies have also been used.[6]

Hira Lal Yadav's song uses the melody of a *nirguṇ bhajan* that was a major commercial hit in eastern Uttar Pradesh in 1982. In addition to borrowing the melody, the words also correspond to the words of the original recording. In the original version, a man says to his wife, "O woman, my heart is taken with your nose ring" (*Jhulanī mē gorī lāgā hamār jiyā*). His wife then answers, "O husband, the nose ring's color is pure" (*Jhulanī kā rang sāncā, hamār piyā*).[7] In the *birahā* version written by the poet Mangal Yadav, a man says to his wife, "O woman, better than your nose ring is this swing" (*Jhulanī se nīk jhulanā hamār gorī*). The song describes the swing as being made by Lord Brahma from various religious and cosmological materials; numerous gods and goddesses, Indian saints and martyrs are then said to have enjoyed themselves on the swing. (Swings, it should be noted, are a major part of rainy season festivities in eastern Uttar Pradesh.)

Refrain: O my beloved, my swing is better than your nose ring.
           The four-faced [Brahma] made this swing.
           He made it on the hood of the serpent king.
           The seat is resting on the turtle's back, my beloved.

Refrain: O my beloved, my swing is better than your nose ring.
            The moon and sun are the two ropes.
            The two mountains associated with the sunrise and sunset are
                on each side.
            The stars serve as flowers, my beloved.
Refrain: O my beloved, my swing is better than your nose ring.
            The fourteen worlds serve as the seat,
            with the ten directions as the doors of the swing.
            The sons of India have swung, my beloved.
Refrain: O my beloved, my swing is better than your nose ring.
            Vishnu swung while Lakshmi massaged his feet.
            Shiva swung while telling Sati the stories.
            From the egg, the parrot swung, my beloved.
Refrain: O my beloved, my swing is better than your nose ring.
            Radha and Shyam swung on the swing in Vrindavan.
            Tulsi, Kabir, and Sur swung on this swing.
            composing each of their creations, one at a time.
Refrain: O my beloved, my swing is better than your nose ring.
            [Mahatma] Gandhi, Subhas [Chandra Bose], and Jawahar
                [Lal Nehru] [swung] as children.
            Bhagat Singh, Udham Singh have swung on this swing [two
                martyrs of the Indian Independence movement who were
                hanged by the British].
            Everyone has to go one day, my beloved.
Refrain: O my beloved, my swing is better than your nose ring.
            Swami, Bihari, and Ramman [gurus of the singer and poet]
                benefited by swinging.
            Hira [the singer] swung with Hori's [another guru's] help.
            Mangal [both "auspiciousness" and the name of the poet] has
                spread in every courtyard, my beloved.
Refrain: O my beloved, my swing is better than your nose ring.

Eventually the *birahā* version became so popular that the singer was
approached by a local record/cassette company and the song was produced
as a commercial recording (on Modern Machinery Mart's Madhur label).
On the recording, the group's "folk" version was "enhanced" with instrumental accompaniment featuring instruments not indigenous to the original folk genre, including the clarinet and the Indian "banjo" (a zither fitted

with typewriter keys). (Chapter 6 in this volume refers to this instrument as a *bulbultarang*.)

From these examples we see many elements inherent in traditional live performance of religious music. These performances occur in settings that offer participants a wealth of contextual associations and meanings. The music of the wandering *bābā*, the communal *kīrtan maṇḍalī*, and the temple *śṛṇgār* festival are part of larger events and processes that confirm one's sense of belonging to a specific community. The music and the event often serve to uphold traditional religious values and customs. Personal contact with the performers, fellow singers, or audience members reaffirms aspects of social ties, obligations, and hierarchies. By words of encouragement, applause, spontaneous monetary remuneration, and even by their mere presence, those in attendance participate directly in a complex performer-audience feedback system.

The Recorded Religious Song

Traditional performed music can be compared to recorded religious music. *Bhajan,* one of the most popular religious genres, has been featured prominently on records and audio cassettes. One of the biggest music companies in India today, Music India Ltd. (previously called Polydor), has focused on this genre by creating a superstar. It promoted the singer Anup Jalota and in time succeeded in establishing him as the most popular singer of devotional music in India today. In what is arguably his most famous song, a Mira *bhajan,* "*Rang De Cunariyā,*" a devotee calls to Lord Krishna, probably at the time of the *holī* festival, saying, "color my *cunarī* [scarf]," not in normal colors like red or green, but in your own color, in a color that will never fade, no matter how often the fabric is washed. The instruments used include *tablā* (a pair of drums), harmonium, hand cymbals, and guitar.

Rang De Cunariyā

Sung: Color my *cunarī* [repeated many times].
[At one point the audience applauds Jalota's vocal artistry.] [A *cunarī* is a large scarf worn over a woman's head and shoulders. Following the practice of double entendre common in Indian religious songs, the *cunarī* can also be understood to refer to the devotee's soul.]

O Shyam [Krishna], my beloved, color my *cunarī*.
Give it such a color that the color will never fade
even if a washerman were to try to wash it all his life.
O Shyam, my beloved, color my *cunarī*. [The audience
applauds.]

spoken: "Shyam, my beloved, color my *cunarī*." Its meaning is
completely clear. [However,] if we go deeper, give it more
attention, then a new meaning appears. The meaning comes
from the color, "*shyam (śyām)*" [midnight blue]. That is,
"color my *cunarī*, o my beloved, with a midnight blue color."
Who is the beloved? The beloved is also "Shyam" [Krishna].
See the beauty of the words here:

sung: Don't color [it] red, don't color it green.
In your very colors color my *cunarī*. [The audience applauds.]
Shyam, my beloved, color my *cunarī*.

Without [having had the *cunarī*] colored I will not go home.

Pa Dha Dha Ni Dha Dha Pa Dha Ma Pa Ga Ma Re Ga Sa Re Ni
Sa Dha Ni Pa Sa.

[The solfege or *sargam* syllables, Sa, Re, Ga, Ma, Pa, Dha, Ni approximate
the Western solfege syllables, Do Re Mi Fa Sol La Ti. A dot below a syllable
signifies a lower octave. A line under a syllable signifies a lowered or flat-
tened note.]

Pa Dha Ni Sa -Sa Na Sa -Sa Ni Sa Re Ni Sa Ni Sa Re Ni Sa
Ga Ga Sa Re Ni Sa Ga Ga Sa Re Ni Sa Ga Ga Ra Ra Sa Re Ni Sa
Ga Ga Re Re Ma Ma Ga Ga Pa Pa Ma Dha Pa Dha Ma Pa Dha
Ni Dha Pa Dha Ma Pa Ga Ma Re Ga Sa Ga Pa. [The audience
applauds during the last moments of this *sargam* section.]

Without [having had the *cunarī*] colored I will not go home
even if my whole life were to pass.
O Shyam, my beloved, color my *cunarī*.

Mira's Lord, the worldly one who holds up the mountain [a reference to an episode in which Krishna saves his devotees from
torrential rains by providing them with shelter under a moun-
tain] . . .

spoken: Here I am presenting a question and its answer. The question is:
sung: What is more transparent than water, what is heavier than earth?

What is more raging than fire, what is blacker than *kājal* [black ash that is put around the eyes]?

spoken: The answer is:

sung: Knowledge is more transparent than water; sin is heavier than earth;

Anger is more raging than fire; and disgrace is blacker than *kājal*. [The audience applauds.]

Mira's Lord, the worldly one who holds up the mountain.

My gaze is locked on the feet of the Beloved, on the feet of Hari [Lord Vishnu], on the feet of Shyam. [The audience applauds.]

O Shyam, my beloved, color my *cunarī*. [The audience applauds as the song ends.]

In this song we find many new contrasting elements. For 99 percent of the people who know this song, there has been no performer-audience interaction. They have never heard the song performed live; they have never met Anup Jalota. As such, they have not participated in the system of direct performer-audience feedback. Many might have heard the song while sitting in a teashop or while passing a store or a temple. Others have gone to a store, bought the cassette, and listened to it whenever they wanted to. Here, audience interaction with the performer has been replaced by consumer interaction with the storekeeper. The storekeeper got the cassette from a dealer. The dealer obtained it from his distributor, who received it from a huge factory outside Delhi. None of these people has ever met Anup Jalota, has ever seen him perform, has ever had the chance to bring him *inām*. In the world of commercial music, many middlemen now stand between the performer and his audience.[8]

A related feature of commercial recordings is the loss of traditional performance contexts. Because so few ever attend live performances of commercially recorded songs, such recordings present music completely divorced from its performance context. The affirmation of social and familial ties inherent in the temple, wedding, and communal examples cited above is thus absent. This loss, however, is often mitigated by a personally imposed context. People have remarked, for example, that they play religious recordings while they do their *pūjā* (private religious ritual) each morning. Recording companies themselves often try to instill a sense of context by releasing recordings of live performances. "Rang De Cunariyā" is one such example. Jalota occasionally speaks to the audience and enthusiastic applause is heard periodically throughout the recording.

The loss of traditional context often changes many of the meanings inherent in a given piece of music. This is especially true for music that traditionally accompanies religious rituals such as *āratī*. *Āratī* is a ceremony in which devotees stand and sing praises to a specific deity. While one or more *āratī* songs are sung, an oil lamp is commonly moved in a circular motion around the statue of the deity and is then circulated among the devotees who symbolically take blessings from the deity by receiving warmth from the lamp's flame. Devotees also commonly receive a dash of colored paste, which they place on their foreheads, another act of symbolically receiving blessings. Many recorded collections of *āratī* songs are now available in the market. When listened to on a cassette player the communal, participatory, and ritual aspects of the songs disappear. The songs are often transformed into mere entertainment.[9]

Further, commercial recordings and the various music media offer a level of dissemination that was not possible when music existed solely in live performance. For example, the Anup Jalota song is widely known in India today. There is great irony in this because such a recording ends up giving millions of people a shared experience, a shared cultural and religious bond, even though many have been sitting alone in their living rooms listening to a cassette. No shared social event offers a sense of community: there was no neighborhood *śriṅgār*. Thus by spreading the musical product to vastly extended audiences, the recording industry gives the specific recordings new levels of power and influence.

As the chapters in this volume demonstrate, many religious objects and symbols in India today are commercially produced and media based. A major example of this in the realm of devotional music is a series of four cassettes that became immensely popular in 1982–83. In these, a singer, Mukesh, presented verses from Tulsidas's *Rāmāyaṇa* (*Rāmcaritmānas*). These cassettes were so famous — in Banaras they were played in temples, in clothing stores, appliance stores, in tea stalls, buses, and so on — that they were surely more popular for a time than the written *Rāmāyaṇa* itself. For over a year, the *Rāmāyaṇa* lived most vividly in cassette form. This is but one of the numerous examples where a technological novelty serves not only to perpetuate but also to further popularize aspects of traditional religious culture. (See also Chapter 9 by Lutgendorf in this volume.)

When religious music becomes a commercial product, one can study patterns of consumption. Cassette companies undertake such studies to maximize their profits. Their efforts lead to additional features peculiar to recorded rather than live music.

In order to try to assure the profitability of new commercial releases, the music industry has created superstars like Anup Jalota. Companies mount extensive campaigns to market their stars. Music India Ltd., for example, arranged a series of concert tours for Anup Jalota, dubbed *bhajan yātrās*, "*bhajan* tours."[10] In addition to Jalota, the other long-established devotional star is Hari Om Sharan. Once stars are established, commercial companies then rely on these individuals for a vast majority of their new releases.[11] The newest such star is Anuradha Paudwal. Having already gained a reputation as a playback singer (a singer whose voice substitutes for that of an actor or actress) in the film industry, she recently began to specialize in *bhajan* singing (Khapre and Laul 1988). As part of its promotional efforts, Supercassettes took the unusual step of inserting advertisements for her past and forthcoming releases inside the plastic packaging of her cassettes.[12]

The superstar phenomenon seems to serve as compensation for the fact that the consumers never meet the performers. Although few have ever seen Anup Jalota, he is known to one and all. People have heard his music so often and seen his picture so many times on cassette covers and poster-sized advertisements that they often *feel* like they know him. Further compensation is provided by the superstars' often exceptional talents: Anup Jalota's voice has a warmth and depth that is matched by few of the local artists one would have a chance to hear live. Nevertheless, significant levels of personal experience and social, communal, and self-validation are lost when live performance is replaced by listening to stars on commercial recordings.

An interesting development regarding the superstar phenomenon occurred when major music companies began to approach well-known classical singers to record cassettes of devotional songs. Among those who responded with recent releases were Bhimsen Joshi, Jasraj, Kumar Gandharva, Kishori Amonkar, Lakshmi Shankar, and M. S. Subbulakshmi.[13] These recordings will undoubtedly raise the prestige of "devotional music" as a whole, giving it classical overtones.

When preparing commercial releases, recording companies commonly manipulate aspects of the musical product and its packaging in order to appeal to either wider or more specific segments of the consumer population. In the commercial *birahā* example discussed above, new instruments were added. Such additions might introduce only minimal nontraditional elements to a specific song if, for example, they are used only to provide an instrumental prelude. Their introduction, however, can radically change the aesthetic of the song if they are used to provide instrumental interludes throughout the piece or nontraditional forms of harmonic accompaniment. In the *birahā* example, the instruments add a prelude and interlude between verses but do not, for the most part, accompany the vocal lines. The effect is to imbue a music that has strong traditional, rural associations with a modern, urban flavor and can thus be seen as an attempt on the producer's part to widen the appeal of the song in urban eastern Uttar Pradesh. The introduction of instruments with a more focused intent occurred in a 1988 cassette of devotional music. Here the singing was accompanied by "bongo, synthesizer and the like." One reviewer commented that the music seemed "out of character for offering devotions to Jagadamba" (a goddess), but concluded that the producers were trying to "cater to the segment of the trendy market. In devotionals too, the music makers must cater to all tastes" (Savur 1988:48).

Changes introduced by the producer also involve the sex of the singer(s) and textual elements. One Banaras music producer experimented with vocal duets involving one male and one female singer. This combination is not traditional in the Banaras area, yet the producer found it highly successful in a few instances. Producers also talk about "cleaning" up the texts to meet their aesthetic and commercial standards.

While producer-generated changes in a given song occasionally have the goal of creating a new and unique sound, the aim is more commonly standardization than experimentation. This is especially true for releases by established superstars and younger aspiring artists. Often artists and producers put together a package that signals an upper or upper middle-class market. Common elements include the use of *tablā,* the drum of Indian classical music, rather than *ḍholak,* the folk drum; the self-conscious use of classical melodic modes (*rāga*s); the occasional use of classical solfège syllables (*sargam*); and the use of English in much of the promotional literature, even when the songs are exclusively in Hindi and related dialects. On cassette covers, for example, it is common to list the Hindi song titles in English transliteration (see notes 10 and 11). A noteworthy (and highly successful) example of the affected use of *rāga*s occurs in the Jalota recording "Main nahin maakhan khayo" (given here as spelled on the cassette insert). In this version of an extremely popular story, Krishna explains to his mother that he could not have eaten the butter his mother had stored away because he was not home all day. He went to graze the cows early in the morning and did not return until evening. At this point in the song, Jalota stops and explains to his audience that it is a specialty of Indian classical music that *rāga*s are associated with specific times of the day. He then says that he will re-sing the text, this time using an early morning *rāga* for the phrase in which Krishna speaks of the morning, and an evening *rāga* for the phrase in which Krishna speaks of the evening. "Perhaps," Jalota says, "it will seem to you that one is indeed early morning and the other evening." The effect of these elements, *tablā, rāga, sargam,* and English, lift the recordings well out of the realm of folk music, giving them significant trappings of classical music, "high" culture, and modern urban life. (This parallels the effect produced by classical singers' recent releases of devotional recordings.) The combination of these elements with traditional religious (and often rural) themes has proved highly successful, as it has generated substantial sales and, thus, profits.[14]

The commercial recording industry is dominated at all levels of production, marketing, and consumption by males (with the notable exception of a small number of female vocalists). While male domination in these realms should come as no surprise to anyone familiar with the public aspect of Indian sex roles, male domination of consumption at home is little acknowledged. Susan Wadley reports that it is the men in western Uttar Pradesh who commonly buy the tape recorders, the cassettes, and the batteries used to run the recorders. "Even at home, women do not commonly have access to the recorders. The recorders get locked up when the men are not around" (personal communication, July 1990). My own experiences in eastern Uttar Pradesh confirm Wadley's observations.

The cassette industry has many unique aspects not shared by other forms of sound media (radios and records).[15] The relative ease and low cost of mass producing cassettes has brought the new industry to virtually every city in India, big and small. One industry observer has commented, "Anyone with two tape decks to string together is in business" (Fera 1989:44).[16] Banaras has several cassette companies, many tucked away in back alleys. One cassette company owner in western Uttar Pradesh proudly showed me one of four machines that were the sum total of his company's production line. Each machine creates six copies of a single cassette at one time. With all four machines running, a worker can make twenty-four copies of an hour-long cassette in one hour.

The biggest cassette company in India today is Supercassettes (with its "T Series" label). Founded around 1980, Supercassettes has some two thousand employees who work three shifts in four separate factories in the industrial townships of Noida and Okhla (outside New Delhi). Using the latest technology, Supercassettes produces between 75,000 and 80,000 cassettes a day (Badhwar 1987:110).

Cassettes have the additional benefit of offering the consumer more music than is found on records. For the same amount of money that one pays for a small 45 r.p.m. record containing four songs, one can purchase a cassette with as many as fifteen songs. When this aspect is combined with the relatively low cost of cassette tape machines, it is clear that cassettes are inexpensive in terms not only of production but also of consumption. The result has been phenomenal growth in the cassette industry in India.

Not surprisingly, the record companies (Gramophone Co. of India with its EMI and HMV labels, Music India Ltd., CBS, etc.) have found themselves losing ground to companies that began as cassette companies, especially Supercassettes and Venus. Specializing in cassette production and cassette technology from their conception, these companies have captured majority shares of the cassette market. Commenting on the film music side of the commercial music industry, Fera writes:

> Five years ago, it was Gramco [Gramophone Co. of India Ltd.] and MIL [Music India Ltd.] which dominated the trade in film music, in terms of both long playing records and cassettes. . . . Till 1969, when MIL was set up, [Gramco] enjoyed a virtual monopoly of film music. Both companies are today in the red, and have been almost eased out of the market they once ruled by [cassette] companies which five years ago were not even registered — Supercassettes and Venus. These companies, which today command a lion's share of the mass markets in film music, do not even figure as members on the rolls of the Indian Phonographic Industries. (Fera 1989:44)

Cassettes have thus paved the way for huge new companies as well as small single-room enterprises.

The plethora of companies, large and small, have produced recordings of a wide variety of music genres (including religious genres) that had previously been recorded either minimally or not at all. For example, there are now cassettes of *bhajan*s devoted to the saint Shirdi Sai Baba, a multiple cassette series of *bhajan*s for *bhagwatī jāgaraṇ*s (all-night goddess rituals popular in and around Delhi), dozens of cassettes of religious discourse (called *kathā*) by an artist from Mainpuri in western Uttar Pradesh, and cassettes of *bhajan*s in all the main regional languages and many of the more prominent dialects of these languages. Cassette recordings of *birahā* are examples of recordings in regional dialects. Set for the most part in Bhojpuri, considered a dialect of Hindi, *birahā* appeared on only a few records, but now are found on many dozens of cassettes. Many of these cassettes feature religious songs (*dhārmik birahā*). Other North Indian genres that received their first major music industry coverage on cassettes rather than records include the epics *Ḍholā* and *Alhā, ras, saṅgīt,* and the Muslim *bayān*.

Cassettes have thus had a great democratizing effect, allowing numerous regional music genres to enter the world of commercial recorded music.

The smallest cassette companies were commonly the first to produce recordings of regional music genres. However, the largest companies soon realized the potential for vast new markets and have recently begun to focus on regional genres.

Another effect of the cassette industry has been that nonfilm genres have been able to make inroads into the realm of popular music. Traditionally, India has not had major advertising campaigns associated with its commercial music. When recording technology was more expensive, recording companies relied on the popularity of the film industry as the main form of advertisement. The vast percentage of commercial music was film music. With the advent of the cassette industry, this changed. The musical product was now so inexpensive that thousands who had never bought records now started buying cassettes. During the first years of the cassette industry, film music remained the uncontested center of attention. Then the first cassette-generated, nonfilm craze appeared: this was for the Urdu-based vocal song the *ghazal*.[17] In the early 1980s, newspapers and weekly magazines were full of articles about the new surge in the *ghazal*'s popularity. A second cassette-generated, nonfilm craze has now appeared and apparently far surpassed the *ghazal* in terms of sheer volume of sales. The new craze, for devotional music, is said to be challenging even film music in terms of sales. Popular publications have responded to the new trend by establishing ongoing columns that review recent releases of devotional music cassettes.[18] Thus the rise of the cassette industry and the recent popularity of religious music in cassette form has focused major attention (artistic, financial, and media attention) on the phenomenon of devotional music.

The new popularity of devotional music is welcomed by record and cassette companies who found film music to be financially "too risky." One recording industry official commented, "Out of 300 new film sound tracks released every year, hardly ten cassettes become popular" (Khapre and Laul 1988). In addition, while film songs' popularity is usually short-lived, commonly selling only in the months immediately after a film's release, devotional music is seen as having a longer "shelf life." As a result, the big recording companies see devotional music as a way to guarantee steady sales and, thus, economic stability. In keeping with this perception, Super-cassettes recently announced that it is shifting its focus from film music to devotional (and classical) music (Khapre and Laul 1988).

To hedge their bets and assure profitability, big cassette companies have taken care to develop special devotional music superstars. The recent fame of Anup Jalota and Anuradha Paudwal, for example, is based on availability of their music on cassette.[19] The phenomenon of classical singers recording devotional music is also cassette based.

The development of the cassette industry introduced additional changes in the social fabric of both the music and religious worlds. For example, cassette technology has affected music pedagogy, aiding (and often replacing) the traditional teacher-student (*guru-celā*) relationship. With cassettes one can listen repeatedly to a given passage of music until one understands its intricacies. In many instances, reliance on a cassette (an "electronic guru") has replaced personal contact with the musician from whom one is learning. In the world of religion a similar change takes place when a family relies on a commercial recording of *satyanārāyaṇ kathā* (a recitation that accompanies a religious ritual of devotion to Lord Satya Narayan) instead of calling on a Brahman priest who traditionally performs the recitation and conducts the ritual. Similarly, Muslim families can now play a commercial cassette of religious discourse (*bayān*) rather than hire a *mullāh* to deliver the same.

Conclusion

In a sense, the new cassette industry is fulfilling the same function as the wandering *bābā:* it is spreading aspects of Indian religious culture to new generations of Indian citizens. Whether contained within a live performance in a traditional setting or in a recent cassette release, the texts of devotional songs continue the practice of retelling and reinterpreting traditional myths, legends, and philosophy. Cassettes work on a more massive scale than was ever possible, even with earlier media technologies.

Ranging from *bhajan*s of nationwide fame to regional genres, the success of commercial devotional music often rests on its ability to mediate traditional, folk, and rural elements with others that symbolize modernity, urban living, and popular or classical art forms. The retention of traditional themes, regional dialects, and folk instruments must thus be weighed against the introduction of popular / classical features such as nontraditional instruments (clarinet, banjo, guitar, *tablā*, etc.), classical *rāga*s and *sargam,* well-known film or classical singers, and the use of English on cassette packaging and publicity.

Judging by their near ubiquitousness, the results of this mediation have a potential popularity that was not possible when music was restricted to live performances. Specific recordings can now function as unifying elements throughout large portions of modern-day India. The *bhajan*s of Anup Jalota or the cassette recordings of the *Rāmāyaṇa*, for example, offer a shared product, a shared religious experience, a shared identity for Indians from a variety of regional and ethnic backgrounds. As such, they can function on a national level somewhat as the *kīrtan maṇḍalī* does on the neighborhood level, that is, to reduce caste and sectarian distinctions. At the same time, local recordings help reinforce regional identity such as one's belonging to Banaras's Bhojpuri culture or western Uttar Pradesh's Braj region.

While many aspects of live-performance contexts are sacrificed, Indian religious music has shown tremendous vitality in recent years. It is clear that religious music can and will keep up with modern trends. By establishing a strong presence on cassettes, religious music, admittedly altered, has achieved an extraordinary surge in popularity.

Notes

1. No attempt has been made to count the number of cassette companies in India today. Cairo, Egypt, had more than 300 legitimate cassette companies in 1981 (El-Shawan 1984).

2. See Henry (1988:160–189) for a detailed discussion of these wandering *bābā*s.

3. Similar female groups also exist but tend to meet for specific holidays and rites of passage rather than weekly.

4. Female devotional singing groups do not generally use loudspeakers.

5. See Marcus (1989) for a detailed introduction to this genre.

6. For example, musicians now commonly use melodies found in men's and women's folksongs, in regional epics, and in popular *ghazal*s and *qawwālī*s. An interesting instance of the use of a *qawwālī* melody finds a Muslim devotional song being reset with Hindu devotional words: The Sabri brothers released the song "Bhar do jholī merī, yā Muhammad; tere dar se na jāungā khālī" ("Fulfill my wishes, O Muhammad; I will not leave your door with my wishes unfulfilled"). The song achieved great fame and was widely copied by Banaras folk musicians. In one example, the words were changed to fit a song about Krishna's birth: "Śyām terī kṣaṭā mādhurī kā, karne darśan sabhī dev dhāye" ("O Krishna, for *darśan* of your sweet beauty, all the gods came running"). This song, by Mangal Yadav, is contained, in its entirety, in Marcus 1995.

7. With its textual ambiguity and wealth of potential for double meanings, this song has all the makings of a *nirguṇ bhajan*.

8. There is, however, an interesting side aspect to this whole phenomenon of performer/audience interaction in the realm of Indian music. One of the ways that audience members interact with a performer is by saying out loud cliché words of encouragement during the performance (*vwā vwā, kyā bāt, bahut khūb, bahut acchā,* and so on). It is interesting to note that many Indians persist in this practice even when listening to commercial recordings. Thus they are carrying on a form of interaction with the performer, even in his absence.

9. Sutton reports just such a transformation in a region of Java, Indonesia, where music for a traditional trance ritual is now listened to on cassette for entertainment alone. It is "enjoyed for its fast tempo, animated drumming, and catchy melodies" (1986:123).

10. See the photograph in Fera (1989:44) of Jalota during one such tour. The curtain behind Jalota has the words "Bhajan Yatra-85 [i.e., 1985], A Live Performance of Bhajans."

11. In the realm of North Indian film music, the star system has resulted in a situation where a small number of singers dominate the industry. The most prominent female vocalist, Lata Mangeshkar, has "made over 30,000 recordings for more than 2,000 films, earning her the distinction in the *Guinness Book of World Records* of having the most-recorded voice worldwide" (Manuel 1988:179).

12. An English-language insert in a 1988 cassette lists seventeen releases in all, including six in the "Hindi film song" category and nine in the "nonfilm devotional" category. The latter include the following titles (given here as spelled on the insert): "Tulsi Bhajnamrit," "Maa Ki Mahima," "Shree Krishna Bhajans," "Jago Maa Jagdambe Vol. 2 and 3," "Aarti," "Meera," "Shree Durga Saptashati" (in Sanskrit), and "Our Lady of Perpetual Succor Novena Service" (in English).

13. Recent releases include the following (titles given as spelled on cassette covers): Bhimsen Joshi and Lata Mangeshkar's "Ram Shyam Gun Gaan Bhajans"; Jasraj's "Soor Padavali-Nitya Kram"; Kumar Gandharva's "Nirgun ke Gun (Hindi Bhajans)"; Kishori Amonkar's "Mharo Praman (Meer Bhajans)"; Lakshmi Shankar's "In a Devotional Mood," which includes *bhajan*s by Mirabai, Sur Das, Jaya Dev, and Rai Das; and M. S. Subbulakshmi's "Meera Bhajans."

14. I thank Susan Wadley for clarifying the issue of standardization both in her personal comments and in Wadley 1983:81–103.

15. I thank Laurie Eisler for providing me with a large number of articles that appeared in New Delhi newspapers and magazines during the winter months of 1988–89. She also reported on interviews she conducted with Delhi cassette store owners.

16. No discussion of the cassette industry would be complete without mentioning the illegal duplication industry. Within a week of the release of a legitimate cassette, it is common to find up to five duplicates available in the market. These have the same musical content as the original but different covers and labels. While these duplicates have contributed greatly to the phenomenal expansion of the cassette industry, they rob performers and producers of their legitimate profits. In the face of this loss of profits, many performers and producers have decided to forego plans for issuing new releases.

17. See Manuel (1988:190), who writes that nonfilm popular music could not really "take off" until the "advent of cheap cassette technology in the late 1970s."

18. See, for example, such a column in *Playback and Fast Forward,* a monthly Indian magazine devoted to music, television, and video. The column appeared on page 48 of the December 1988 issue.

19. On Jalota's importance to Music India Ltd., Fera comments, "Over the last six years, it is common knowledge in the industry that MIL has been able to stay afloat largely on the strength of two of its successful nonfilm artists — Pankaj Udhas [a *ghazal* singer] and Anup Jalota" (1989:46).

References

Badhwar, Inderjit. 1987. "A Supersuccess Story." *India Today* (April 30):110–112.

Fera, Ivan. 1989. "The Last Waltz." *Illustrated Weekly of India* (February 5):44–47.

Henry, Edward O. 1988. *Chant the Names of God.* San Diego: San Diego State University Press.

Khapre, Shubagi, and Brian Laul. 1988. "Why T-Series Opt for Basic Music." *Playback and Fast Forward* (December).

Manuel, Peter. 1988. *Popular Musics of the Non-Western World.* New York: Oxford University Press.

Marcus, Scott L. 1989. "The Rise of a Folk Music Genre: Biraha." In *Culture and Power in Banaras: Community, Performance, and Environment, 1800–1980,* ed. Sandria Freitag, pp. 93–113. Berkeley: University of California Press.

———. 1995. "Parody Generated Texts: The Process of Composition in *Biraha,* a North Indian Folk Music Genre." *Asian Music* 26(1) (Fall/Winter): 93–146.

Savur, Sumit. 1988. "Devotional." *Playback and Fast Forward* (December):48.

El-Shawan, Salwa. 1984. "The Cassette Industry and New Arabic Music in Cairo, Egypt." Paper presented at the annual meeting of the Society for Ethnomusicology.

Sutton, R. Anderson. 1986. "The Crystallization of a Marginal Tradition: Music in Banyumas, West Central Java." *Yearbook for Traditional Music* 18:115–131.

Wadley, Susan S. 1983. "Popular Hinduism and Mass Literature in North India: A Preliminary Analysis." In *Main Currents in Indian Sociology,* Vol. 5, *Religion in Modern India,* ed. Giri Raj Gupta, pp. 81–103. Delhi: Vikas Publishing House.

Section 3

Visual Media

Susan S. Wadley

Introduction

As we suggest in the general introduction to this volume, there is something special about media that transmit moving visual images. If the eye is not the window of the soul, we may at least concede that moving images have a unique capacity to engage the emotions and imagination of viewers. The technologies underlying moving images are historically the latest of those considered in this book. It is true that cinema was invented in the nineteenth century, but its maturity as a medium was achieved only in the twentieth century, largely as a consequence of developments in electronics. Television and video recording are based on still later technologies. Indeed, the future of images of the sort transmitted by television and videocassette recorders is very much an open one. No one yet knows what will ultimately result from the fusion of television-type viewing systems and systems for the transmission and storage of digitally encoded information.

Cinema arrived in India in the late nineteenth century. The first film, brought from Europe, was shown at Watson's Hotel in Bombay on July 7, 1896. Other films were shown about the same time in Calcutta. A Bengali, Hiralal Sen, produced the first commercial films in India, shorts depicting scenes from Bengali drama. The first feature film was made by Dhundiraj Govind Phalke and opened in Bombay in 1913.

After 1913, the Indian film industry grew rapidly, and by 1931 over half the feature films released in India were Indian-produced. Now India has the largest film production industry in the world, with some eight hundred feature films released yearly. Cinema halls are found in most towns above fifty thousand in population, and temporary halls are created at district fairs, where a wide rural audience is reached. Despite minimal charges, however, the cinema is still a luxury for many Indians.

From the early days of Indian cinema, religious films were part of India's cinematographic culture, and this phenomenon is treated in Steve Derné's essay. His analysis suggests that the importance of the religious film may be less than meets the eye, but that the role of religion *in* film is significant indeed.

Cinema audiences are overwhelmingly male; television, which is available in the home and does not require the mobility that viewing cinema does, is more accessible to females, although more prohibitively expensive for the masses. Moreover, until the influx of cable television — through privately run networks and drawing on programming beamed by satellites from around the world following the Persian Gulf War in 1991 — viewing was limited to government channels run by Doordarshan.

All-India Radio (AIR) began television programming in New Delhi in 1959. Only in the early 1970s were stations added in Bombay, Calcutta, Madras, and other major centers. In 1976, television programming was separated from AIR and made an independent organization called Doordarshan. Currently, Doordarshan has 274 transmitters, providing television service to some 80 percent of India's population. Programming often includes both excerpts from popular films as well as showings of complete feature films. Hence television is an important outlet for India's feature film makers. In the late 1980s, more innovative programming began, including the immensely popular productions of the major epics, the *Rāmāyaṇa* and *Mahābhārata*. Phil Lutgendorf's contribution to this volume deals with the televised serial of the *Rāmāyaṇa,* which became an extraordinary cultural (and political) event.

The 1980s saw the advent of video, in both individual residences and commercial establishments. It is now possible to travel long distances in a "video bus," watching a movie instead of the countryside. Shops renting videos have sprung up throughout India, often attached to electrical appliance stores, but also in local groceries and other small shops. Here too the main fare is Indian-made feature films, but videos of ritual events and news stories are also available.

In the late 1980s, the increasing availability of camcorders has led to a transformation in the uses of video technology, removing it from the hands of professionals. John Little's analysis of the use of video in the Swadhyaya movement shows us how valuable this technology can be in transmitting the charisma of a sectarian leader and maintaining the cohesion of a far-flung religious movement. In 1990, the most popular videos, in northern India at least, were privately circulated prints of the events at Ayodhya surrounding the ultimately (and violently) successful attempts of Hindus to reclaim what they believe to be Rama's birthplace from what was, until its destruction, a mosque. We see, therefore, that the intersection of religion and video technology is entering new phases, unanalyzed in this volume.

Steve Derné

8. Market Forces at Work: Religious Themes in Commercial Hindi Films

Commercial Hindi films produced in Bombay and Madras are widely watched by modern Indians. Among the many market factors that influence Hindi filmmakers' presentation of religious images are censorship; a nationwide market with diverse religious, ethnic, and language groups; and a taxation policy that makes profits problematic. The financial pressures that force filmmakers to appeal to the full breadth of the Hindi film market encourages them to lure religious-minded Indians with explicitly religious "mythological" films and to intercalate subtle religious motifs into the crazy salad of popular "social" films.

The religious themes introduced in ostensibly "social" films tend to draw on a repertoire of mythological images that have been proven to offend neither conservative Hindus nor government censors. Thus filmmakers create a "film religious culture" that develops around a standardized repertoire of mythological images presented as merely part of the "mix" of rousing fights, provocative dances, slapstick humor, nationalist sentiment, and family dynamics that makes up secular Hindi films. Market pressures lead filmmakers to produce this mixed bag of "something for everyone," presenting religious themes not as the center of attention but in the context of diverse secular themes.

While it establishes mythological models by repeatedly referring to them and presents religious themes on a cluttered canvas in a way that could shift the religious eye, the Hindi film is not a source of change in the actual content of religious stories. Religious elements in social Hindi films tend to be noncontroversial — as might be expected, given government censorship policies — as well as condensed and inexplicit — as might be expected in a market that includes not just Hindus but also Muslims, Christians, and Sikhs. Moreover, because Hindi films include provocative dances and crude humor, they are denigrated as vulgar, tasteless entertainment, and Indians do not approach most films with the reverence accorded to more primarily and explicitly religious cultural forms. While Indians usually do not consider thematic alterations that originate in a denigrated medium legitimate sources of change in respected religious traditions, the presentation of standardized religious elements as just part of a diverse mixture seen by a tremendous variety of Indians *is* new and may contribute to spreading particular images across a wide range of groups and to subtly altering the field to which Indians bring religious concerns.

The Commercial Formula Film in Hindi

India's first silent film was made in 1912 and its first "talkie" in 1931. Indian films were so popular that the country became the world's third-largest film producer in 1938, and since 1971, India has produced the most feature films in the world (Vasudev and Lenglet 1983:317, 326). In the 1980s, the film industry produced between 700 and 900 films per year (*India West* 1988). On an average day, 15 million Indians enjoy watching Indian films in the nation's 11,000 cinema halls (Kakar 1989:26). Inexpensive booklets recounting a film's "dialogue and songs," cassette tapes that include a film's songs and sometimes its dialogue, and more recently videotapes are vehicles that today bring films into the homes of modern Indians.

Although films are produced in nearly a dozen Indian languages, the Hindi film dominates in audience size and investment stakes. In several recent years Tamil, Telugu, or Malayalam films have outnumbered Hindi films (Singh 1983:29; *India-West* 1988), but only the latter are screened throughout the country. As film journalist Bikram Singh (1983:29) puts it, "the Hindi film is to India what the Hollywood film is to the world."

This study focuses on commercial Hindi films designed for broad-based appeal rather than on regional language films or Hindi "art films" that do not usually aim for or reach mass audiences. This study is based on my own analysis of the most popular films of 1986, on interviews with urban Hindu men, on film reviews by Indian critics, and on published analyses of Hindi films and the industry by scholars, critics, government officials, and people in the industry itself.

In connection with another study (Derné 1995a) examining urban Hindu men's ideas about family life, I did fieldwork and conducted in-depth interviews in Banaras with comfortably well-off male caste Hindus, most of whom live in households that include more than one married couple. In the course of these interviews, conducted in 1986 and 1987, I asked men about their leisure activities — a line of questioning that often led to a discussion of Hindi filmgoing. I asked men about whom they saw films with, what appealed to them in Hindi films, and why they did or did not approve of the medium. While this chapter focuses on my 1986–87 research, I also briefly refer to interviews and fieldwork I conducted with male filmgoers in Dehra Dun in 1991 (see Derné 1995b). While my 1986–87 interviews were framed around family life, my 1991 interviews were framed around filmgoing. Despite this difference, both studies suggest that filmgoers reject religious changes presented in films. Except where noted, the interviews I cite are from my 1986–87 interviews about family life.

FILMGOING EXPERIENCES FOR DIVERSE GROUPS OF INDIANS

To be a hit, a film must include distinctive elements that appeal to the many diverse groups that attend Hindi films. Young unmarried men make up the Hindi film's largest audience; many of them attend films more than once a week. A twenty-four-year-old single man told me, for instance, that he sees films "10, 15, or 20 times a month. When I have time, I see them." Some of the two hundred responding to a question posed by a Hindi film fan magazine admitted to viewing films two or three times a week (Khare 1985:143), and some of the male filmgoers I interviewed in 1991 declared that they watched as many as forty movies a month. Young unmarried men enjoy attending films with one another. During the "interval" and before and after films, men often gather at tea stalls surrounding cinemas to smoke cigarettes, drink tea, eat *pān*, and enjoy talk and laughter with other young men. The young single males who attend with their friends tend to sit in the inexpensive, crowded seats on the floors of the theater, where they occasionally shout or dance suggestively in the dark, usually during the popular dance and fight scenes. One unmarried twenty-six-year-old described his preference in films as the kind "the world likes," namely, "films with fights and with songs."

Although they attend far less often, young husbands also value filmgoing as an escape from the pressures of joint-family living. Of the twenty-four married men I asked in 1986–87, nineteen occasionally see films with their wives. One married twenty-six-year-old living with his wife and child in a small joint family says that since marrying he does "not have [male] friends," although he admits to "familiarity with some people." He says he does not like films now but that he "sometimes" sees films with his wife: "If I see a film, it is with my wife. Otherwise, I will not see a picture." Those men attending films with family members usually watch from the more expensive balcony to protect women and children from the antics of the young men in the cheap seats on the floor below. Whereas unmarried men prefer unrestrained dance and fight scenes, married men profess to enjoy films that consider problems of family life. Men responding to the Hindi film fan magazine questionnaire indicated that while they would be embarrassed to see crude films in the company of their wives, they do not mind seeing social films with them (Khare 1985:145). A thirty-five-year-old married Brahman who lives with his parents, wife, and several small children told me, for instance, that he enjoys seeing films with his wife, but that he prefers "social films, which are related to the whole family." He described the films he likes as "about the mother, father, paternal uncle [*cācā*], children, and others [*aur bhī*] in a family that is completely joint [*pūrā sanyukt*]." When I asked him whether he liked to see films that feature dancing by the popular heroine Sridevi, he replied abruptly, "No, it is not like this." (He and his wife had recently seen Sridevi's *Nagina,* but they did not focus on her dancing as the element that had drawn them to the film.)

Married and single women also attend films often, albeit less frequently than men. While rarely constituting even a fourth of the audience, women were always present in the urban cinemas I was in. Women attend fewer films (Hartmann et al. 1989:215–216) partly because husbands, brothers, and fathers fear that the dances and songs will seem too vulgar (Khare 1985:144–154), because the protected balcony seats cost more, and because of the occasional difficulty of arranging a male family escort. The presence of women in theaters and the substantial sections that women's magazines devote to film reviews and to film industry gossip indicate women's importance as a market for Hindi films. Several of the men I interviewed told me that their wives, who often have little scope for interactions outside the home, were always pressuring their husbands to take them to see films. Occasionally men resent the pressure. One twenty-seven-year-old living with his wife and parents hoped that "when video came," the "problem" of taking his wife to the theater would be solved. Although he hoped his wife could enjoy films on a television inside the home, he lamented that "little by little, my family has had enough of the video. They want to see movies on a bigger screen." Because women nearly always sit in the more expensive seats, because they persuade their husbands and whole families to attend particular films, and because they are thought to make up much of the repeat audience necessary to make a film a hit (Mitra 1987:45), women have a greater effect on the film market than their relative numbers would suggest and may lead producers to design films calculated to appeal to women.

The market for Hindi film includes not just urban middle-class men and women in the Hindi-speaking region but nearly all groups in Indian society. Producers try to lure Muslims and Hindus, Brahmans and Untouchables, rickshaw-wallahs and white-collar professionals, villagers and urbanites, as well as non-Hindi speakers, whether Calcutta intellectuals, college students in Madras, or street urchins in Bombay, many of whom see films but may not be fluent in Hindi (Lutze 1985:4; Vasudev 1978:76–77; Mitra 1987). To achieve such appeal, filmmakers use techniques to transcend a limited market. They employ standard formulas and well-known stories and emphasize spectacle and special effects that can overcome language barriers. To allow any viewer to identify with the film's heroes and heroines, filmmakers create characters not easily identified as members of particular regions or castes (Karnad 1983:221) and often use an urban upper-class background where caste and regional differences disappear in a Westernized uniformity (Vasudev 1978:76–77). Dances and fights are designed to appeal to young unmarried men, family themes are included for married men, slapstick humor for children, religious themes for the devout, and a variety of female characters for women. The heroine of *Nagina* (1987) helps her husband despite her mother-in-law's opposition; in *Ram Teri Ganga Maili* (1986), the loyal wife struggles to maintain her purity, and in *Jai Santoshi Ma* (1975), the virtuous wife shows unbending devotion to the goddess Santoshi Ma.

GOVERNMENT TAXATION AND DUTIES

The government places heavy burdens on the film industry through taxation and foreign-exchange restrictions (H.C. 1986). Heavy duties on raw film artificially increase the cost of production, and entertainment taxes are excessive. With stars demanding huge fees (Karanjia 1983), Hindi films must attract a huge, heterogeneous audience to make a profit. The filmmaker and scholar Aruna Vasudev argues that such financial pressure makes box-office success an imperative (1978:116). Because of Hindi films' production costs, financiers and distributors, rather than directors and scriptwriters, have the greatest influence on a film's shape (Karnad 1981:105–106).

Censorship and Filmmakers' Caution about Religious Alterations

Given this financial pressure, a film's timely release — assured by quickly obtaining government certification — is essential. Filmmakers are very concerned about censorship since as many as half (Mohamad 1988:10) get into trouble with censors. Hindi films' wide reach makes censors believe that nothing in them should offend any religious, communal, or regional group (Vasudev 1978:116), so censorship policies give voice to vocal, conservative Hindus.

Militant Hindus sometimes oppose films they find offensive to religious sensibilities. Vasudev (1978:xiv) reports an instance in which such pressure forced a filmmaker to change the names of a hero and heroine from Rama and Sita. In 1987, filmmakers likewise were pressured into changing the name of a film from *Kaliyug Ki Ramayana* (The *Rāmāyaṇa* of the Dark Age) to *Kaliyug Aur Ramayana* (The Dark Age and the *Rāmāyaṇa*) and finally to *Kaliyug Aur ???* (The Dark Age and ???). The magazine *Filmfare* reported that "traditional Hindu organizations" objected to "the film's 'unholy' reference to the great epic" and insisted that the names of the main characters be changed from Rama, Lakshmana, and Sita.[1]

Inappropriate family themes are also the target of protest. In 1954, thirteen thousand housewives presented an antifilm petition to the prime minister, prompting the Rajya Sabha to pass a motion asking the government to consider banning Indian films altogether. One woman speaking at the debate complained that a then-popular Hindi film portrayed an aunt in an unfavorable light, which would lead children to assume that all aunts are cruel (Vasudev 1978:107). Infrequent theatergoers continue to complain that films do not teach appropriate moral lessons about interactions among family members, a reaction I heard from several men in their fifties and sixties (also see Hartmann et al. 1989:203). For instance, one father I interviewed said, "If boys and girls are together seeing the world and the bad films, sex automatically arises [and] they will go astray." Filmmakers avoid departures from religious orthodoxy because these might offend religious groups, delay the film's approval by the censorship board, or prevent its distribution through intimidation of theater owners (Sarkar 1975:24).

Religious Elements in Hindi Films

Because of religion's continuing hold on modern Indians, financially pressed filmmakers faced with the imperative of appealing to a heterogenous group produce films that include religious themes among other diverse elements. Hindi filmmakers appeal to Indians by using traditional dramatic forms, by making explicitly religious "mythologicals," and by introducing subtle religious themes even into social films.

RELIGIOUS INFLUENCE ON HINDI FILMS' FORM

Traditional dramatic styles dominate Hindi films. Folk plays present lengthy familiar stories with complicated digressions, players characterized as either good or evil, and interludes of song and dance. The Hindi filmgoer comes to expect many of these same elements in film. Many scholars have noted that the song and dance essential to *every* Hindi film draws on traditional forms like *jātrā, nautaṇkī, līlā,* and *tamāśā* (Sarkar 1975:16; Barnouw and Krishnaswamy 1980:70–72). Exaggeration, extravagant speeches and sentiment, elaborate digressions, and the black-and-white depiction of characters derive from *Rāmāyaṇa* and *Mahābhārata* readings and performances (Sarkar 1975:14; Kakar 1989). Hindi filmgoers' expectation of three-hour extravaganzas may have been cultivated by lengthy performances of traditional dramas (Karnad 1983:277; Sarkar 1975:14).

The "predictability" essential for Hindi films is also linked to traditional dramatic forms (Karnad 1983:221). The Hindi filmgoer's pleasure at viewing familiar, formulaic plots is similar to the *rāmlīlā* aficionado's pleasure at repeated viewings of the well-known *Rāmāyaṇa* story. Delhi scholar Ashis Nandy argues that like *rāmlīlā,* "a Bombay film aims at presenting a not-so-unique combination of themes that have been witnessed hundreds of times before" and are derived from other movies or from traditional tales. Filmmakers actually expect the viewer to "experience . . . a feeling of *déjà vu*" (Nandy 1981:90–91; see also Saari 1985:23).

PRESSURES TO MAKE MYTHOLOGICALS

Mythological films—versions of familiar stories from the *Rāmāyaṇa* or *Mahābhārata*—initially helped attract audiences to the new medium of film and continue to lure them today (Dharap 1983; Raina 1983). Because the audience is familiar with the stories' outline, mythologicals were particularly suited to introducing audiences to unfamiliar new media like silent films, talkies, and television. Until 1923, 70 percent of films were mythological, although the percentage of that type of film production declined to 22 percent in 1935 and remained less than 10 percent throughout the period following independence. In the 1970s, mythologicals averaged only about 5 percent of yearly films (Dharap 1983:80–81). Yet mythologicals continue to be produced, partly because they draw in new audiences of urban women who increasingly view films and new village audiences that are added each year as cinemas expand into rural areas (Dharap 1983:82; Karnad 1981:106). But filmmakers emphasize familiar stories, counting on spectacle and special effects to bring in new viewers.

RELIGIOUS INFLUENCES IN SOCIAL FILMS

While mythologicals like *Jai Santoshi Ma* (1975) are occasionally big hits, they are now far less important, and most money is in ostensibly secular, social films that also have the greatest influence on spreading religious images across regions, castes, and class groups. Nearly every social film utilizes mythological imagery—somehow made harmlessly secular (Kakar 1981; O'Flaherty 1981; Lutze 1985; Vasudev 1983).

Hindi films consistently link female characters to mythical models, most often as the perfect wife who, like Sita, acquiesces to the demands of an often undeserving husband. Since its inauguration in 1979, the feminist magazine *Manushi* has regularly reviewed Hindi films, lamenting that they constantly portray women as doormat Sitas. Long-time editors Ruth Vanita and Madhu Kishwar complain that commercial films have a

> hallowed tradition of glorifying women's patience in suffering. Like Sita and like Kannagi, countless heroines have put up with maltreatment, beatings and injustice, continuing to shower service and smiles on the husband and tears at the shrine of Sri Krishna. (Vanita and Kishwar 1985:46)

In *Naseeb Apna Apna* (1986), for instance, the heroine's husband Kishan (played by Rishi Kapoor) abandons the heroine in a railway station and establishes a household with another woman. His wife, Chando (played by Radhika), seeks out her husband and lives as a servant in his household. With a tear in her eye, Chando sings:

Whether he be bad or good, my husband is my god . . .
Only he is my world; only he is my life
I am only devoted to him; only him do I worship . . .
Wherever he be, and whatever he is,
My husband is my god.[2]

As feminist Jyoti Sanghera (1980:51) wrote of an earlier film, *Naukar,* film producers "pronounce most unabashedly" that " 'a wife is a glorified servant and a husband should never forget this.' "

Devoted wives lucky enough to have loyal husbands are also celebrated in recent films. In the 1987 hit *Nagina,*[3] the heroine Rajni (played by Sridevi) uses magical powers to save her husband from several dangers, even as her mother-in-law puts obstacles in her path—a theme that surely appeals to many Indian wives (see Harlan 1992). Rajni celebrates the often problematic role as "daughter-in-law of [her husband's] family [*khāndān*]." In the climactic struggle with the villain, Rajni asserts that the "power [*śakti*] of a virtuous wife [*satī, pativrata*]" is even greater than the magical powers of the villain snake-charmer, Bhairavnath (played by Amrish Puri).

This image is balanced by those of destructive women (Vasudev 1983; O'Flaherty 1981). *Manushi* writer Shobha Sadagopan notes, for instance, that in every third film the "image of woman as Sita," as "demure, passive, self sacrificing sister, mother, daughter, or wife" is balanced with the "vamp who smokes, drinks, and wears pants" (1979:47). Characteristics of female villains are sometimes based on mythological models. O'Flaherty notes, for example, that the sexual voracity, age, and wealth of the villainess in the Hindi film *Karz* are classical mythological characteristics and that "like the demons in Sanskrit texts," this villainess resumes her true form only at the moment of death (1981:26–27).

Mythological male models — the courageous Rama, the hot-headed but loyal brother Lakshmana, the playful Krishna, the evil Ravana — also are invoked constantly in Hindi film. The struggle between a virtuous Rama and an evil Ravana often can be seen in the contest between hero and villain in Hindi film. In those like *Karma* (1986) and *Mr. India* (1987), the villain's camp has all the luster of Ravana's castle in Lanka. A modern-day action star often needs strength and cunning like Rama's to foil a Ravana-like villain (see Lutze 1985:9–11). Playful Krishna types also sometimes appear. Parallels with Krishna mythology are apparent in Raj Khosla's *Mera Gaon Mera Desh* when the hero hides in a tree and watches village girls bathing in a river (Lutze 1985:11). In *Toofan* (1989), Amitabh Bachchan played two characters, both based on mythical models. As Toofan, Amitabh is a powerful figure "identified with Hanuman," while "as Shyam, he is a Krishna figure . . . indulging in mischief, fun and frolic" (Vanita 1989:43).

Filmmakers use mythological models both to attract filmgoers and because the models remain salient for filmmakers themselves. G. P. Sippy, who produced 1975's *Sholay*,[4] said that the figures of Rama and Ravana "are somehow brought [into every film], and the story is woven around those characters" (1983:299–300). Raj Khosla, maker of the important social film *Do Raste* and the successful action film *Mera Gaon Mera Desh,* also consciously uses the mythological parallels, which have influenced his understanding of family relationships:

> I've been listening to the stories of *Rāmāyaṇa* and *Mahābhārata* from my mother. [When I was a child], I used to go to the village and [like Krishna] . . . watch girls take their bath. . . . I was playing Krishna myself [and this was portrayed in my *Mera Gaon, Mera Desh*]. As far as Ram [Rama] is concerned . . . I have the image of my elder brother in my own house. . . . [The *Rāmāyaṇa*

and the *Mahābhārata*] are in our blood. They have to come in our film if we
are making a film which is truthful, which has to do with our lives. You cannot
escape these two classics . . . in any film. Somewhere a shade will come.
(Khosla 1985:39–40)

Khosla uses the mythological images ingrained in his psyche to appeal to
Indians who watch films through religiously informed eyes.

Though religious themes are prominent in Hindi film, they are nonetheless often vague and condensed, perhaps because so many of their viewers are Muslims — and because filmmakers believe that Muslims constitute
much of the repeat-view audience (Mitra 1987:45). Even without explicit
mythological references, a Hindi film often provides clues that it could be
seen through a religious lens. Most films begin with an invocation — recitation of a verse from a respected religious text like the *Bhagavad Gītā* against
a stereotyped religious backdrop — before proceeding to the film production company's glitzy logo. Hindi films also tend to include passing references to Hindu religion, such as depictions of the shrines of gods and goddesses, women worshipping at temples, and Hindu weddings. O'Flaherty's
analysis of *Karz* rightly argues that such references stir "deep mythological
resonances" (1981:25) in religiously minded viewers, encouraging them to
see the film characters as incarnations of mythological models.

Indeed, there is good evidence that audiences tend to see the family
relationships portrayed in Hindi films in terms of mythological models.
Pfleiderer and Lutze (1985a) showed films including Raj Khosla's *Do Raste*
to villagers and urbanites in several locations in North India. While viewers
often protested that they could learn nothing from these films, they nonetheless were pleased to find familiar characters. One villager was delighted
that the elder daughter in *Do Raste* conformed to Sita's model, saying she
"was like a typical Indian woman; she could be compared to . . . Sita of
ancient times" (Pfleiderer 1985a:69). In *Do Raste,* an educated woman
causes discord between her husband and his brother. Village audiences saw
this as paralleling fights said to occur occasionally within the village, citing
the *Rāmāyaṇa* to bolster their argument that husbands must discipline their
wives to prevent internecine quarrels (Pfleiderer 1985a:67–69).

Religious Themes in Hit Films of 1986

Subhash Ghai's *Karma* and Raj Kapoor's last film, *Ram Teri Ganga Maili,*
were the most popular films of 1986.[5] Both films alert viewers to religious

themes by opening with a recitation from classical texts and by depicting temples and other religious images. While both make explicit references to mythological models for their characters, in each film, religious themes are only part of the Hindi film mixture of dances, fights, slapstick humor, and family themes.

KARMA

Karma, an action adventure in the *Sholay*[6] mold, focuses primarily on efforts of the patriot Rana (played by Dilip Kumar) to capture the Ravana-like Dr. Deng (played by Anupam Kher), a terrorist out to destroy India. Deng escapes from jail, kills Rana's children, and leaves his wife, Rukmani (played by Nutha), speechless from the shock. With the approval of a government minister, Rana trains three convicted killers to capture Deng. They are also helped by Dharma, a man once jailed for killing a corrupt government official who had ruined Dharma's chances to get medicine for his brother. In an early film scene, Rana compares Deng and Dharma in terms that prepare the audience for Deng's Ravana-like characteristics. While Dharma is described as a victim of circumstances who has lived "with honor [*izzat*]" since serving his time, Deng is portrayed as a "demon [*rākṣas*]" whose annihilation is the "duty [*kartavya, dharma*]" of every citizen of India.

Other religious allusions are made throughout the film, further preparing the audience to see the heroes as Rama-like in their attack on Deng. Twice a cow is shown looking on as Deng's men kill Rana's children, a reference that makes little sense unless we recognize the cow's role as designed to spark religious thinking. Rana prays at the temple of the goddess Parvati before he and his men leave for battle, and Rukmani applies a *ṭīkā* [mark of blessing] to their foreheads, with the temple clearly in the background. Later Rukmani (who still cannot speak but communicates with Rana by shaking her bangles) expresses over the phone her fears about Rana's safety. To reassure her, Rana reminds her of the *ṭīkā* she had applied, implying that their success is assured.

While the unstated parallels are clear enough between the *Rāmāyaṇa's* Rama/Ravana struggle and that in *Karma* between the virtuous Rana and the evil Deng, the film also refers explicitly to the great epic. When Deng torments Rana by coming to the hospital room where he lies injured from his gun battle with Deng's men, Rana tells him that his own soldiers by now have reached Deng's hideout, which he refers to as "Ravana's Lanka." Deng embraces the allusion, informing Rana that "Sita-mata, too, has been taken to Lanka," inviting Rana to look out the window and see that he has captured the heroine, Radha (played by Sridevi), along with Rukmani. The parallels to the *Rāmāyaṇa* become even clearer as the heroes must rescue a Sita-like heroine from the evil Deng who, Ravana-like, tries to force Radha to marry him.

Karma likens the struggle between Rana and Deng not only to that between Rama and Ravana in the *Rāmāyaṇa* but also to the contest between the Pandavas and the Kauravas in the *Mahābhārata*. Rana tells Dharma that to "change these criminals into soldiers, it is necessary to provide rules [*niyam*] and discipline [*anuśāsan*]." Dharma agrees, likening the fight to the one described in the *Mahābhārata* and noting that "it is very necessary that the Pandavas have the strength to fight the Kauravas."

The heroines in *Karma* also are modeled explicitly on mythological images. Audiences are clued to this by the heroines' religiosity. Two of the men trained by Rana to fight Deng, Johnny (Gyaneshwar, played by Anil Kapoor) and Birju (played by Jackie Schroff), develop romantic relationships. Johnny is first alerted to the presence of his beloved-to-be, Tulsi (played by Poonam Dillon), when he hears her singing after prayer at Shiva's temple. Tulsi's religiosity is apparent when she rebuffs her *cācī* (paternal uncle's wife) who had taken her to task for doing *pūjā* instead of household chores. Although her *cācī* tells Tulsi she will never get a husband by doing *pūjā*, she is unconcerned, announcing that the day before Shiva had come to her in a dream. Birju is similarly impressed by Radha's religiosity. When she walks by on her way to the temple, he asks whom she is worshipping. Radha's friends joke about whether it is Rama or Krishna, but she tells Birju that she is really worshipping Santoshi Ma, to which all present shout, "Jai Santoshi Ma"[7] (Victory to Santoshi Ma).

Later, the two heroines are explicitly linked to mythological models. After Birju tells Tulsi that Johnny admires her but cannot make her his wife because he lacks money, Tulsi gets her mother's jewelry and offers it to Johnny. Her assistance is explicitly modeled on that of Sita to Rama; she tells Johnny, "When Ram-ji had some trouble didn't he make Sita-ji his helper?" Although Johnny is a somewhat reluctant husband-to-be, he is moved by this comparison to Sita. The audience sees that Tulsi's words ring in Johnny's head as he tries to sleep at night. Radha is similarly linked to her mythological namesake when Johnny and the third hero, Kairu (played by Naseerudin Shah), tease Birju that his attraction to Radha is as strong as the mythological Krishna's relationship with his beloved Radha. "Why don't you become Radha's Krishna, and therefore make Kittam Kittu [Radha's uncle] our relative?" Johnny jokingly asks Birju.

The mythological references in *Karma* are only part of a mixture that includes secular elements. Four provocative dances are prominent in the film: one by the three heroes at a party by Radha's uncle, dances celebrating the love of Birju and Radha and of Tulsi and Johnny, and Radha's dance before the villain Deng. Fight scenes are also important, including two stirring battles between Rana's and Deng's men, Deng's original escape from Rana's prison, and several fights between the heroes and Radha's uncle's men. Themes of familial harmony are apparent in the deep love of Rana and Rukmani and in Rana's affection for Birju and Johnny, whom he treats as his children at the end of the film. But Rana's objections to their romances also attest to the existence of family tensions, as does Dharma's obligation to kill his own brother Jakka, who turns out to be allied with Deng's men. Slapstick humor is apparent in Rana's teasing lovesong to his wife and when Radha deceives Birju into thinking she has a twin sister.[8] Appeals to nationalist sentiments are made in an opening Independence Day celebration and a concluding ceremony in which Johnny and Birju are forgiven for their past crimes and rewarded for helping to capture Deng. Both ceremonies feature stirring songs and garlanded photos of Nehru, Gandhi, and others.

This use of mythical models in an ostensibly secular story helps create a semi-secular national "public culture" that provides standardized images. The powerful film medium — reaching educated and illiterate, rural and urban, high caste and low, Hindu and Muslim, across many regions — may create an unprecedented homogeneity in the images that move diverse groups of Indians. Future research should focus on how Indians use these images to understand diverse realms of social life, from political struggles (Mohamad 1988) to gender relationships. Although *Karma* does not substantially change the surface content of classical images, the condensed mythological references appear in a secular context that may lead Indians to use these images in unexpected ways.

RAM TERI GANGA MAILI

Ram Teri Ganga Maili focuses on exposing corruption in those who pretend to have holiness, purity, and virtue, be they politicians, priests, or parents. The film contrasts such false claims to purity with true virtue, and it draws a parallel between a pure village girl, Ganga (played by Mandakini), and the holy river Ganges (called *gangā* in Hindi). While these religious themes are central, they are presented on a canvas that includes controversial, often denigrated elements.

Ram Teri revolves around Narendra's love for the pure Ganga. Narendra's father, Jiva Babu (played by Kulbushan Kharbanda), is closely associated with the villainous politician Bhagvat Chaudhari (played by Raza Murad), who pretends to champion a cleanup of the Ganges. Their alliance is cemented when Chaudhari arranges to have Jiva's factory burned so that the latter can collect the insurance money. Narendra (played by Rajiv Kapoor) overhears their villainous talk. He is very close to his *mausā* (maternal uncle), Kunj Bihari (played by Sayed Jafferi), and to his grandmother, Dadi Ma. With their support, Narendra embarks on a college trip to Gangotri to see the clean, pure river Ganges, promising to return with some of its water for his Dadi Ma.

In Gangotri, he falls in love with Ganga, presented as a loyal woman who will treat her husband as a god. She at first had mistaken Narendra's name, and when told it is Narendra ("king" in Hindi), she declares that since meeting him she had wondered whether he was a human [*insān*] or a god [*devtā*]. Although Ganga has been betrothed to another, she marries Narendra. When he leaves Gangotri for his home in Calcutta, Ganga declares that she will wait by the road for him, whether or not he returns quickly as promised. But in Narendra's absence, his parents arranged his marriage to Chaudhari's only daughter, Radha. When Narendra tries to return to Gangotri for Ganga, Chaudhari calls the home minister and has Narendra arrested on trumped-up charges. In the ensuing months, Chaudhari and Jiva Babu prevent Narendra from leaving Calcutta. Ganga, who has given birth to a son, remains devoted to Narendra and resolves to seek him in Calcutta, as her "child would never forgive" her "if he has no name." Making the long trip down the river Ganges to Calcutta, she maintains her purity despite advances from priests, being sold into prostitution, and finally being made a dancing girl in Banaras. When she finally reaches Narendra, she tells him that she "didn't come to demand anything of you. The aim of my life, was to reach you and give you your son."

The concern with purity is apparent in the film's title, *Ram Teri Ganga Maili* (Rama, Your Ganga Is Polluted), in the many scenes of people doing *pūjā* in the great river at holy places like Banaras, and in the practice of carrying Ganges water to people's homes. Often the claim to honor of those doing *pūjā* and carrying Ganges water is clearly shown to be false — a priest bathing in the river tries to rape Ganga, a passenger traveling with Ganga refuses to let her use her Ganges water to relieve her child's thirst, and Chaudhari's claims to purity and correctness are obviously a hoax. To contrast these with real, unself-conscious purity, the film repeatedly draws parallels between Ganga, the village girl, and Ganges, the holy river. When Narendra first meets Ganga, declaring that he is going to take Ganges home in his metal pot, she laughs, tells him her name ("Ganges"), and asks if he is a man or a god. Similarly, when Dadi Ma, who has fallen sick, weakly asks for Ganga and Narendra brings her the sacred water in a metal pot, she replies, "Not this, silly [*paglā*] — your Ganga, my *bahū* [daughter-in-law]."

Parallels also are drawn between Ganga and the mythological Sarasvati, Draupadi, and finally Sita. On her way to Calcutta, Ganga steps off the train in Banaras to get water for her son. When the train pulls out suddenly, Manilal, who had heard Ganga singing on the train, lures her to a *koṭhā* — a place where women are trained in singing and dancing so they can be sold to wealthy customers. Even as he does so, Manilal recognizes her as goddesslike, praising her as an "invaluable jewel" whose voice is a "manifestation of Sarasvati." Ganga fears she will be destroyed by the *koṭhā;* she lacks even Narendra's Calcutta address and despairs of ever finding him.

Chaudhari comes to Banaras to take a mistress [*rakhail*] who will soothe his heart [*dil bahalā denā*] after Radha has married, and he chooses Ganga. When discussing the purchase, the minor character Chamanlal comments that "Krishna had come to save Draupadi's honor [*lāj*]," but no one would come to save the honor of a prostitute [*raṇḍī*]. (In the *Mahābhārata,* the Pandavas gambled away their wife, Draupadi — a Hindu figure of ideal womanhood — but when the mythological victors try to publicly disrobe her, Krishna makes new clothes appear as the old ones are torn off.) When Ganga declares that she has already given her shame [*lāj*] to her Krishna [*apne mohan*], Chamanlal replies, "Don't try to make yourself a devoted wife [*satī savitrī*] in the flow of words." Although Chamanlal thinks Ganga is a *raṇḍī* who will not be saved like Queen Draupadi, her Krishna, Narendra ("king"), emancipates her from Chaudhari.

Narendra's *mausā,* Kunj Bihari, knows of his relation to Ganga, but Narendra's mother has convinced him that her son must be told Ganga is dead to avoid ruining the family. On his way to Banaras to hire dancing girls for Narendra's wedding to Radha, Kunj meets his old underworld acquaintance, Manilal, and learns of Ganga's subsequent fate. He goes to see her, and Ganga asks to be taken to Narendra immediately, but Kunj replies:

> Daughter, I could take you to Narendra now, but then those people, because of their own lechery [*aiyāśī*], would not recognize you as [their] daughter-in-law. Until Narendra can accept [*apnānā*] you in front of the whole world, they will call your son ill begotten [*harām*].

You have already taken the difficult test of fire. Now it is time for your Rama to take his test.

Finally, then, Ganga is compared to Sita. Kunj arranges for her to dance at Narendra's and Radha's wedding, where Narendra too passes his test. Discovering Ganga to be alive, he rushes to her over the objections of Jiva and Chaudhari. The former condemns Narendra for raising a hand against his father for the sake of this woman of the market [*bāzārū laṛkī*], but Narendra replies that Ganga is his "wife, the *bahū* [daughter-in-law] of this *khāndān* [family]."

The themes of purity and salvation appear again in the film's final scenes. Chaudhari shoots and wounds Ganga, and she and Narendra realize that they must leave. Kunj tells him:

Narendra, you are the ocean and Ganga is the stream. In the confluence [*sangam*], where the ocean and the Ganges meet, there is salvation [*mukti*].

The final scene of the film shows Ganga, Narendra, and their son rowing out into the Bay of Bengal, completing their trip from the pure Ganges at Gangotri down the increasingly polluted river and being reborn in the sea, at the holy confluence of the Ganges and the ocean.

Ram Teri Ganga Maili draws parallels between the heroine, Ganga, and Saraswati, Draupadi, Sita, and the river Ganges and it develops an extended theme comparing the purity and virtue of Ganga to the corruption and falseness of the politician Chaudhari, Narendra's father, and those whom Ganga meets on her journey. But these religious themes are drawn on a secular canvas that includes politics, boys on a college fieldtrip, and the imperative of running Jiva's factory at a profit. Fights (between Narendra and Jiva, between Narendra and a college schoolmate), dances (featuring Narendra and Ganga together and her as a dancing girl), and some slapstick humor (a person falling on banana peels) are also important elements in the film. The canvas also includes controversial scenes some regard as lewd (even *mailī!*).[9] The scenes in which Ganga's breasts are exposed through her thin *sāṛī* as she bathes under a waterfall, in which she breastfeeds her child, and in which Narendra kisses her all caused controversy in film magazines, and were often discussed by people I met.[10] *Filmfare* noted that these scenes were important to the film's success but only part of the Hindi film mix:

All over the country, they flocked to the theatres with enthusiasm . . . to sit in rapt attention for three hours, to shower their appreciation, wolf whistles and small change on the film. . . . The man on the street doesn't attempt to camouflage the fact that it was Mandakini who lured him to the theatre. But once inside, he realized that there was more to the film than her half-clad state. There was grandeur, lavishness, catchy songs, well-choreographed dances and the best [dialogue] this side of Salim Javed. (*Filmfare* 1986a:66–67)

Even in *Ram Teri*, then, religious themes are presented in the context of the distinctive, controversial mixture that makes up Hindi film. Observers of the changing Indian religious scene should give attention to potential consequences of presenting religious themes in such a context. (I speculate about some of these consequences in my conclusion.)

Audience Rejection of Religious Alterations in Hindi Film

Prompted by religious cues to recognize orthodox religious themes, audiences nevertheless tend to reject cinematic departures from religious convention — possibly because the film medium is denigrated in Hindu society. People approach different cultural objects differently. Hindus who regard epics like the *Rāmāyaṇa* as an authoritative guide to action may dismiss films as meaningless entertainment at best. A twenty-six-year-old married man told me that by reading Tulsi's *Rāmcaritmānas,* Indians "receive good teaching about how one should behave with one's parents, *bhābhī* [elder brother's wife], and *bahū* [daughter-in-law], and how one should behave with one's *devar* [husband's younger brother]." In sharp contrast, critics, conservatives, the educated (Vasudev 1978), and older people tend to regard films as promoting vulgarity, "intoxications," and neglect of family responsibility. "From childhood on," Khare argues, "Indians are discouraged from seeing films." Indians, he says, believe that films preach "lascivious and immoral behavior," propagating "smoking, drinking, [and] vulgar speech and manners" and arousing "passion" and "sexual promiscuity" (Khare 1985:142). "Critics and columnists," Ashis Nandy argues, have "a heyday decrying the inconsistency and irrationality of the big film hits of their time" (1981:89).

Even filmgoers often see them as mere meaningless entertainment. Many whom I interviewed were somewhat embarrassed about seeing films, which they know are regarded as morally suspect. A twenty-nine-year-old who lives with his wife and parents admits to seeing films a couple of times a month. Yet, he told me, "I get nothing out of films. When I have no work, I go and sit in the cinema. I spend five rupees and nothing seems good." Pfleiderer's (1985b:115–118) study of urban film audiences likewise found that many Indians were embarrassed about attending Hindi films, which they regarded as very low quality. A twenty-three-year-old Uttar Pradesh student responded to a questionnaire by lamenting that although "at first I saw [Hindi films] for entertainment, now it has become a habit (like smoking cigarettes)" (Pfleiderer 1985b:117). A twenty-one-year-old male student denigrated the films he saw a few times a month, saying that he never goes alone because he needs someone with whom to share the boredom (Pfleiderer and Lutze 1985b:233).

Filmmakers and filmgoers minimize films as mere fantasies with nothing to teach about daily life. One commercial film director said, for instance, that he is "interested in touching the heart of the common man, leading the audience into a world of fantasy and telling them stories like one tells children" (Ghai 1991:6). The male filmgoers I interviewed in 1991 agree. One twenty-three-year-old college student told me that he sees films for "amusement [and] to refresh the mind when it becomes bored." An unmarried twenty-two-year-old living with his parents in a joint family said that "films are a fantasy world that is very different from reality." For him, films provide "a little entertainment for three hours. Whenever I want, I can pass the time for three hours away from my problems." Devoted letters to film magazines, similarly, focus on films as a relieving fantasy. One letter writer from Bangalore wrote, for instance, that "people go to see films to ease their minds and relax, forgetting all their problems" (Nagendra 1991:6). The Hindi film's image as morally dubious and the audience's approach to them as mere entertainment militate against film innovations being taken seriously as a positive contribution to respected religious traditions.

RESPONSES TO INNOVATIONS IN MYTHOLOGICALS
Although in recent years mythological films have appealed largely to rural Indians, the 1975 hit *Jai Santoshi Ma*[11] was widely watched by urban audiences as well (Mitra 1987; Das 1981:43). Filmmakers are usually wary of taking liberties with mythological themes for fear of provoking adverse audience reaction, but here the theme of goddess-dispute is an innovation; in the Hindu religious tradition, all goddesses usually are seen as one (Kurtz 1992). The film focuses on Satyavati's devotions to Santoshi, a new "daughter" of Ganesh. Satyavati prays to her, asking to be married to Birju,

and when her prayer is answered, Satyavati fulfills her vow by offering great devotion to Santoshi Ma. The goddess's fame spreads so that even Brahma, Vishnu, and Shiva receive *prasād* offered to Santoshi Ma, and their three venerable wives (Brahmani, Lakshmi, and Parvati) become jealous. Although they punish Satyavati with misfortunes, she continues her devotions to Santoshi Ma. Ultimately the three goddesses relent, saying that they were only testing Satyavati's devotion.

Jai Santoshi Ma was a huge success, but according to Stanley Kurtz (1984, 1992) its innovation — the goddess-dispute theme — has not been taken seriously by most devotees of Santoshi Ma cults, who focus more on printed stories than on the film as a guide to worship. Even the goddess's most ardent devotees, Kurtz (1984) argues, are skeptical of the goddess-dispute theme, seeing it as tainted by purely commercial considerations. The film spread Santoshi Ma worship to rural and urban Indians of diverse castes and regions, but its effect on mythic content was limited by resistance to innovation presented in the denigrated film medium.

RESPONSES TO INNOVATIONS INTRODUCED IN SOCIALS
Ram Teri Ganga Maili presents a love marriage that overcomes the resistance of the young husband's family. Despite the film's success, very few of the men I interviewed accepted its message. Instead, they drew on their commonsense understanding that love marriages inevitably fail and concluded that the one celebrated in the film could never succeed (see Pfleiderer 1985a:72–74, for a similar example). For example, a twenty-six-year-old whose marriage had just been arranged told me that the hero and heroine's marriage in *Ram Teri*

> will not remain successful. Because the boy and the girl are not of the same caste, they will have no prestige, and will not be able to live in the society. There is nowhere that the couple can live.

Several other men condoned Jiva Babu's attempts to stop Narendra's marriage. A twenty-nine-year-old eldest son living with his wife, parents, and siblings commented that Jiva's attempt to stop the marriage "was proper. This marriage will not succeed in the Indian environment. In this atmosphere, everyone will see it as a love marriage. Such a marriage has no future."

Even filmgoers I interviewed in and around movie houses in 1991 distanced themselves from cinematic celebrations of love marriages. "Without parental consent," as one man said, "a marriage cannot be successful."

Others warned that boys only take advantage of girls: "It is just one-sided," one young man said. "Boys do this behavior for amusement." Another young man emphasized the problems that parents would face:

> In love stories, a boy and a girl like each other and there is excitement. They marry for love, but they fail to see that in the future even their parents must face the problems the marriage causes.

An unmarried twenty-one-year-old who enjoys love stories nevertheless talked of the incompatibility of love and joint-family living:

> Mostly love marriages are not successful because as long as you have mutual love [*pyār*] you will want to marry, and you will want to remain in that true way of mutual love. But after the marriage it cannot be obtained in the familial situation. Most girls think that the boy will love them the way he loved her [*pyār karnā*] before marrying her. But that can never be.

Despite cinematic fantasies, young male filmgoers continue to disapprove of love marriages, to focus on parental authority, and to emphasize the incompatibility of love with joint-family living.

One reason films do not transform men's understandings may be that films remind viewers of cautionary tales about the costs of abandoning one's parents for love. Kathryn Hansen (1992:169) argues that while nineteenth-century *nauṭankī* theater celebrated the love that "fully stretches and exercises the human heart," *nauṭankī* theater also emphasized the "hard wall of opposition erected to hold back this mighty emotional flood." Similarly, recent Hindi film love stories continually remind viewers of the costs of marrying for love. In recent hits like *Maine Pyar Kiya* (1989) and *Dil* (1990) the hero and heroine must give up financial support of their families to follow their love. As the hero's father told his son in *Dil:*

> Because you have married the daughter of my enemy you can no longer live in this house. Before you go, think about how very hard it is to earn enough to eat. You have become so totally blinded by love [*pyār*] for this mere girl that you are going to give up everything.

In *Ram Teri* it is a love marriage that starts the chain of events that lead Ganga to be sold as a dancing girl and shot at Narendra's wedding. Like *nauṭankī* theater (Hansen 1992:149), Hindi films also portray "romantic love" as only possible "beyond society's boundaries" "in the barren wilderness or in heaven." In *Ram Teri,* Narendra and Ganga meet in the faraway hills and after they are reunited they abandon society by leaving Narendra's relations behind: The final scene shows Narendra, the wounded Ganga, and their child rowing out into the Bay of Bengal.

The cultural world surrounding Hindi films similarly reasserts the dangers of love marriages. Advice columnists who write in Hindi film fan magazines often warn young readers against marrying for love. One twenty-four-year-old Delhi filmgoer wrote that he was in love with a woman other than the one his parents had chosen for him. The columnist advised him that he should

> marry the girl your parents have chosen. If you marry the other one you will not be prepared to endure her improper pressures. . . . Although you like the girl it wouldn't be right to marry her. In the coming time, your beloved will marry in another place. (*Filmī Kaliyān* 1991:74)

While films celebrate love, both films and film culture remain restricted by conventional paradigms, perhaps unwittingly reinforcing the popular belief that love is incompatible with family honor and joint-family living (see also Hansen 1992:199–206). While films side with lovers over society, they nevertheless remind audiences of the impending loss of family support, which young men often cite as a reason that they would never marry for love (Derné 1995a).

Like Kathryn Hansen's (1992:260) study of *nauṭankī* theater, this chapter suggests that while popular culture may reflect "moral tensions posed by dilemmas of everyday life," it does not transform audience understandings. Like the romantic tales of *nauṭankī* theater, Hindi films' celebration of love indicates the "tension that arises between a pair of lovers and their families" (Hansen 1992:145). But because Hindi films are not respected as an authoritative guide to action and because films remind viewers of the consequences of marrying for love, cinematic celebrations of love marriages do not prompt viewers to change traditional beliefs that custom should guide interactions among family members and especially that children should please their parents by consenting to an arranged marriage. This resistance to films' authority contrasts strongly with the attitude toward respected religious texts like Tulsidas's *Rāmcaritmānas*. For instance, a fifty-four-year-old head of a large joint family told me that the reason he did not "like love marriages" is that the proper "system of marriage is that done by Rama and [Sita]." This man explicitly relied on the "big description of this marriage in the *Rāmcaritmānas*." "It is important," a married twenty-six-year-old concurred, that in marriages "we follow the example of him whom we call Bhagvan Ram [Rama]." It is no surprise, then, that cinematic departures from Hindu social and religious tradition are rejected by an audience that sees film as mere entertainment, and degraded entertainment at that.

Conclusions

The market forces that shape Hindi films ensure that religious themes will be introduced, vaguely, in most of them. Filmmakers enlist such themes to appeal to a large, heterogeneous audience that also wants dances, fights, family themes, and slapstick comedy. Hence religious themes in Hindi film are only part of a mixture with diverse elements.

Hindu conservatives and government censors discourage religious innovations in Hindi films. Filmmakers comply by using religious imagery that will not be too offensive, and so a pantheon of "acceptable" gods tends to be invoked repeatedly in films. While contributing to standardization of mythological images, Hindi film is not the source of alterations to the content of religious stories. Mythological references are often condensed and inexplicit, constructed to avoid controversy. Since Indians regard film as a denigrated medium, moreover, those innovations sometimes introduced into mythological stories are rejected by audiences.

While Hindi filmmakers are driven by market considerations to promote religion but not religious change, the presentation of religious images in a very secular, degraded context may prompt changes in Indian religion — changes for which observers should be alert in coming years. Will religion's status as a special realm suffer by being made ordinary in Hindi films? Might cinematic innovations — such as the goddess-dispute theme in *Jai Santoshi Ma* or the hint in *Ram Teri* that Rama also should undergo a test of fire — be picked up in *kathā*s and in other venerated genres that are treated as authoritative guides? Are critiques of mythological models like those offered by *Manushi*'s editors more acceptable, and hence more powerful, when directed at images presented in Hindi films? While audiences say they reject cinematic departures from tradition and filmmakers are cautious about straying too far from mythological stories, the presentation of mythological models along with denigrated secular elements may prove to spur important — and still evolving — changes in Indian religion.

Acknowledgments

The U.S. Department of Education supported this research with Foreign Language and Area Studies fellowships, which financed my study of Hindi, and with a Fulbright-Hays Doctoral Dissertation Research Abroad grant, which funded the 1986–87 research. The American Institute of Indian Studies provided a senior fellowship that funded the 1991 research. Awadesh Kumar Mishra, Nagendra Gandhi, Parvez Khan, and Ramchandra Pandit assisted me in conducting and translating the 1987 interviews. Narender Sethi and Vimal Thakur assisted me in conducting and translating the 1991 interviews. Davidson College provided funds for research assistance and the purchase of videotapes of Hindi films. The University of North Carolina at Charlotte and Hobart and William Smith Colleges assisted me in paying the administrative fee to the AIIS. Stacy Rooker aided me in searching recent Indian periodicals for articles on the film industry. Bharat Krishnamurthy helped in translating scenes from recent Hindi films and in identifying mythological figures depicted in films, and offered helpful insights about the Hindi film industry and the Hindi film scene. Bill Mahoney assisted my interpretation of Hindu mythology. Lawrence A. Babb, Lisa Jadwin, Philip Lutgendorf, and Susan Wadley made helpful suggestions on earlier versions of the essay. Parts of this work were presented at the University of California, Berkeley, the University of Chicago, Cornell University, and Nazareth College.

Notes

1. See *Filmfare* September 16–30, 1987, pp. 20–21. More recently Hindu fundamentalists stalled the screening of a television serial, *The Sword of Tipu Sultan* (Baweja 1990:92).

2. Kishan finally shifts his affections to Chando, praising her devotion despite her suffering and proclaiming that even *bhagvān* (God) could not forgive his sins.

3. Mitra (1987:42) reports that the film was "the astounding success story of recent years."

4. *Sholay* is one of the seven biggest hits in Hindi film history (see *Filmfare* 1986a:70). A twenty-year-old respondent to Pfleiderer and Lutze's survey (1985b: 228) noted that children enjoy repeating a famous scene from *Sholay*. During my fieldwork, I witnessed children mimicking that scene (described in note 6) from the film, then a decade old.

5. *Ram Teri Ganga Maili* was the biggest hit of 1986 (Kakar 1989:30) and one of the seven biggest of all time (*Filmfare* 1986a:80). *Filmfare* called *Ram Teri* the "decade's biggest blockbuster" (1986a:66) and the "lone mammoth hit in the indus-

try" (1986b). *Karma* was recognized as a "box office bonanza" (Tripathi 1989:90–91), and, like *Ram Teri,* it played for more than a year in many Indian cities (Mitra 1987:42).

6. *Karma* takes a bow to *Sholay,* making explicit reference to the famous scene in which the villain tells his dependents that although they have been eating his salt, now they will have to eat a bullet (see Pfleiderer and Lutze 1985b:228). In *Karma,* the villain tells his dependents that if they work, they will eat bread; if not, they will have to eat a bullet. *Karma* makes other references to famous Hindi films; see notes 7 and 8.

7. Birju makes awed reference to the fifty weeks during which the film *Jai Santoshi Ma* played in Bombay.

8. Believing her stunt, Birju refers to this as a "double role" like those he had seen in Bombay films.

9. *Filmfare* reported that Doordarshan rejected a proposed serial starring Mandakini "on the grounds that television was for family viewing." Although the producer assured that "Mandakini's neckline would be raised to respectable heights, . . . as far as Doordarshan was concerned, Mandakini was *mailī*" (1986 or 1987 clipping in author's possession). Film magazines constantly asked Mandakini about the three controversial scenes (e.g., *Mādhurī* 1986:16; *Cineblitz* 1987:83).

10. The waterfall scene was most celebrated on movie posters. Several people who knew I had seen the film several times commented that I must have been intoxicated by these scenes.

11. *Jai Santoshi Ma,* which still plays in revival, is one of the seven biggest hits in Hindi film history (*Filmfare* 1986a:70).

References

Barnouw, Erik, and S. Krishnaswamy. 1980. *Indian Film,* 2d ed. New York: Oxford University Press.

Baweja, Harinder. 1990. "Communal Casualty." *India Today* (February 28): 92.

Cineblitz. 1987. "Mandakini Grilled." *Cineblitz* (September):80–85.

Das, Veena. 1981. "The Mythological Film and Its Framework of Meaning: An Analysis of *Jai Santoshi Ma.*" *India International Centre Quarterly* 8, no. 1:43–55.

Derné, Steve. 1995a. *Culture in Action: Family Life, Emotion, and Male Dominance in Banaras, India.* Albany: State University of New York Press.

——. 1995b. "Popular Culture and Emotional Experiences: Rituals of Filmgoing and the Reception of Emotion Culture." *Social Perspectives on Emotion,* volume 3, ed. C. Ellis and M. G. Flaherty. Greenwich, Conn.: JAI Press.

Dharap, B. V. 1983. "The Mythological or Taking Fatalism for Granted." In *Indian Cinema Superbazaar,* ed. A. Vasudev and P. Lenglet, pp. 79–83. New Delhi: Vikas.

Filmfare. 1986a. "A Wet Dream, Yes, But. . . ." *Filmfare* (May 1–15):66–70.

——. 1986b. "Ravindra Jain: Toward the Big Time." *Filmfare* (October 16–31).

Filmī Kaliyān. 1991. "*Kāse Kahūn.*" *Filmi Kaliyān* (August): 70–74.

Ghai, Subhash. 1991. "Theme for a Dream" [Interview]. *Times of India Sunday Review* (14 July 1991):6.

H. C. 1986. "The 'Film Bandh' and After." *Economic and Political Weekly* (November 22):2030–2031.

Hansen, Kathryn. 1992. *Grounds for Play: The Nautanki Theatre of North India.* Berkeley: University of California Press.

Harlan, Lindsey. 1992. *Religion and Rajput Women: The Ethic of Protection in Contemporary Narratives.* Berkeley: University of California Press.

Hartmann, Paul, B. R. Patil, and Anita Dighe. 1989. *The Mass Media and Village Life: An Indian Study.* London: Sage.

India-West. 1988. "Feature Film Production Declined in 1987, Tamil Cinema Topped Charts." *India-West* (February 19):38.

Kakar, Sudhir. 1981. "The Ties That Bind: Family Relationships in the Mythology of Hindi Cinema." *India International Centre Quarterly* 8, no. 1:11–22.

———. 1989. *Intimate Relations: Exploring Indian Sexuality.* Chicago: University of Chicago Press.

Karanjia, B. K. 1983. "The Star System: Another Kind of Nonsense, Another Profound Humanity." In *Indian Cinema Superbazaar,* ed. A. Vasudev and P. Lenglet, pp. 84–88. New Delhi: Vikas.

Karnad, Girish. 1981. "Comments from the Gallery" [including an interview with Girish Karnad]. *India International Centre Quarterly* 8, no. 1:97–108.

———. 1983. [Interview.] In *Indian Cinema Superbazaar,* ed. A. Vasudev and P. Lenglet, pp. 216–228. New Delhi: Vikas.

Khare, Vishnu. 1985. "The *Dinman* Hindi Film Inquiry: A Summary." In *The Hindi Film,* ed. B. Pfleiderer and L. Lutze, pp. 139–148. New Delhi: Manohar.

Khosla, Raj. 1985. "The Maker's View." In *The Hindi Film,* ed. B. Pfleiderer and L. Lutze, pp. 31–45. New Delhi: Manohar.

Kurtz, Stanley. 1984. "The Goddesses' Dispute in *Jai Santoshi Ma:* A Mythological Film in Its Cultic Context." Paper presented at the convention of the American Academy of Religion, December 8–11, Chicago.

———. 1992. *All the Mothers Are One: Hindu India and the Cultural Reshaping of Psychoanalysis.* New York: Columbia University Press.

Lutze, Lothar. 1985. "From Bharata to Bombay: Change in Continuity in Hindi Film Aesthetics." In *The Hindi Film,* ed. B. Pfleiderer and L. Lutze, pp. 3–15. New Delhi: Manohar.

Mādhurī. 1986. "Cumban carcitāē kyā kahatī hāī." *Mādhurī* (April 27):10–19.

Mitra, Sumit. 1987. "The Return of Big Budget Cinema." *Sunday* (August 9–15):39–48.

Mohamad, Khalid. 1988. "Fatal Attraction: The Politician as Villain." *Illustrated Weekly of India* (November 13):8–17.

Nagendra, C. R. 1991. "Timely Story" [Letter to the Editor.] *'g'* (July):6.

Nandy, Ashis. 1981. "The Popular Hindi Film: Ideology and First Principles." *India International Centre Quarterly* 8, no. 1:89–96.

O'Flaherty, Wendy Doniger. 1981. "The Mythological in Disguise: An Analysis of *Karz.*" *India International Centre Quarterly* 8, no. 1:23–30.

Pfleiderer, Beatrix. 1985a. "Rural Audience Reactions." In *The Hindi Film,* ed. B. Pfleiderer and L. Lutze, pp. 58–78. New Delhi: Manohar.

———. 1985b. "An Empirical Study of Urban and Semi-Urban Audience Reaction to Hindi Film." In *The Hindi Film,* ed. B. Pfleiderer and L. Lutze, pp. 81–130. New Delhi: Manohar.

Pfleiderer, Beatrix, and Lothar Lutze, eds. 1985a. *The Hindi Film: Agent and Re-Agent of Cultural Change.* New Delhi: Manohar.

———. 1985b. "Appendix C: Samples of Letters in Response to the *Dinman* Inquiry." In *The Hindi Film,* ed. B. Pfleiderer and L. Lutze, pp. 227–248. New Delhi: Manohar.

Raina, Raghunath. 1983. "The Context: A Socio-Cultural Anatomy." In *Indian Cinema Superbazaar,* ed. A. Vasudev and P. Lenglet, pp. 2–18. New Delhi: Vikas.

Saari, Anil. 1985. "A Critic's Notes." In *The Hindi Film,* ed. B. Pfleiderer and L. Lutze, pp. 46–57. New Delhi: Manohar.

Sadagopan, Shobha. 1979. "Women in Indian Film: Another Commodity." *Manushi,* no. 1 (January):47.

Sanghera, Jyoti. 1980. "*Naukar:* Guidebook for Husbands." *Manushi,* no. 5 (May–June):51.

Sarkar, Kobita. 1975. *Indian Cinema Today: An Analysis.* New Delhi: Sterling.

Singh, Bikram. 1983. "The Commercial: A Reality Disturbed." In *Indian Cinema Superbazaar,* ed. A. Vasudev and P. Lenglet, pp. 28–32. New Delhi: Vikas.

Sippy, G. P. 1983. [Interview.] In *Indian Cinema Superbazaar,* A. Vasudev and P. Lenglet, pp. 281–300. New Delhi: Vikas.

Tripathi, Salil. 1989. "Anil Kapoor: Joker in the Pack." *India Today* (March 31):90–91.

Vanita, Ruth. 1989. "Film Review: Toofan." *Manushi,* no. 53:43–44.

Vanita, Ruth, and Madhu Kishwar. 1985. "Review of Bahu Ki Awaz." *Manushi,* no. 28:46.

Vasudev, Aruna. 1978. *Liberty and Licence in the Indian Cinema.* New Delhi: Vikas.

———. 1983. "The Woman: Vamp or Victim?" In *Indian Cinema Superbazaar,* ed. A. Vasudev and P. Lenglet, pp. 95–100. New Delhi: Vikas.

Vasudev, Aruna, and Philippe Lenglet, eds. 1983. *Indian Cinema Superbazaar.* New Delhi: Vikas.

Philip Lutgendorf

9. All in the (Raghu) Family:
A Video Epic in Cultural Context

> Rama incarnates in countless ways
> and there are tens of millions of *Rāmāyaṇa*s.
> — Tulsidas[1]

Introduction

On January 25, 1987, a new program premiered on Doordarshan, India's government-run television network. Broadcast on Sunday mornings at 9:30 A.M., it represented an experiment for the national network, for it was the first time that the medium of television was to be used to present a serialized adaptation of one of the great cultural and religious epics of India. The chosen work was the *Rāmāyaṇa* — the story first narrated in Sanskrit some two millennia ago by the poet Valmiki, and retold numerous times in succeeding centuries by poets in every major regional language, most notably, for North India and for Hindi, in the sixteenth-century epic *Rāmcaritmānas* ("The Holy Lake of Rama's Acts") of Tulsidas. The television adaptation, produced and directed by Bombay filmmaker Ramanand Sagar, was itself an epic undertaking: featuring some three hundred actors, it was originally slated to run for fifty-two episodes of forty-five minutes each, but had to be extended three times because of popular demand, and eventually grew into a main story in seventy-eight episodes, followed after an interval of several months by a sequel incorporating the events detailed in the seventh book (the *Uttarakāṇḍa,* or epilogue) of the Sanskrit epic.

Long before the airing of the main story concluded on July 31, 1988, Sagar's *Ramayan* had become the most popular program ever shown on Indian television, and something more: a phenomenon of such proportions that intellectuals and policymakers struggled to come to terms with its significance. Why and how, observers wondered, had this serial — almost universally dismissed by critics as a technically flawed melodrama — elicited such a staggering response? Did its success point once again to the enduring power of sacred narrative to galvanize the masses, or was it, rather, a cue to the advent of a new force in Indian culture: the mesmerizing power of television? Inevitably the airing of the serial provoked lively debate over such topics as the relationship of folk and elite traditions, the marketing of religion and art, the politics of communalism and of government-controlled mass media, and indeed over the message of the *Rāmāyaṇa* story itself.

In seeking to make a modest contribution to this debate, I first present a brief account of the making and airing of the serial and of its public reception, and then consider its relationship to the *Rāmcaritmānas* epic (its principal literary source) and to older and ongoing traditions of performance. The concluding section of the chapter examines some critical responses to the serial and the debate it engendered over the impact of television on Indian culture.[2]

Sunday Mornings with Rama

To suggest that the making of a television serial began several millennia ago may appear to risk mimicking studio promotional hype, yet it must be observed that the success of India's most popular serial derives largely from the enduring appeal of the narrative tradition on which it draws. Although the textual and historical problems associated with Valmiki's Sanskrit rendering of the Rama story have fascinated generations of scholars, only recently has significant research focused on the developments that, from the eleventh century onward, contributed to the proliferation of the devotional cult of Rama in northern India, and created a religious climate in which its ultimate vernacular vehicle — the epic *Rāmcaritmānas* — could acquire throughout much of the region the status of preeminent text for religious performance (Whaling 1980; Bakker 1986; van der Veer 1988). Elsewhere I have traced some of the factors contributing to the adoption of this text by ever wider audiences for both ritual and entertainment purposes; factors that included the patronage of *rājā*s and *zamīndār*s in the post-Mughal period and of urban mercantile groups during the latter half of the nineteenth century, as well as the advent of print technology, the rise of literacy among the middle classes, and the ongoing effort to define an orthodox Hindu identity (Lutgendorf 1989, 1991a). One result of these trends was the proliferation of increasingly standardized genres of *Mānas* (*Rāmcaritmānas*) performance: ritualized recitation (*pāṭh*), oral exposition (*kathā*), and dramatic enactment (*rāmlīlā*). All three involve sustained, episodic recitation of the text and use it as a foundation for creative elaboration. As will be shown, the conventions and interpretive strategies of these still-popular genres are reflected in the screenplay of the television serial.

Another background against which the success of the serial must be viewed is the history of motion pictures in India, particularly the film genre of "mythologicals." Drawing on the story traditions of the epics and *pur-āṇas* and imbued with the emotional piety of regional devotional traditions, mythological films have been part of Indian cinema since the beginning. The pioneer of the Bombay cinema, the Maharashtrian Brahman Dadasaheb Phalke, was inspired by a film on the life of Jesus to create a series of mythologicals beginning with *Rajah Harishchandra* (1912) — the first feature-length film made in India — and including *Lanka Dahan* (The Burning of Lanka, based on an episode from the *Rāmāyaṇa,* 1917) and *Krishna Janma* (The Birth of Krishna, 1919). Although film had been on the Indian scene since 1896 (when the Lumière Brothers *cinématographe* was unveiled at Watson's Hotel in Bombay), the actors and themes of early foreign-made films failed to engage the deepest sympathies of the Indian audience. In Phalke's films, however, "the figures of long-told stories took flesh and blood. The impact was overwhelming. When Rama appeared on the screen in 'Lanka Dahan,' and when in 'Krishna Janma' Lord Krishna himself at last appeared, men and women in the audience prostrated themselves before the screen" (Barnouw and Krishnaswamy 1980: 15). The devotional behavior of the audience — so striking to a foreign observer — would remain a common response to the screening of religious films and, as we shall see, to the television "Ramayana." Yet the worship of the "flesh and blood" (or celluloid or video) image, far from being a consequence of the "revolutionary" impact of film, was a response with a long indigenous pedigree, rooted in the ritualized but complete identification of actor with deity that is central to Hindu folk performance.

Over the years, a modest number of mythologicals scored as major hits with nationwide audiences — two of the most notable were versions of the *Rāmāyaṇa:* Vijay Bhatt's *Ram Rajya* (1943; the only film, it is said, that Mahatma Gandhi would consent to see) and Homi Wadia's *Sampoorna Ramayana* (1961). The stronghold of such pictures, however, has not been the Hindi film capital of Bombay, but regional production centers that cater to less urbanized audiences.[3] As was the case in the American film industry, where the 1950s and 1960s saw a flurry of epic religious films, mythologicals have tended to come in clusters, as one successful film generated a series of spinoffs. But while the occasional low-budget effort has produced an unexpected windfall — the best example is *Jai Santoshi Ma* (1975), which, through presenting a new goddess whose time had clearly come, became a runaway hit with women and one of the highest-grossing films of the period — the genre as a whole has seemed riskier than most formulas. Although an audience for such films obviously existed, it was also evident that it was not the regular filmgoing crowd of young urban males at whom the majority of releases were targeted.

The advent of television did not initially create conditions favorable to the screening of religious narrative. During the 1960s and early 1970s, television sets in India served principally as technological novelties to adorn upper-class sitting rooms, where they provided, for a few hazy hours each night, a droning rendition of the day's news (read in Sanskritized Hindi by a newscaster who always looked directly into the camera — a sort of All-India Radio with a face) and drably edifying cultural programming. The 1970s saw a steady increase in the number of sets and transmission centers, and the advent of color programming, yet the standard audience complaint about Doordarshan remained that it was overwhelmingly dull. The addition of a weekly program of song and dance clips from hit movies (*Chitrahaar*, which immediately became the most popular program on television) and of a Sunday afternoon feature film sparked viewer interest, but also confirmed that the appeal of television was largely as an adjunct to the existing film industry, and that the distinctive potential of the small screen had yet to be realized.

In the early 1980s, two related developments transformed Doordarshan: the advent of commercials and the commissioning of serialized dramas from independent studios. Maintaining the national network as a noncommercial preserve had proved a costly proposition, and powerful private-sector interests were eager to pay to reach consumers over the airwaves. The decision to accept commercials in turn forced the network to provide more varied and entertaining fare, since sponsors required assurance that audiences would indeed be watching. The new commercials themselves were highly entertaining: financed with high budgets and conceived by advertising directors who kept up with the latest American trends, they burst on the screen in fifteen-minute blocks, sparkling with humor, catchy music, and dazzling special effects, but their glossy look only made the regular programming appear more tired in comparison.

At the same time, Doordarshan began to face competition from videocassette recorders and a burgeoning market in rental movies, which gave viewers the option of switching off the state-controlled channel in favor of taped programs of their choice. The impact of the VCR on Indian culture during the last decade warrants closer examination — it has, for one thing, given Bombay films the truly mass exposure they never enjoyed when confined to cinema halls — but at least one effect of the machines was to jolt the officials in Mandi House (Doordarshan's New Delhi headquarters) into the realization that they were in danger of losing their audience, and with it, revenues from private sponsorship, unless they were prepared to offer programs that could compete more successfully with the fantasies of the cinema.

The first such effort was Kumar Vasudev's *Ham log* (Us), a soap opera about a group of families in a middle-class neighborhood. In place of the larger-than-life heroes of the cinema, it introduced a set of believable characters with whom viewers were invited to identify. The runaway success of this fledgling effort prompted the network to commission a whole crop of serials and miniseries, of which the most popular were *Buniyaad* (Foundation, a melodramatic family saga directed by Ramesh Sippy) and *Nukkad* (Streetcorner). Though official parlance blessed such efforts with the newly coined Sanskritic genre name *dhārāvāhik* ("serialization"), the Hinglish word *sīriyal* effortlessly entered popular speech. By any name, serials had come to stay, and during the mid-1980s more than a dozen were airing during any given week. The relative popularity of each was reflected in viewer polls, advertising rates, and the eagerness with which sponsors sought ten-second slots in the blocks of commercials preceding each episode. A new industry was created, employing directors and technicians as well as many stage and cinema actors.

With the rapid proliferation of serials and the liberalization of bureaucratic policies on programming, the subject matter of shows began to display more imagination and diversity. During 1986 two miniseries aired that drew on folklore and mythology: *Vikram aur vetal* (King Vikram and the Vampire, based on the folktales preserved in the Sanskrit *Kathāsaritasāgara* and in Hindi-Urdu *kissā* texts) and *Krishna avatar* (Lord Krishna, loosely based on the *Bhāgavata purāṇa*). Although both were well received by viewers, neither enjoyed enough success to eclipse the popularity of established serials like *Buniyaad,* nor did the religious content of the Krishna series provoke much controversy.

The creator of *Vikram aur vetal* was Ramanand Sagar (born Ramchand Chopra), a veteran producer-director who, together with his five sons, ran a production company responsible for several hit films, including the high-grossing musical *Arzoo* (Desire) and the espionage thriller *Aan-khen* (Eyes) — but never, incidentally, for a mythological. Sagar's Natraj Studios fell on lean times in the late 1970s after a string of failures, prompting the director to turn his attention to television. While producing a second miniseries entitled *Dada-didi ki kahaniyan* (Grandpa and Grandma's Stories), Sagar approached Doordarshan officials with a proposal for an extended serialization of the *Rāmāyaṇa*. By his own account a lifelong devotee of the Tulsi *Mānas,* Sagar claims to have been involved for some twenty-five years in a group that met regularly to recite and discuss the Hindi epic. His proposal was for a detailed treatment in fifty-two episodes, to be based primarily on the Tulsidas version but also drawing on the Sanskrit *Rāmāyaṇa,* the Tamil and Bengali versions of Kamban and Krittibas, and other regional retellings. Initially vetoed by Mandi House, the proposal was revived and resubmitted, but its approval was apparently delayed by concern that the airing of such a serial would arouse communal sentiments (Mazumdar 1988:2). Even when the project was finally given the go-ahead in 1986, it is certain that neither the bureaucrats nor Sagar himself had an inkling of the response it would generate. Significantly, it was assigned a languid time slot at the start of the weekly holiday, when prior network experience indicated few viewers would be watching.

Sagar assembled a cast that combined relatively unknown principals (such as Arun Govil as Rama, Sunil Lahri as Lakshman, and the twenty-year-old Dipika Chikhlia as Sita) with veteran character actors (former wrestler Dara Singh — the serial's monkey-hero Hanuman — had appeared in some two hundred action-adventures). At the secluded hamlet of Umbergaon, on the Gujarat coast some three hours north of Bombay, Sagar laid out "Vrindavan Studios," where the entire crew lived for two weeks each month for the duration of the project.

The serial premiered with a framing narration that situated it in the long tradition of *Rāmāyaṇa* stories in various languages and thus introduced the theme (to be reiterated many times) of the *Rāmāyaṇa* as a symbol of national unity and integration. The story itself opened with a parliament of frightened gods petitioning Vishnu, recumbent on his serpent-couch on the Milky Ocean, to take human form and put a stop to Ravan's depredations; this in turn led to scenes of King Dashrath's fire sacrifice and the birth of Rama and his brothers. Early episodes, while not exactly hurried, moved at a moderate pace through the first of the epic's seven books, showing scenes of Rama and his brothers' childhood, some highly original interpretations of their education in a spartan ashram, and the familiar story of Rama and Lakshman's adventures with the sage Vish-vamitra, culminating in the young hero's winning of Sita as his bride.

The rest, as they say, is history. Despite mostly acerbic reviews in the English-language media, condemning the serial as a crude commercialization and decrying its production values and sluggish pace[4] and a few equally harsh critiques in the Hindi press,[5] the popularity of the serial rose steadily throughout its first six months on the air. In the absence of anything like Nielsen ratings for India, the most telling statistics come from advertising revenues. During its first month, *Ramayan* lagged behind the serials *Buni-yaad* and *Khoj,* the weekly Hindi film, and the film-clip revue *Chitrahaar* in the number of advertising spots sold. But it caught up quickly, and the average of fifteen commercials per episode during February jumped to thirty-two by April. In June, *Ramayan* was earning more revenue than any program except *Chitrahar,* and it passed this competitor the following month. By August, Sagar's program was generating an eighth of the total income of national television. Doordarshan was flooded with requests from some 135 advertisers anxious to pay Rs. 40,000 per ten-second slot to have their products plugged at *Ramayan* screening time, and in September the number of commercials was increased to forty. From that point on, *Rama-yan* consistently outgrossed every other program, generating an estimated weekly income of 2.8 to 3 million rupees for the network (*Illustrated Weekly of India* 1987:17).

What all this translates into in audience numbers is harder to say with accuracy. Conservative estimates of Doordarshan's daily viewership during the period range from 40 to 60 million, but the response to the *Ramayan* serial was unique. Many sets were mounted in public locations and drew in large numbers of people not normally exposed to television; hence the most popular episodes may have been seen by 80 to 100 million people — roughly an eighth of India's population. This figure may seem modest by Western standards (the Superbowl reportedly engages the attention of 40 percent of Americans, while the Academy Awards telecast draws an international audience of some 300 million; Read 1985:153, 163), but it must be appreciated in terms of the limited number and distribution of television sets in India and the restricted availability of electricity. In fact, it represents an unprecedented regional response to a communicated message.

This response had tangible effects that were repeatedly noted in the press. The spread of "Ramayan Fever" (as *India Today* termed it) generated a flood of newspaper and magazine articles ranging from critical analyses of the serial's content to sensational accounts of its fans' behavior. Throughout most of the serial's run, *Ramayan*-related news appeared with almost daily regularity in local papers. Many reports described the avidity with which successive episodes were awaited and viewed, emphasizing that, for millions of Indians, nothing was allowed to interfere with *Ramayan*-watching. Visible manifestations of the serial's popularity included the cancellation of Sunday morning cinema shows for lack of audiences, the delaying of weddings and funerals to allow participants to view the series, and the eerily quiet look of many cities and towns during screenings — a reporter in Mirzapur observed, "Bazaars, streets, and wholesale markets become so deserted they appear to be under curfew" (*Dainik Jāgaraṇ* 1988c:7). Other articles reported the decline of traffic on national highways during broadcasts, as truck and bus drivers steered their vehicles to teashops equipped with television sets, where driver and passengers piled out to watch the episode. On occasion, trains were delayed when passengers refused to leave platform sets until a broadcast was over.[6]

Many articles described the devotional activities that developed around the weekly "auspicious sight" (*darśan*) of epic characters:

> In many homes the watching of *Ramayan* has become a religious ritual, and the television set . . . is garlanded, decorated with sandalwood paste and vermillion, and conch shells are blown. Grandparents admonish youngsters to bathe before the show and housewives put off serving meals so that the family is purified and fasting before *Ramayan*. (Melwani 1988:56)

Local press reports detailed instances of mass devotion: a Banaras newspaper reported on a sweetshop where a borrowed television was set up each week on a makeshift altar sanctified with cow dung and Ganges water, worshipped with flowers and incense, and watched by a crowd of several hundred neighborhood residents, who then shared in the distribution of 125 kilos of sanctified sweets (*prasād*), which had been placed before the screen during the broadcast (*Dainik Jāgaraṇ* 1988b:3). Such ritualized public viewings were not uncommon: throughout the country, crowds gathered in front of video shops to watch display sets, and some community groups undertook to place sets in public areas. During the final months of the serial, electronics shops reported a dramatic surge in television sales and all available rental sets were engaged for the crucial Sunday morning slot — sometimes by whole villages that pooled their resources to allow residents to see *Ramayan*. Sporadic incidents of violent protest resulted from power failures during the weekly screening, as when an angry mob in the Banaras suburb of Ramnagar (home of North India's most acclaimed *rāmlīlā* pageant) stormed and set fire to an electrical substation (*Dainik Jāgaraṇ* 1988a).

The duration of the serial itself became a cause célèbre. Doordarshan initially contracted for fifty-two episodes, but as the story unfolded it became clear both that the audience did not want it to end on schedule and that the pace of the narrative would not allow it to; indeed, by late summer of 1987 it appeared that a termination the following January would leave viewers stranded somewhere in the fifth of the epic's seven books. The slow pace consistently annoyed critics, who complained that Sagar was deliberately drawing out the story to increase his profits, but a public outcry coupled with the financial windfall from advertisers prompted Mandi House to grant two extensions of thirteen episodes each. But as the battle for Lanka raged during June and early July of 1988, concerns were again voiced as to whether the series could end on schedule. At the request of Doordarshan officials, Sagar promised in writing that he would conclude with a special one-hour telecast on July 31.[7] The airing of the final installment was marked by festivities in many parts of the country. Sunday newspapers carried full-page articles on the serial, featuring photos of its stars and headlines like "Farewell to 'Doordarshan Ramayan'" (*Āj* 1988b:6). In Banaras, many neighborhoods were decorated with saffron-colored pennants and festive illuminations, while residents celebrated Rama's enthronement by distributing sweets, sounding bells and conches, and setting off fireworks (*Dainik Jāgaraṇ* 1988d:3). In the Maharashtrian city of Nagpur, canopies were erected at principal intersections and color sets installed to allow those without televisions to witness the spectacle (*Indian Express* 1988:5). Other municipalities reported homes decorated with earthen oil lamps to welcome Rama's return, prompting one reporter to call it an "early Divali" (similarly, the slaying of Ravan several weeks before had been observed in some areas as an out-of-season *daśahrā festival; Times of India* 1988:3).

Yet amid the descriptions of rejoicing, there were intimations of grief and loss as viewers anticipated the first of many Sundays without Rama and Sita. These sentiments found expression in the press a week later, detailing the stages of what one columnist called "the national withdrawal symptom." The front-page headline of *Jansattā* on August 9 announced, "Without *Ramayan* Sunday Mornings Seem Empty." Noting that people throughout the country passed their first *Ramayan*-less Sunday "with difficulty," the article reported responses to the show's absence by people in various neighborhoods of the nation's capital. These ranged from a betel seller in Shakarpur who observed, "After so many months, I'm finally getting some business on Sunday morning!" to a clothseller in Karolbagh who explained why he had sent his in-shop television set back home by asking, "Why watch television now that *Ramayan* is over?" Anticipating a promised sequel, a woman shopping on Chandni Chowk no doubt summed up the feelings of many devoted viewers: "At least we only have to wait two months. Then Ram will return! Mother Kausalya waited fourteen years for Ram to come back, but I don't know if we can manage for even two months" (*Jansattā* 1988b:1).

The Kathā and the Camera

Clearly, viewer perceptions of the pace and duration of the Sagar *Ramayan* varied greatly. While reviewers in the English-language press complained about the agonizingly slow advance of the narrative — "what with taking practically five episodes to kill Bali and another five to behead Kumbhakarna" (Mazumdar 1988:2) — such criticism was less common in Hindi publications, and many viewers protested that the epic was ending too quickly. When asked by *India Today* why he could not fit the events of Valmiki's final book into the original sequence, Sagar himself ingenuously replied, "I had no time. I was given only seventy-eight episodes, fifty-two to begin with. . . . So much had to be omitted" (cited in Jain 1988:81).

Perceptible beneath the various responses were varying conceptions of the *Rāmāyaṇa* itself. The English-language critics repeatedly referred to it as a "literary treasure" that Sagar was butchering by dragging it out to enhance his own and the network's profits. Such critics, who often made reference to C. Rajagopalachari's three hundred-page retelling, or R. K. Narayan's even shorter synopsis, could note that films like *Sampoorna Ramayana* had reduced the whole story to three hours, and that the modern ballet *Ramlila,* presented in Delhi each autumn, offered the epic to urbanites and foreign tourists as a four-hour spectacle. For audiences accustomed to such handy condensations, the pace of the serial was irksome indeed.

Yet there exist other performance genres in which revered scriptures like the *Mānas* are treated less as bounded texts than as outlines for imaginative elaboration, and if a storyteller's patrons and audience are willing (as Sagar's were), such performances can be extended almost indefinitely. Indeed, the television version's rambling main narrative, weighing in at just under sixty hours, is far from being the longest popular serialization. The *rāmlīlā* of Ramnagar, which tells roughly the same story, averages three hours per night for thirty-one nights, and has been playing to enraptured audiences for a century and a half. And an oral expounder like Ramnarayan Shukla, who proceeds through the epic in daily installments at the Sankat Mochan temple in Banaras, may take more than seven hundred hours (i.e., two years or more) to complete a single "telling"—a feat that makes Sagar's effort seem like a condensation. Since, as I will argue, the *rāmlīlā* and *kathā* traditions have greatly influenced the style and content of the television adaptation, summarizing some of their conventions would be useful here.

In Vaiṣṇava *kathā* (narration or storytelling), a performer, usually called a *kathāvācak* or *vyās*, is invited by an individual patron or community to retell or discourse on a sacred story; a performer who specializes in the Tulsi *Mānas* (the most popular text for *kathā* in North India today) is sometimes called a *Rāmāyaṇī*. Until recently, such storytellers were often hired on a long-term basis to narrate the entire epic in daily installments, usually in the late afternoon when the day's work was done. However, most patrons now favor shorter programs of fixed duration (such as nine, fifteen, or twenty-one days), in which an expounder discourses on only a small section of the text. In both styles of *kathā,* the source text serves merely as the anchor for an improvised verbal meditation that may include almost endless digressions and elaborations, interspersed with relevant quotations from any part of the epic as well as from other revered texts. Tour-de-force performances in which a single line is expounded for days on end are not uncommon and are often cited by devotees as evidence of the talent of a favorite expounder.[8] Another characteristic of such narration is its tendency to "domesticize" epic characters through the retelling of incidents in a highly colloquial style and with details absent from the source text. In addition, events in the story often serve as springboards for homely excursus on matters mystical, philosophical, and even political. Though little studied by academic scholars, *kathā* performance remains a principal form of both religious instruction and popular entertainment in many parts of India.

Rāmlīlā—which occurs mainly at the time of the annual *daśahrā* festival—is similarly extended and episodic, but here the emphasis shifts from hearing to seeing as oral exegesis is replaced by visual and iconographic realization of the narrative. The famous Ramnagar production (see Schechner and Hess 1977) is often termed a "visible commentary" by its aficionados, who emphasize the opportunity it affords for the experience of divine *darśan*. *Rāmlīlā* is closely related to another Vaiṣṇava performance genre: *jhānkī* ("glimpse" or "tableau"), in which consecrated persons or images (usually boys, but sometimes figures of painted clay) are dressed and made up as divine characters and placed in settings intended to evoke mythic scenes. These tableaux are presented for contemplation by audiences, often to the accompaniment of devotional singing (Hein 1972:17–30).

In the more elaborate *rāmlīlā* cycles, as in other Indian performance genres, great importance is given to facial expression and gesture. Actors are chosen for their physical appearance and trained in all aspects of delivery. The boys in Ramnagar undergo a two-month apprenticeship durin; which they are taught to identify completely with their epic roles. Such training is thought to facilitate the process whereby the divinity manifests in the body of the actor — an essential element in the theology of Vaiṣṇava performance. And although most *rāmlīlā* plays, like *kathā* performances, are based on the *Mānas,* they too may include episodes not found in the text as well as creative interpretations of its verses. Such elaborations often result in scenes and dialogues much enjoyed by the audience.

Whatever else he may be — movie moghul and shrewd businessman — Ramanand Sagar appears to have a genuine enthusiasm for the *Mānas* and a taste for *kathā.* His reported participation in an ongoing study group must have exposed him to many interpretations of the text, and his interest in the popular expounder Morari Bapu is reflected in his use of excerpts from the latter's performances to introduce several of his marketed cassettes. As the serial unfolded and as he prepared a permanent edition for international release, Sagar became increasingly concerned with his own role as storyteller, frequently appearing in the introductory or concluding portions of each cassette to comment (in typically rambling *kathāvācak* style) on the events being presented.[9] Like Tulsidas he sought to place himself in a long tradition of *Rāmāyaṇa* narrators, claiming little originality for his screenplay (the credits for each episode cite ten *Rāmāyaṇa*s in various languages). Yet Sagar also realized that he was creating a powerful, independent retelling — he remarked to one reporter that "video is like writing Ramayan with a camera" (cited in Melwani 1988:56) — and in the final, extravagant episode of July 31, he took the ultimate step of placing himself in the narrative, hovering cross-legged on a lotus in the sky above Ayodhya to join assembled deities in singing the praises of the newly crowned Rama. Critics dismissed this as tasteless self-aggrandizement, but viewers apparently took it in stride; wasn't he everywhere being hailed as the "Tulsidas of the video age"?

In both *kathā* and *rāmlīlā,* performers enter a consecrated condition.

The oral commentator, no less than the young Brahman actor, purifies himself through dietary and devotional practices and performs rituals before ascending the expounder's dais, where he is garlanded and worshipped as a temporary incarnation of Veda Vyas, the archetypal orator of sacred lore. Sagar was mindful of such conventions, and his widely publicized changes in life-style — renouncing alcohol and tobacco and instituting a vegetarian regimen for the film crew — though mocked as hypocritical posing by critics, revealed his concern to accede to his audience's standards for epic performers.

The iconography of the serial combined *rāmlīlā* conventions with the visual vocabulary firmly established through a century of mass-produced religious art. For the consecrated boys of *rāmlīlā*, Sagar substituted adult actors and actresses carefully chosen to reinforce popular conceptions of each character's appearance. In casting his principals, the producer aimed for "exactly that Ram, that Sita, which is in the hearts and minds and perhaps in the souls of millions of people" — and, one might add, on the walls of teashops and the pages of comic books (Melwani 1988:56). That he was extraordinarily successful is attested to by numerous posters and calendars featuring garishly colored stills from the serial, or costumed close-ups of Arun Govil with his now-famous enigmatic smile.

The "humanizing" influence of television's close focus imposed its own restrictions on iconography, and certain stock conventions were dispensed with — thus Rama and Bharat did not appear with blue complexions (though Vishnu did in his brief appearances). Yet the depiction was hardly "realistic" in other respects. The costumes and wigs of Rama and Lakshman during their long forest exile, for example, remained immaculate and perfectly arranged (down to a dandified curl at each temple) and their faces clean-shaven, a stylization that bothered critics reared on more naturalistic theater (R. K. Narayan quipped that the brothers "look like Wiltech [razorblade] ads"; cited in De 1988:5). Hanuman and his legions were depicted according to long-established convention, with muscular but hairless human bodies and only long, padded tails and stylized masking about the mouth and nose to suggest a simian status; their wives were shown as fully human women.[10] Sets and costumes adhered to the garish standard of film mythologicals, which itself reflects poster art and the conventions of the *nauṭankī* tradition and of nineteenth-century Parsi theater. This too provoked criticism — Simran Bhargava (1987:70) in *India Today* quipped that "Raja Janak's palace looks like it's been painted with cheap lurex paint and the clothes look like they've been dug out of some musty trunk in

Chandni Chowk's costume rental shops" — yet Sagar made considerable use of outdoor footage, including many impressive sequences of Rama's wanderings through the countryside.

The poor quality of special effects was another fixation of critics, and those accustomed (as some urban Indians now are) to the standards of post–Steven Spielberg Hollywood would indeed find only laughable the pulsating, garishly tinted "divine weapons" and the hovering demons of the television serial, which adhered to a technical standard closer to that of early *Star Trek* or *Dr. Who*. Cost containment was undoubtedly a factor (though some scenes — such as the burning of Lanka — were admirably executed), and Sagar may have shrewdly perceived that the bulk of his audience, accustomed to the modest stagecraft of *nauṭankī* and *rāmlīlā*, would be sufficiently dazzled by cheaper effects. He must also have realized that special effects, per se, were not crucial to maintaining viewers' interest in the saga, and this leads me to an observation concerning the overall focus of the production. The emphasis in *Ramayan* was squarely on "seeing" its characters. Not "seeing" in the quick-cut, distracted fashion in which modern Western audiences take in their heroes and heroines, but drinking in and entering into visual communion with epic characters.[11]

To most viewers, *Ramayan* was a feast of *darśan,* and its visual aesthetic clearly derived from an indigenous standard. Scenes and dialogues were long (interminable, critics said) and aimed at a definitive portrayal of the emotional state of each character. This was conveyed especially through close-ups (and in moments of intense emotion, repeated zoom shots — a convention favored in Hindi films), so that much of the time the screen was dominated by large heads, either verbalizing or silently miming their responses to events. Every nuance of emotion of every character — each *bhāv* of classical aesthetic theory — was conveyed visually, and in scenes involving many characters (such as the assembly in Chitrakut, when Bharat begs Rama to return to Ayodhya), the camera focused in turn on the face of each principal to record his or her response — grief, surprise, anger, calm — to each new development. Though appallingly overstated by contemporary Western standards, this technique is consonant with the mime or *abhinay* of indigenous genres like Kathakali and Bharat Natyam, in which the audience is expected to focus intently on the performer's facial expressions and gestures. The television screen is particularly suited to this kind of close-up mime, and Sagar exploited its potential to allow his viewers an experience of intense communion with epic characters.

Notable too was the production's tendency to periodically halt the flow of its narrative to focus on stylized, posterlike tableaux, accompanied by devotional singing. This convention has a long history, and both *Rāmāyaṇa* texts and *rāmlīlā* plays are usually divided into sequences of episodes, each of which is associated with a striking visual image, often presented in popular art as a visual distillation for the contemplation of devotees. In the *rāmlīlā,* such moments as Sita's placing the marriage garland around Rama's neck, Hanuman's carrying the two brothers on his shoulders, and Rama's worshipping a Shiva *liṅga* before crossing the sea all necessitate halting the action of the play. Magnesium flares are ignited to guarantee distant viewers a glimpse of the auspicious tableau, and the crowd responds with devotional chanting and cries of "Rājā Rāmcandra kī jay!" (Victory to King Ramchandra!). This custom is, in turn, a visual translation of Tulsi's practice of halting the narrative at such intense moments, by abandoning the storytelling meters of *caupāī/dohā* in favor of the more musical *chand,* which lovingly elaborates on the auspicious tableau set up in the preceding stanza.

These conventions are straightforwardly adapted in the television version, and each of the scenes noted above occasions a halt in the prose dialogue, as verses are sung and the camera frames a leisurely tableau of the auspicious scene. If the technique allowed Sagar to slow down the pace, it also reflected his understanding of audience expectations. In contrast, the impatient responses of critics (such as Mimi Vaid-Fera's exasperated query [1987:16], concerning the scene of Hanuman's transporting Rama and Lakshman, "Does one really have to watch Hanuman's enlarged frame against a changing backdrop for the next few minutes, in order to appreciate his strength?") suggest ignorance of the *Rāmāyaṇa* performance tradition. To the modern critic, apparently, all scenes are created equal—a view that accords well with the secular notion of time as a succession of discrete and equal moments. In the perception of *Ramayan*'s devoted audience, however, some scenes and characters have more intrinsic potency than others and so must be held up to view longer.

As an original and substantial retelling of the *Rāmāyaṇa,* Sagar's screenplay presents both continuities with past versions and original elaborations of the kind common to *kathā* and *rāmlīlā* performances. For the most part, the narrative follows the Tulsi *Mānas,* though it occasionally favors an interpretation of Valmiki or Kamban. Yet, as *rāmlīlā* producers know, there is a vast difference between a poetic narrative and a performance script, and hundreds of interpretive decisions must be made in the representation of each scene. Such decisions are not made arbitrarily, but are guided by the thrust of traditional exegesis. Similarly, the conventions of *kathā* allow an expounder freedom to improvise on the text, yet this interpretive latitude is not unlimited, but is constrained by his training and by the audience's expectations and knowledge of the story. Certain characters and incidents have always received special attention, often because they have raised moral issues or aroused "doubts" (*śankāē*) that each reteller must address. The extended run of the serial gave Sagar license to explore many episodes in the kind of depth in which they are treated by traditional commentators, and to pose original "solutions" to problems that have troubled audiences for centuries. Below I examine one such character, the portrayal of whom reflects both tradition and innovation and also suggests the impact of the television medium on the telling of the story.

Kaikeyi Redeemed

The motives of Queen Kaikeyi—Dashrath's tempestuous junior wife and Prince Bharat's mother, whose early love for Rama is poisoned by jealousy of her co-wives and who becomes implacably bent on his ruin—have always been problematic for the *Rāmāyaṇa* tradition, since they suggest a darker side to the epic's rosy picture of the royal family; Valmiki's treatment still hints at deception on the king's part, or worse still, rivalry among the brothers. The requirements of the narrative raise uncomfortable questions that have vexed storytellers and audiences for centuries: if Rama is so good and Kaikeyi loves him so dearly, how can she suddenly turn against him and betray him? and how is the story subsequently to deal with this maternal traitor in its midst?

Broadly speaking, we detect in many retellings a concern both to exonerate Kaikeyi from responsibility for the demands and to depict her as subsequently repentant, if not fully redeemed—a concern made all the more compelling by the greater theological weight given to the story and its characters in most vernacular versions. Tulsidas first resorts to *deus ex machina* and has the gods, anxious to get on with the business of slaying Ravan, derange the mind of Kaikeyi's hunchbacked maidservant (2.12). Later, he remarks several times on Kaikeyi's contrition (e.g., 2.252.5–6; 7.6a,b), and has Rama take pains to show her special respect (e.g., by saluting her first, when greeting the three mothers in the forest; 2.244.7–8). For the most part, however, he simply ignores her, merging her into a composite portrait of "all the queens." This approach is carried out visually in the Ramnagar *rāmlīlā,* in which, after Dashrath's funeral, the three queens appear together like a spectral chorus, clad in white and veiled; their individual personalities are not further developed and Kaikeyi's emotional state is left to the audience's imagination.

Popular lore has been kinder to Kaikeyi, however. A story that I have several times heard in *kathā* programs has Rama, when granted a boon following his victory over Ravan, tearfully request that Bharat withdraw his disavowal of his mother. And in 1983 I was told a "wonderful, secret story" by a Banaras bank clerk in which it was revealed that the young Rama, in his desire to fulfill his mission on earth, himself compelled her to request the boons, since he knew that she alone in the palace loved him enough to obey even his most painful order. Concluded the amateur expounder, "Yes, and you know, it's in the *Rāmāyaṇa!* . . . well, in *some Rāmāyaṇa.*"

"Television's strongest point," Neil Postman has remarked, "is that it brings personalities into our hearts, not abstractions into our heads" (Postman 1985:123). And if, as this critic complains, the nature of the medium tends to "personalize" every kind of program, from news documentary to religious sermon, how much more powerful is its influence on the serialized narrative or soap opera, in which the acts and feelings of a limited cast of characters are explored at close range through repeated installments. Unlike the *rāmlīlā,* television can leave little to the imagination; if principal characters are to be shown on the screen, they will be shown close up, and their emotional responses cannot be avoided. Consequently, the depiction of Kaikeyi presented Sagar with a challenge: to make believable her transformation from loving mother to cruel enemy, and then to reintegrate her successfully into the family (and into the hearts of viewers) — in short, to redeem her.

Kaikeyi's portrayal by Padma Khanna exemplifies the serial's overall excellent casting and fine (if not always subtle) acting. Manthara is played by Lalita Pawar, a veteran character actress known for her portrayal of villainous women. Although in most written versions of the story Kaikeyi's maid is unheard of until early in Book Two, when she appears on the palace balcony to fume over the preparations for Rama's consecration, Sagar inserts her into the palace milieu right from the first episode, when she hobbles ecstatically into Dashrath's chamber to announce Prince Bharat's birth. The audience feels a thrill of anticipation — here is the woman who is destined to destroy the king — yet the effect is also to humanize Manthara and to underscore her powerful loyalty to Kaikeyi and her clan. This theme is further developed during several scenes depicting the women's response to the news of the princes' impending marriages. While the queens rejoice together for all their sons, Manthara can chortle only over "My Bharat! My Bharat's wedding!" In a telling and (to my knowledge) entirely original scene, she orders lamps lit in private celebration of Bharat's good fortune, and when Kaikeyi protests that "Didi (*dīdī*)" ("elder sister," an affectionate reference to Kausalya) is seeing to all the festive arrangements, the hunchback replies scornfully, "'Didi, Didi'—you always talk about Didi! What she does, she does only for her Rama. You have to look out for your own son" (episode 10). At this point, Kaikeyi dismisses this sour remark with obvious impatience, yet the audience perceives that the seed of dissidence and jealousy is already being sown.

For the most part, the powerful confrontations that follow as the events of Book Two begin in episode 12—between Manthara and Kaikeyi, between the latter and the king, and so on—closely follow Tulsidas (who in turn follows Valmiki here), and it is only after the princes and Sita have departed for the forest, the king has expired of grief, and Bharat has returned to learn the awful truth, that Sagar's efforts to absolve Kaikeyi resume in earnest.

There is the scene of Dashrath lying in state on a flower-bedecked bier (invoking the now-familiar imagery of the formal obsequies of India's national leaders) as courtiers pay their last respects. Each of the queens comes forward to place a handful of flowers at his feet, and Kaikeyi weeps profusely, wringing her hands in apparently sincere grief. However, she resumes her haughty and obstinate air during her confrontation with Bharat, but his unexpected denunciations gradually weaken her, until, when he renounces his bond to her and leaves vowing never to set foot in her chamber again, she collapses weeping; the camera lingers on her pathetic, crumpled figure in the deserted room.

A significant innovation follows, just after the court scene in which Bharat refuses the throne and presents his plan to journey to the forest to search for Rama. As noted earlier, Tulsi tells us nothing of the individual queens' reactions to these events, noting only that "all the queens were upset" (2.186) and that, shortly later, "they all mounted palanquins and set out" (2.187.8). But in the serial, as the determined Bharat strides from the hall, he encounters a tearful Kaikeyi in the corridor. He coldly addresses her as "Queen Kaikeyi" (having earlier vowed never again to call her "Mother"). She begs to be allowed to accompany him to the forest, to ask Rama's forgiveness for her sins. When he coldly refuses, she weeps piteously. Then Kausalya appears and, touched by Kaikeyi's desperation, takes pity on her former rival and orders Bharat to relent — he of course must bow to the will of Rama's mother. The scene concludes with the powerful image of Kausalya and Kaikeyi weeping in each other's arms (episode 22). Kaikeyi's redemption is well under way.

En route to Chitrakut, the townspeople are shown debating the issue of Kaikeyi's guilt. The last speaker expresses deep sympathy for her, "How she must be repenting now, poor thing!" (episode 23). On first meeting Rama, Kaikeyi breaks down and pleads for forgiveness, saying that she is to blame for everything. Rama replies that what has occurred is due to fate (episode 24). This might appear to be adequate absolution, but the camera's portrait of the queen's remorse — and of her gradual reintegration into the family — continues unabated. During the emotional assembly scene, the camera repeatedly scans the queens' faces as they listen to Bharat, Rama, and Vasistha debate the terms of the exile, until at last, unable to restrain herself, Kaikeyi speaks up — as she never does in Valmiki or Tulsi — to declare publicly her own willingness to withdraw the boons (Rama counters that only the king himself could take or give back boons; episode 24).

When in due course it is settled that Rama will remain in the forest and Bharat return to the capital to reign as regent, every viewer reared on Valmiki and Tulsi would expect to turn away from Ayodhya once and for all to follow the unfolding adventures of the princes and Sita in the forest. Instead, Sagar cuts back repeatedly to contrast scenes in the palace with the doings of the three principals. These scenes further develop our sympathies for the home-bound family members, especially the women, and in one lengthy and innovative scene Kaikeyi pays a visit to her son's ascetic ashram on the outskirts of the city. Bharat, scribbling royal edicts before Rama's enthroned sandals, first ignores her and then coldly addresses her as "Queen Kaikeyi." When she pleads with him to call her "Mother," he replies that "Queen Kaikeyi killed my mother," and cruelly reviles her. By this point, viewers' sympathies are likely to be with the queen. Telling her son that the comforts of the palace torture her, she begs to be allowed to come live with him, to do penance for her sins. Bharat sternly orders her to return to the city, but allows just the slightest hint that perhaps, by enduring her sentence in the palace, she may eventually be freed of guilt. As a mournful chorus sings of her pain, the queen collapses into a palanquin and is borne back to the city, where the camera follows her as she wanders through the empty corridors of the palace, alternately weeping and laughing — a sort of Hindu Lady Macbeth (episode 26).

All this is innovation, true, but with a traditional basis. Sagar's portrayal of Bharat's rigid and guilt-ridden personality accords well with the image presented in the *Mānas* (a Banarsi friend of mine once called Bharat "Tulsi's 'portrait of an obsession'"); his prolonged treatment of Kaikeyi's redemption-through-suffering satisfies popular longing to salvage Dashrath's youngest queen. The viewer's curiosity about the domestic aftermath of the banishment is more than satiated, and he is left with a feeling of intimate knowledge of the royal family. Female viewers are presented with a story in which women are more pervasively present and forcefully active than in most written versions. More than ever, this ultimate soap opera emerges as a family saga, in which the members of the sundered royal clan are shown as united in their emotions even though physically apart. Thus it will come as no surprise, in episode 28 (when the princes and Sita are deep in the Dandak forest) to find the camera whisking us back to Ayodhya to focus on the loneliness of Lakshman's wife, Urmila,[12] and later, to show us Kausalya standing at the palace window, visibly graying as she endures her long vigil of awaiting Rama's return.

These scenes reflect Sagar's exploitation of a narrative convention common in modern prose literature, which developed to its logical conclusion with the advent of film. The oral storyteller generally unfolds his narrative by focusing listeners' attention on a single location and withdrawing to a narrative frame in order to announce the transition to another scene, as when Tulsidas informs us, "I've told of Rama's lovely journey to the forest; now hear how Sumantra came back to Ayodhya" (2.142.4). Such shifts are usually kept to a minimum, and it is almost as if the storyteller (and with him the audience) must physically accompany some character — Sumantra on his return to Ayodhya, Bharat on his journey to Chitrakut, Hanuman on his quest for Sita — in order to move about within the geography of the tale. In contrast, much modern fiction has preferred an invisible narrator who takes the form of an omnipresent eye. But in substituting images for words, film and television provide ultimate license to this eye, and the quick cuts and fades possible in these media all but eliminate any experience of scenic transition — the very abruptness of the change becoming a new convention that is exploited by directors. What this means for narrative is that the storyteller becomes so otiose that he disappears entirely, for the great illusion of the camera is that the viewer himself is the eyewitness narrator. Hence film and television partake of — indeed aim for — the quality of collective fantasies: of dreams that myriad dreamers can believe that they share.[13] To further this illusion, the camera's eye anticipates and indulges our every curiosity: thus it records Rama's conversation with Sita on their wedding night (episode 11), shows us the thoughts that flash through Dashrath's mind as he lays dying (episode 20), reveals the reaction of Bharat's wife, Madhvi, to his self-imposed exile (episode 26), and so on. This approach contrasts sharply with that of a performance genre like *rāmlīlā*, which (as Richard Schechner has observed) is multidimensional, elusive, and can never be experienced in its totality by any one viewer.[14]

The example of Kaikeyi could be supplemented with many others — for instance, with the characterization of Rama's demon adversaries, who are similarly humanized by the voyeuristic eye of the camera, and emerge as complex, tragically flawed titans — much in contrast to their two-dimensional treatment by Tulsidas, but again, in keeping with a major strand in their folk conceptualization. Such examples help explain how Sagar, like many a *Rāmāyaṇī* before him, successfully sustained his audience's interest, week after week, in a slow-moving story, the plot of which they already knew, by making them look forward to the manner of its telling.

Critical Perspectives

I regard the Sagar serial as an independent *Rāmāyaṇa:* an original retelling in a new medium that affords distinctive capabilities to a storyteller. Such innovations have occurred before — the *rāmlīlā* is a good example — and they have not occurred in a vacuum, but have arisen out of existing forms, often through the intervention of patrons concerned to project a particular cultural vision. A similar phenomenon is occurring with the twentieth-century medium of video, and it is notable that during roughly the same period that *Ramayan* was being aired in India, audiences in China were viewing a government-sponsored serialization of *Hong Lou Meng* (The Dream of the Red Chamber), the voluminous novel of aristocratic life during the Qing dynasty. In the West, such projects stand out less strikingly in the flood of television programming, yet Soviet television's treatment of Tolstoy's *War and Peace,* BBC serializations like *Middlemarch,* and the ABC miniseries *Jesus of Nazareth* all reflect a desire on the part of national elites to translate their cultural classics into the new mass medium.[15] To dismiss such efforts as a pastiche of cultural elements — as when critics label Sagar's work a kitsch blend of Tulsidas, the *rāmlīlā*, calendar art, and mythological films — is as unsatisfyingly reductionist as viewing the *Mānas* itself, for example, as a blend of Valmiki's plot, the nondualist philosophical stance of the *Adhyātma rāmāyaṇa,* and the devotional fervor of the *Bhāgavata purāṇa.* These ingredients are all present in the Hindi epic, of course, but its vast appeal derives more from its original exploitation of the new medium of melodious and idiomatic Hindi verse. An effective analysis of Sagar's *Ramayan* must consider not only the various influences reflected in the production, but its distinctive exploitation of the video medium.

In the ongoing debate among intellectuals throughout the world over the value and effects of television, both sides are inclined to stress the revolutionary nature of its impact. Media enthusiasts like Marshall McLuhan and detractors like Neil Postman both posit the transformation of a typographical universe into one dominated by moving images, and either speak glowingly of an "information explosion" and a leap to "electronic literacy," or sound ominous warnings of a "trivialization" of discourse and "passivization" of audiences. English-educated intellectuals in India generally share with their Western counterparts an attitude of disdain for the vulgarly accessible mass medium.[16] Yet if one looks at literature on the impact of television, one finds that it is primarily based on the Euro-American experience and may be of questionable relevance to the Indian situation. Having noted some of the continuities the *Ramayan* serial shares with older genres of epic-based performance, my discussion below examines some assumptions that seem implicit in the criticisms directed at it within India, with a view to developing a more balanced and culturally relevant assessment of its impact.

Commercialization and Commodification

The Illustrated Weekly of India began its cover story on *Ramayan* with the charge, "Ramanand Sagar's teleserial is a commercial proposition, the sole purpose of which, despite the director's protestations, is to make money." Terming the series "a blockbuster like none other on the idiot box, the ultimate grosser," the author suggested that the aesthetic deficiencies of the serial were directly related to its director's avaricious motives (*Illustrated Weekly* 1987:9). Articles in the English-language press emphasized the commercial success of the production, quoting statistics on the unprecedented revenues it generated. The fact that Sagar and his sons refused to release details of their earnings irritated reporters and led to much speculation on their actual gain, which was estimated at roughly Rs. one crore (roughly 500,000 dollars). The sources of this profit were analyzed in detail: the actual production budget, the sale of the official cassette version both within and outside India, and the franchising of serial-related spinoff products, such as children's toys, comic books, and audio cassettes.[17]

Implicit in much criticism of the selling of the serial was the assumption that it represented an assault on a hitherto pristine and uncommercial tradition — no article that I have seen raised the possibility that the *Rāmāyaṇa* had ever been "marketed" before. Yet this epic has clearly been supporting a large (if decentralized) industry on the Subcontinent for many centuries. I refer not only to the marketing of printed *Rāmāyaṇa* texts during the last one hundred and fifty years (such as the numerous competing editions of the *Mānas,* each claiming to present the "authentic" version), but to the whole complex of professional and semi-professional performers: expounders and singers, professional *līlā* troupes, and priests and *sādhu*s who perform ritual recitations for a fee. The expenditures involved in such performances are often not insignificant — some *Mānas* expounders are lavishly rewarded by their patrons, and the commerce generated by the *rāmlīlā* (itself a costly enterprise employing large numbers of people) represents an important factor in the economy of Ramnagar — but we need not restrict ourselves to the cold currencies of our age. For, as Pierre Bourdieu reminds us, other forms of wealth must be taken into account in reckoning the "worth" of traditional activities: unquantifiable elements such as social status, prestige, and political influence that often interact with (are obtained from or translated back into) material wealth (Bourdieu 1977:171–183).

I venture no judgment as to whether the "marketing" of a story like the *Rāmāyaṇa* is "good" or "bad"; I only propose that it is not new and has always been inseparable from the dissemination and performance of the epic. The introductory cantos of the Sanskrit *Rāmāyaṇa* represent the poet Valmiki taking an existing story tradition and transforming it into an elegant poetic composition, which is then publicly performed by trained bards, who receive lavish praise and generous gifts for their efforts. Yet we tend to assume that the bards' motives are not "solely" commercial; they are obeying their teacher, praising a king, and sharing a great work of art — Bourdieu might observe that they are generating large amounts of "symbolic capital," and that Ramanand Sagar is doing the same.

But isn't there an essential difference, one may ask, between Lav and Kush's live singing and rows of shrink-wrapped cassettes with shimmering mylar labels? Walter Benjamin, writing in the 1930s, argued that original works of art possess an "aura" that is dissipated through mechanical reproduction (Benjamin 1955:223). Others (the present author included) have

warned that the process of "commodification" inherent in modern consumer societies lessens the participatory experience by turning audiences
into passive consumers (Butsch 1985:65–66; Lutgendorf 1991b). I re-
examine the question of audience passivity below; here let us note the
Sagars' efforts to promote their cassettes (in an ironic twist on Benjamin's
notion of "aura") as potent religious artifacts:

> As Sagar points out, no consumer can mistake the pirated version for the
> original. The originals are beautifully packaged, with almost a religious aura
> about them. Each tape is surrounded by a rosary, wrapped in a red satin
> bag. . . . As Prem Sagar says, "We want people to preserve it. It gives out good
> vibrations; no one has received it without touching it to their foreheads."
> (Melwani 1988:57)

Such hype is aimed at the middle-class householder (especially the nonresi-
dent Indian), who would like to pass on the *Rāmāyaṇa* tradition to his
Nintendo-playing children and who hopes that the presence in his home of
orange videocassettes with an "almost religious aura" will help effect this.
The same consumer is addressed by other companies marketing various
reifications of the *Rāmāyaṇa,* such as Shree Geeta Press of Chandigarh (not
to be confused with the famous Gita Press of Gorakhpur, the name of
which it has apparently pirated), which places a full-page advertisement in
the international edition of *India Today* for a Rs. 100 edition of the *Mānas*.
The ad announces that Tulsidas's epic is both "a scripture, epitomizing the
teachings of the Vedas, Smrities & Purans" and also "an art, highly developed to compete with the greatest epic poems of world" (*India Today*
1986:22), thus reassuring overseas buyers that the epic of their motherland
is not only holy, but also (like athletic equipment and concert pianists)
"world class." This too is a kind of "aura," drawing on symbolic capital's new
international currency. It is clearly very different from Benjamin's romantic
notion of the lingering presence of an individual creative genius, but is it
wholly unlike, say, the more impersonal "aura" of authority claimed by
Tulsidas for his common-language epic, through the invocation of an im-
memorial tradition of exalted narrators?

Video-latry

To both Indian and foreign reporters, one of the most striking features of
the public response to *Ramayan* was its religious dimension: the cere-

monies of worship that developed around the weekly broadcasts and the spontaneous expressions of reverence that greeted the public appearances of the stars. News stories described the purificatory *pūjā* of television sets, the burning of incense before the screen, and pious fans' prostrations before Arun Govil and Dipika Chikhlia (Rama and Sita). More critical responses, especially in English-language publications, ranged from bemused condescension at the incongruity of "worshipping" an electronic gadget, to disgust at what was seen as an embarrassing cultural anachronism; wrote Arvind N. Das (1988:6) in *The Times of India,* "Through the electronic Ramayana . . . the Indian juggernaut is moving at a frenetic pace—backwards." In an interview in *The Illustrated Weekly,* one reporter pressed Dipika to evaluate the religious response of viewers.

> *Reporter:* In the mofussil [provincial] towns, and even in the cities people have a bath and do pooja [pūjā] of their television screens before watching the serial. Do you think this is right?
> *Dipika:* There's no right and wrong about it. It's a matter of their belief. We haven't asked them to do it, it's the way they feel.
> (*Illustrated Weekly* 1987:15)

Notable is the reporter's disdain for what she regards as rustic religious customs, now seeping back from provincial towns into "the cities." Such critics are often out of touch with the religious customs of their own urban neighbors, and choose to overlook, for example, the purificatory *pūjā* of motor vehicles, printing presses, and other mechanical devices, which is common throughout the country. Equally prevalent is the custom of bracketing religious performances with auspicious rites. When a *kathāvācak* is preparing to expound the *Rāmāyaṇa,* care is always given to the seat he is to occupy, which must be purified in order to be worthy of the divine sage, Veda Vyas, who will speak through the storyteller. Similarly the crowns, ornaments, and weapons of *rāmlīlā* actors are worshiped before the start of the pageant. Since the *Ramayan* serial became a weekly in-house *kathā* or *rāmlīlā* for millions of families, the television screen became the new seat of the storyteller and ritual stage for the *līlā,* and its perch in the family sitting room had to be sanctified.

Of course, a more reflective critic might also have noted that backward Indians are not the only people who "worship" television sets. Behind the modern secular smile of condescension lies a joke at our own expense, for the television set became the central altar of the American home some three decades ago—the main focus of the living room, displacing the hearth/fire altar as the nucleus around which family members gathered for communion and sustenance. It is only a highly compartmentalized notion of religion that blinds us to the ritual dimensions of such activities. Neil Postman's assertion that television is unsuited to religious experience because it is "so saturated with our memories of profane events, so deeply associated with the commercial and entertainment worlds that it is difficult to be recreated as a frame for sacred events" (Postman 1985:119) suggests the over-facility of the conventional sacred/profane dichotomy; in any case it is clearly inapplicable to the Indian situation. Millions of Hindus did indeed feel a need to sacralize their television screens each week in order to make them "a frame for sacred events," yet they apparently found no more difficulty in doing this than they do in sacralizing their town squares for *rāmlīlā* plays each October, their kitchens for monthly *ekādaśī* rites, or piles of cow dung for *govardhan pūjā*.

And Now, the "Couch Pakoṛā"?

Television, like religion, is frequently assailed by critics as an "opiate" that deadens and desensitizes its devotees; Robert MacNeil called it, "the soma of Aldous Huxley's *Brave New World*" (Postman 1985:111). Many Indian intellectuals similarly despise the "idiot box" and feel particularly disturbed by the presentation of "fundamentalist" religious material through its hypnotic medium. A critic in *The Times of India* explained the appeal of *Ramayan* — even to those who should have known better — by invoking the tube's power to lull.

> What about the Westernized elite which is not basically religious but nevertheless almost religiously viewed Ramayana in spite of making snide comments about its poor production? The answer . . . is to be found in a complex situation where mass culture, the search for roots, entertainment and education have all got mixed into an addictive and soporific compound which reinforces intellectual passivity. That this compound is available without much effort by the recipient adds to its ethereal charm as the medium itself becomes the message. (Das 1988:6)[18]

Such facile analysis, effortlessly (and without citation) incorporating the *mahāvākya* or "great sentence" of the pre-eminent Western media pundit of the 1960s, typifies the knee-jerk reaction to the serial of many English-language critics. Yet how applicable is this warmed-over approach to the

Indian situation? The technology of mass media may be much the same everywhere, but their utilization and impact depend on specific conditions — even specific "ways of seeing" — which vary in culture-dependent ways. In his perceptive study, *Amusing Ourselves to Death,* Neil Postman bases much of his critique of television on a historical analysis of the impact of literacy and publishing in the United States during the eighteenth and nineteenth centuries, arguing that Americans were the most print-oriented people in the world and that their cultural emphasis on the printed word influenced all forms of public discourse. His most damning case against television is that it leads to the trivialization of information and the reduction of all forms of discourse to "entertainment." Yet he is careful to point out that this effect derives in part from the specific circumstances of American television: the fact that it is available twenty-four hours a day on multiple channels and is presented mainly in tiny segments jarringly juxtaposed with commercial messages or (in news programs) contrasting bits of information.[19] It is the constant bombardment of decontextualized information through a relentlessly amusing visual format that Postman views as promoting desensitization and passivity, rather than the act of "viewing" itself — for although they lack direct contact with performers, television viewers need not be more "passive" than audiences at other mass events.

For most Indian viewers, the *Ramayan* serial was not simply a program to "see," it was something to *do* — an event to participate in — and this participation was nearly always a group (extended family, neighborhood, village) activity. Audience participation included pre- and post-performance rituals, cheers of *"Rājā Rāmcandra kī jay!,"* and distribution of sanctified food. In addition, each episode became a prime subject of conversation throughout the week: Was each character portrayed properly? Were the special effects up to standard? How did the screenplay depart from the *Mānas* or the Valmiki *Rāmāyaṇa*? Such matters were endlessly debated, and everyone had an opinion. Moreover, some viewers made their opinions known through a dialogue with the storyteller that, in its own way, resembled the dialectic that goes on in *kathā* sessions. Since Sagar's crew often worked on episodes until just before screening time, it was sometimes possible to incorporate audience feedback with little delay. The scene in which Rama and Lakshman are temporarily overpowered by a serpent weapon wielded by Ravan's son Indrajit, and lie helpless and wounded on the battlefield, was regarded by many viewers as a catastrophe comparable to an eclipse of the sun (some devotees took ritual baths, as during an eclipse, for protection during the Lord's period of helplessness). When

Sagar chose to extend it for two broadcasts, he was deluged with letters and was forced to make an on-screen apology the following week for this undue extension of a painful and inauspicious scene. His sense of audience expectations was usually more on target, however. One feature article included an account of a day's shooting in which, as Rama completed a poignant speech on how sorely he missed Sita, Sagar, wiping his eyes with a handkerchief, rushed from behind the camera to embrace his actor, exclaiming, "Vāh, beṭā, vāh!" ("Superb, son, superb!"), while an onlooker chimed in, "The whole country will cry next Sunday" (Vaid-Fera 1987:13).

Clearly, the impact on Indian culture of the proliferation of television needs to be carefully studied, particularly as programming schedules continue to expand, the bombardment of commercial messages increases, and VCRs provide bored viewers with a wider range of choices. Yet such research must be informed by cultural specifics: by the fact that Indian typographic technology is only a little more than a century old and has never produced the kind of print-saturated culture that developed in the United States; that "oral literacy" (in which people who cannot read and write are familiar with and sometimes creators of sophisticated bodies of literature) remains prevalent; that great religious significance attaches to the act of seeing (*darśan*) and hearing (*śruti*); and that a wide range of oral performance genres continue to flourish. All these factors contribute to creating an environment in which the advent of television may produce less jarring discontinuity and cultural alienation than it has in the United States.

Homogenization, Hegemony, and the Multiform Text

The fact that a single version of the *Rāmāyaṇa,* accorded high status by virtue of being aired on state-run television, was presented to an audience of unprecedented size was viewed by many critics as the single most ominous aspect of the production, for it was seen as not only threatening the nation's modern "secular" ethos but as overwhelming and obliterating a vibrant and multivocal cultural tradition. In short, such critics assumed that Sagar's opus was the *Rāmāyaṇa* to end all *Rāmāyaṇa*s. Wrote Hindi critic Sudhish Pachauri, "The Ram story is the people's story. But this folk story has never had a single form nor has everyone recited and understood it in one distinct, regulated context" (1987). While conceding that the Tulsidas version also achieved a normative status in earlier centuries, another critic observed that "the people . . . added to it their own concerns and gave it their own colors which came out when it passed through the prisms of the many versions of the Ramlila. The text was one, discourse remained many and de-construction retained the possibility of plurality." But such deconstruction is no longer possible, he continued, because the impact of the Sagar *Ramayan* "has put paid to Ramlilas. Indeed the purveyance of Ramayana through television has destroyed the very concept of *līlā*" (Das 1988:6).

This grim prognosis for the fate of *rāmlīlā* plays in post-Sagar India was echoed by other writers, and only the passage of time will permit us to judge its validity. Clearly, standardized and mass-produced recordings of religious performances offer both convenience and technological glamour and have been adopted for a variety of uses; what is less certain is the impact such usage has on genres of live performance. The audio cassettes of the sung rendition of the *Mānas* by the film singer Mukesh were immensely popular in the early 1980s and became the Muzak-of-choice for broadcast at a wide range of religious functions. Yet I found *Mānas* singing to be still alive in Banaras in 1990, coexisting with the booming amplification of Mukesh, and I hesitate to conclude that the presence of electronic media spells the doom of other forms of performance — an assumption often made with reference to American culture (where each new technological advance is characteristically touted as epoch-making) but which may not even hold true there.[20]

A sensitive statement of concern over the prospect of cultural homogenization is contained in an essay on the serial by historian Romila Thapar. She is particularly concerned with the fact of state sponsorship of the production, which she sees as raising troubling questions.

> Were we perhaps witnessing an attempt to project what the new culture should be, an attempt to expunge diversities and present a homogenised view of what the Ramayana was and is? . . . Where culture is taken over by the state as the major patron, there the politics of culture is inevitably heightened. It is therefore often easier for the state as patron to adopt a particular cultural stream as the mainstream: a cultural hegemony which frequently coincides with the culture of the dominant social group in the state. (Thapar 1989:72)

In this instance, Thapar sees the dominant group as "the middle class and other aspirants to the same status" and argues that the "received version" (i.e., definitive text) of the *Rāmāyaṇa* popular among this group — the *Rāmcaritmānas* — is being projected as an expression of "mainstream national culture." But, she warns, such cultural hegemony "requires the marginalising and ironing out of other cultural expressions" (Thapar 1989:74). Much of her essay is devoted to tracing the diversity of the *Rāmāyaṇa* tradition over the past two millennia, through Buddhist, Jain, and tribal variants, and through individual oral performances, as well as through such influential texts as the epics of Valmiki and Tulsidas. She emphasizes that the changes introduced in the numerous retellings "were not simply variations in the story to add flavor to the narrative. They were deliberate attempts at taking up a well-known theme and using it to present a new point of view arising out of ideological and social differences in perspective" (Thapar 1989:72). While conceding that the Doordarshan serial is an effective evocation of "the world of middle class fantasy," she pronounces emphatically that "the TV version is not a folk genre" (apparently the middle class, however large, can never be "the folk"), and she too warns that its popularity may ruin the *rāmlīlā* (1989:74).

Sagar's *Ramayan* does display what may be termed a mainstream *sanā-tanī* (orthodox) iconography and ethos, but this reflects only another step in a long historical process. Tulsi's epic was already an attempt at a grand synthesis of Vaiṣṇava and Śaiva traditions, as well as of orthodox and heterodox currents of devotionalism. Embraced by ever wider audiences, it did indeed largely supplant earlier versions of the story (including that of Valmiki), but itself became the basis for endless reinterpretation, as the patronage of aristocratic and commercial elites led to the creative proliferation of its performance genres. At the same time the tradition acquired greater standardization through the impact of new technologies for the mass reproduction of images, texts, and sounds. A certain homogenization has been one result of this process: visually speaking, the characters and settings of the Sagar serial look much like those of the *Amar Chitra Katha* comic books, which in turn look like poster and calendar art.[21] Ashish Nandy warns that such standardization "impoverishes all the imagination and fantasy which is associated with the Ramayan," adding, "This serial leaves no scope for fantasy. Every motion is right there. There is no scope for new interpretations" (*Illustrated Weekly* 1987:14–15). Yet I hope that some of what I have written above may help assuage this fear. As a visual statement, the serial is unavoidably explicit (as the *rāmlīlā*, too, is forced to be) about many matters that written texts could treat in more ambiguous terms, and it often attempts to avoid controversy by projecting positive and humanized characters. Yet in so doing it has offered new interpretations that have already become the subject of lively public debate.

Although urban intellectuals now idealize the diversity and creativity of "folk performances," for the most part they neither patronize nor even observe them — they are more likely to watch television or go to the cinema. If they did view local genres in detail, they would find such performances as the celebrated *rāmlīlā* of Ramnagar (and perhaps even tribal tales and village folksongs) to be bound up in local networks of power and hegemony — to duplicate, in fact, at the local level what the television version is accused of doing nationally. They would also find such performances, by and large, exceedingly dull, for most folk stagings of the epic are lengthy, slow-moving, highly contextualized, and very demanding of their audiences. The intelligentsia might enjoy an artistic documentary on the Ramnagar *rāmlīlā*, but an airing of the complete thirty-one-day cycle, even were it possible (what would one show of a "play" that goes on in many locations simultaneously?), would make even Sagar's sluggish staging look like an action-packed synopsis. Most critics are content to champion "the folk" and their ways from afar, and no longer choose to invest the time and effort needed for immersion in the local "received text," without which, as one Banaras connoisseur playfully remarked to me, "our *rāmlīlā* is probably the most boring play in the world!" (Singh interview).

Thapar's view of the television serialization as a "received text" seems to reflect the Sagar company's own hopes in marketing the cassettes. Ads display the numbered boxes in an impressive array that resembles a set of encyclopedias and beckons to the consumer with a message of reified and enduringly packaged culture: "Treasured for over 10,000 years. Enshrining ideals that are ageless. Teaching lessons that are timeless."[22] In interviews, the producer reminds us that "videocassettes can be kept in your library, like valuable books, to be referred to always" (cited in Melwani 1988:56–57). Beneath the hype and novelty of the new medium, however, are limitations as well as possibilities. A video *kathā* can be shown to large audiences and has great visual appeal. Yet it is not as "accessible" as may at first appear: it requires costly technology and a steady supply of electricity. The twenty-eight cassettes are heavy, bulky, and fragile. To view a favorite scene may require much fast-forward or rewind searching through a cassette, and in this respect the serial compares unfavorably to a printed text — a pocket edition of the *Mānas* offers the whole epic in a compact format and can be instantly opened to any scene — and still more so to the remembered/memorized version that many still carry "in their throats."[23] The serial makes frequent reference to this text, quoting it in sung excerpts and even sometimes (with charming reflexivity) in speeches, as when Dashrath, assuring Kaikeyi of his faithfulness to his promise, quotes a *Mānas* verse:

The way of the Raghus has ever endured —
Give up your breath but not your word. (2.28.4)[24]

As is the case with *rāmlīlā* audiences, television viewers well acquainted with the *Mānas* are able to derive more pleasure from the serial, and there seems no reason to assume that the video and written texts cannot continue to coexist in their respective spheres.

When critics bemoan the serial as a vulgarization of a "literary treasure," they invoke the *Rāmāyaṇa* as one of the Great Books in a Mortimer Adler model of human culture: a reified monument to be enshrined on a shelf and periodically cited as a cultural reference point, and perhaps occasionally even "read." They overlook the fact that millions of people recite, sing, enact, and in their own words retell the epic every day, generating a powerful cultural metatext that functions at every point along a shifting spectrum that outside observers chart with such terms as "folk" and "classical," "elite" and "popular." The Tulsi *Mānas,* for example, was long scorned by Sanskrit *paṇḍit*s as a crude popularization of the elegant classic of Valmiki, concocted to please the sensibilities of illiterates. Yet the same text, patronized by royal dynasties, expounded by scholars, and celebrated in voluminous commentaries, has come increasingly to be viewed as a hoary masterpiece of India's "classical" heritage.

Those who have come to view the *Rāmāyaṇa* as a text rather than a tradition are understandably concerned over Sagar's casting of it into a "permanent" visual form.[25] Should their fears prove correct and this effort come to stand, in time, as the definitive and exclusive version of the story, then the making of the serial would indeed represent a sad impoverishment of a multiform tradition. But I still doubt whether the advent of video technology can produce such a rapid sea-change in Indian culture. Instead, I suggest that the bulk of the audience will continue to regard the Sagar *Ramayan* — like the Tulsi *Mānas* and the Valmiki *Rāmāyaṇa* — as an enthralling but not exclusive rendition of a story that is itself more a medium than a message. They will continue to argue the production's merits and flaws, its innovations and continuities, and to be aware of numerous variations that find no place even in its protracted screenplay. They will continue, in short, to owe primary allegiance to what A. K. Ramanujan liked to call the "meta-Ramayana," incorporating the versions of countless tellers but never fully encompassed by any one of them. This meta-Ramayana includes, for example, the story of Rama and Sita's romance in a flower garden (told by Tulsi and Sagar but not by Valmiki), of Shabari's sampling the fruits she offers to Rama, and Hanuman's writing Rama's name on the stones of the monkey-bridge (told by Sagar but not by Tulsi); it also includes the stories of Ahi Ravan, and of the self-immolation (*satī*) of Indrajit's wife, Sulochana (told by none of these three, yet known to every North Indian villager). The tale that contains all these — and more — is alive and well, and unlikely to succumb quickly to the assault of either intellectuals or cameramen. If nothing else, the success of the Sagar serial has once again forcefully demonstrated that the *Rāmāyaṇa* remains, throughout much of the Subcontinent, a principal medium not only for the expression of individual and collective religious experience but also for public discourse and social and cultural reflection.

Notes

1. *Rāmcaritmānas,* 1.33.6. All references to the epic are to the popular Gita Press version (Poddar 1938; reprinted in numerous editions). Numbers refer to book (*kāṇḍ*), stanza (understood as a group of lines ending in a numbered couplet), and individual line within a stanza. When a stanza concludes with more than one couplet, these are indicated with roman letters (e.g., 12a, 12b, etc.). Throughout this chapter, the term "*Rāmāyaṇa*" is used to refer to the overall tradition of stories about Rama. The title of the Sanskrit epic of Valmiki is similarly transliterated *Rāmāyaṇa,* and the Hindi epic of Tulsidas is generally referred to (as in Hindi sources) as "the *Mānas.*" Proper nouns from Indic languages are transliterated without diacritics and certain common romanizations are used — e.g., "Doordarshan" for *dūrdarśan.* The more familiar "Rama" is used instead of "Ram."

2. I am grateful to Cynthia Ann Humes, who collected articles on the serial for me (with the help of a newspaper vendor in Mirzapur, Uttar Pradesh) while carrying out research at the Vindhyachal Devi temple in 1987–88. I am also indebted to Chitranjan Datt of Landour Language School, who assisted me in translating several articles.

3. A film often cited as one of the finest and most popular of the genre was the Marathi-language *Sant Tukaram* (1936). In the 1960s and 1970s, the Telugu film industry churned out a steady diet of mythologicals, featuring the star whose portrayal of epic characters in forty-two musicals (he played Rama in six films, Ravana in three others, and in one — through the miracle of the camera — both roles at once) earned him the leadership of a political party — N. T. Rama Rao.

4. *India Today*'s critic carped that "everything seems to be wrong with *Ramayan* . . . [it] has all the finesse of a high school function" (Bhargava 1987:70). *The Illustrated Weekly* (1987:9) complained that the serial had "destroyed the spirit and the superb literary quality of the original, in its obsession for the megabuck." A critic in *Economic and Political Weekly* termed it "a poorly acted, still more poorly produced, lurid dramatisation of the epic" (Deshpande 1988:2215).

5. For example, Pachauri in *Jansattā* (1987); I am grateful to Monika Thiel-

Horstmann for alerting me to this article. While condemning the series as a vulgar commercialization likely to inflame communal violence, Pachauri, like many other Hindi critics, devotes much attention to what he sees as misinterpretations of the *Mānas* text—a line of attack used by few English-language writers (perhaps because they have not read Tulsidas?). This criticism does not seem especially well-informed, however; thus Pachauri mocks the "flower garden" scene of Rama and Sita's first meeting (episode 6), claiming that it shows Rama as "a flirtatious dandy" and is inspired by the love scenes of Bombay films. "Tulsi," he primly asserts, "disposed of Lord Ram's romance in two verses." This is patently untrue: the garden scene in the *Mānas* occupies nearly a hundred lines and, precisely because of its romantic content, has become one of the most beloved passages in the epic.

6. Reported in "The Ramayan Phenomenon," an article apparently reprinted from an unidentified magazine and included in a promotional brochure distributed by Sagar Enterprises.

7. This decision gave rise to a tumultuous controversy over the deletion of Valmiki's seventh book, the *Uttarakāṇḍa,* which led to strikes, political agitation, High Court cases, and the eventual commissioning of a sequel series of twenty-six episodes that aired during 1989. Fascinating though it was, the controversy is beyond the scope of this chapter.

8. The renowned early nineteenth-century expounder, Ramgulam Dvivedi, is said to have once discoursed on a single line from Book One for twenty-one days. I myself witnessed a seven-evening performance by the Banaras expounder Shrinath Mishra, based on one line from Book Seven (see Lutgendorf 1989, 1991a).

9. He was not the first director of a religious film to assume this responsibility—cf. Cecil B. DeMille's opening speech, before a golden curtain, at the start of *The Ten Commandments* (1956).

10. All such details have a long history and reflect an ongoing controversy over the precise nature of Rama's *vānar* allies, who as incarnations of deities in simian guise both are and are not "monkeys."

11. American movies and television in recent years have favored constant visual stimulation, often at the expense of dialogue and extended character development. The trend is especially striking if one compares films of the 1920s and 1930s with those of the past two decades; in the latter, camera angles constantly shift, scenes often last only seconds, and character is conveyed through a few expressive close-ups and terse exchanges; the style has become such a convention that we may no longer notice it. According to Neil Postman, the average length of time during which a single image remains on the American television screen is only three and a half seconds (Postman 1985:86). The commercial success of MTV in recent years, with its numbing flood of decontextualized images, has further upped the ante on visual stimulation throughout the media.

12. Though barely mentioned in the Valmiki and Tulsidas versions, Urmila receives much attention in folk traditions, and her renunciation is often said to exceed that of her husband. Sagar develops this theme through several scenes.

13. They thus disguise their manipulative intent, for (as Susan Sontag has argued) their storytellers hide from us and pretend to impartiality, even while they

remain as partisan as other artists and seek, through carefully ordered images, to influence our thoughts and feelings (Sontag 1973:22–24).

14. For example, the spectator has to choose whether to be with Sita in the Ashok Grove or (several miles away) with Rama and Lakshman in the forest of Kishkindha (Schechner 1983:284). Some might argue that the camera's assumed omniscience lulls the dreamer/viewer into passivity and impoverishes his own imagination. I return to this question in my conclusion.

15. An American company plans to create "The New Media Bible," consisting of 225 hours of video (Postman 1985:96).

16. For example, *The Illustrated Weekly* invariably labeled it "the idiot box," though it could not overlook its appeal even to its own readers, and, under this heading, had for several years been offering color photos of television starlets, obviously in demand for pin-up purposes.

17. The budget was estimated to have been Rs. 400,000 per episode, though Sagar claims to have spent most of this on production costs. Videocassettes market in India for about Rs. 325 each or Rs. 7,000 for the series; the North American distributor, Ramimex International of Jamaica, New York, asks $779.74 for the set. However, while sales of serial-related items were reported to be brisk, the Sagars' profits were reduced by the weak enforcement of Indian copyright laws and the resultant piracy of images, logos, and audio and videotapes. Despite efforts to give a distinctive cachet to the authorized tapes, and a printed warning that "IT IS NOT ONLY A CRIME BUT ALSO A SIN TO PIRATE RAMAYAN CASSETTES," illegal versions lifted directly from the broadcasts began appearing in shops long before the first Sagar cassette was released, and sold for less than a third of its price. Thus the *Ramayana* serial functioned as a kind of cottage industry exploited by numerous petty entrepreneurs — streetcorner video dealers, small-town printers, even jewelry and cosmetic companies that made unauthorized use of serial styles and logos.

18. See also the Hindi article by Satyendra Shrivastav, "Rāmāyaṇ ke nām par afīm" (Opium in the Name of *Rāmāyaṇa;* 1988:5).

19. For example, a report on a catastrophic famine is juxtaposed with singing actors munching hamburgers, then immediately followed by an "upbeat" sports story (Postman 1985:chaps. 6–7).

20. For example, even the slick, packaged culture of commercial rock music coexists with thousands of aspiring neighborhood bands, and new styles continually develop out of the rich matrix of amateur talent.

21. J. S. Hawley (1989) reports that Sagar hired some of the *Amar Chitra Katha* artists as costume and set designers, to achieve a look that would be acceptable to his audience.

22. Advertisement for the international edition, c. June 1988.

23. Hindi speakers declare a memorized text to be *kaṇṭhasth,* "situated in the throat."

24. Similarly, when lecturing Ravana, Vibhishan quotes a *Mānas* verse on the dangers of following the advice of sycophants (5.37), prefacing it by stating, "*śāstra* declares . . . " (episode 49).

25. Though it is worth noting that the mere translation to a visual format is not necessarily objected to, but only the "vulgar" middle-class idiom of the production; thus Sunil Bandopadhyay suggests that Doordarshan redeem itself by giving "a huge amount of money to Satyajit Ray to make an *authentic* version" of the Sanskrit epics (*Illustrated Weekly* 1987:20; emphasis mine).

References

Āj. 1988a. "*'Rāmāyaṇ'* ke daurān parīkṣāẽ na ho" (Exams Not to Be Held During 'Ramayan') (May 26): 4.
———. 1988b. "Alvidā 'Dūrdarśan rāmāyaṇ'" (Farewell to 'Doordarshan Ramayan') (July 31): 6.
Bakker, Hans. 1986. *Ayodhyā*. Groningen: Egbert Forsten.
Barnouw, Erik, and S. Krishnaswamy. 1980. *Indian Film*. New York: Oxford University Press.
Benjamin, Walter. 1955. "The Work of Art in the Age of Mechanical Reproduction." In *Illuminations,* ed. Hannah Arendt. New York: Harcourt, Brace and World.
Bhargava, Simran. 1987. "Ramayan: Divine Sensation." *India Today* (April 30): 70.
Bourdieu, Pierre. 1977. *Outline of a Theory of Practice*. Cambridge: Cambridge University Press.
Butsch, Richard. 1985. "The Commercialization of Leisure." In *The Critical Communications Review, Vol. III: Popular Culture and Media Events,* ed. Vincent Mosco and Janet Wasko. Norwood, N.J.: Ablex.
Dainik Jāgaraṇ. 1988a. "'Rāmāyaṇ' ke mauke par bijlī jāne se upakendra par patharāv, āgjanī" (Stoning and Arson at Electrical Substation Due to Power Failure During 'Ramayan') (March 21): 3.
———. 1988b. "Rāmāyaṇ dekho, mālpuā pāo" (Watch Ramayana and Get Sweets) (June 6):3.
———. 1988c. "Dhārāvāhik Rāmāyaṇ: hiy kī pyās bujhai na bujhāye" (The Ramayana Serial: The Heart's Thirst Is Still Unsatisfied) (July 31): 7.
———. 1988d. "'Rāmrājyābhiṣek par 21 man dūdh kī khīr bāṇṭī gayī" (One Ton of Milk-sweets Distributed for Ram's Royal Consecration) (August 1): 3.
Das, Arvind N. 1988. "Electronic Religiosity: Meaning of Goswami Ramanand Sagar." *Times of India* (August 6):6.
De, Aditi. 1988. "The Man From Malgudi." *Indian Express Magazine* (October 2):5.
Deshpande, G. P. 1988. "The Riddle of the Sagar Ramayana." *Economic and Political Weekly* (October 22):2215–2216.
Hawley, John Stratton. 1989. Personal communication, February 24.
Hein, Norvin. 1972. *The Miracle Plays of Mathura*. New Haven: Yale University Press.
Illustrated Weekly of India. 1987. "The Ramayan" (November 8–14):8–17.
India Today. 1986. (*advertisement*) (March 15):22.
Indian Express. 1988. "*Fanfare marks 'Ramayana' end*" (August 2):5.
Jain, Madhu. 1988. "Ramayan: The Second Coming." *India Today* (August 31):81.

Jansattā. 1988a. "Sāgar ko yakīn thā kī Rāmāyaṇ baṛhegī" (Sagar was confident Ramayan would be extended) (August 1):7.

——. 1988b. "Binā 'Rāmāyaṇ' ravivār kī subah sūnī-sūnī sī" (Without 'Ramayan' Sunday Mornings Seem Empty) (August 9):1.

Lutgendorf, Philip. 1989. "Ram's Story in Shiva's City." In *Culture and Power in Banaras,* ed. Sandria Frietag, pp. 34–61. Berkeley: University of California Press.

——. 1991a. *The Life of a Text: Performing the* Rāmcaritmānas *of Tulsidas.* Berkeley: University of California Press.

——. 1991b. "The 'Great Sacrifice' of Ramayana Recitation." In *Contemporary Ramayana Traditions: Written, Oral, Performed,* ed. Monika Thiel-Horstmann. Wiesbaden: Otto Harrassowitz.

Mazumdar, Debu. 1988. "Mandi House Had Rejected Ramayana." *Indian Express* (August 1):2.

Melwani, Lavina. 1988. "Ramanand Sagar's Ramayan Serial Re-Ignites Epic's Values." *India Worldwide* (February):56–57.

Pachauri, Sudhish. 1987. "Savāl to rāmkathā ke istemāl kā hai" (The Real Question Is of the Use of the Rama Story). *Jansattā* (August 6).

Poddar, Hanuman Prasad, ed. 1938. *Śrī Rāmcaritmānas.* Gorakhpur, U.P.: Gita Press.

Postman, Neil. 1985. *Amusing Ourselves to Death.* New York: Penguin Books.

Read, Michael R. 1985. "Understanding Oscar: The Academy Awards Telecast as International Media Event." In *The Critical Communications Review, Vol. III: Popular Culture and Media Events,* ed. Vincent Mosco and Janet Wasko, pp. 153–178. Norwood, N.J.: Ablex.

Sagar Enterprises, Inc. 1987?. "The Ramayan Phenomenon." Reprinted article contained in a promotional brochure.

Schechner, Richard. 1983. *Performative Circumstances from the Avant-Garde to Ramlila.* Calcutta: Seagull Books.

Schechner, Richard, and Linda Hess. 1977. "The Ramlila of Ramnagar." *Drama Review* 21 (September):51–82.

Shrivastav, Satyendra. 1988. "Rāmāyaṇ ke nām par afim" (Opium in the Name of Ramayan). *Svatantra Bhārat* (August 3):5.

Sontag, Susan. 1973. *On Photography.* New York: Farrar, Straus and Giroux.

Thapar, Romila. 1989. "The Ramayana Syndrome." *Seminar 353* (January):71–75.

Times of India. 1988. "Early Divali" (August 9):3.

Vaid-Fera, Mimi. 1987. "Hare Rama! Hare Sagar!" *Imprint* (October):6–17.

Van der Veer, Peter. 1988. *Gods on Earth.* London: Athlone Press.

Whaling, Frank. 1980. *The Rise of the Religious Significance of Rama.* Delhi: Motilal Banarsidass.

INTERVIEW

C. P. N. Singh (Banaras), 1983.

John T. Little

10. Video Vacana: Swadhyaya and Sacred Tapes

It is Sunday morning in a Chicago suburb. At the River Park District Hall, about three hundred Indian immigrants have gathered for a religious service. The children, divided according to age and in separate rooms, are memorizing Sanskrit *śloka*s and learning the rudiments of their parents' faith. The adults, divided into two halls according to whether they prefer Hindi or Gujarati, are seated in front of televisions, one on the women's side of the room and another on the men's. An image of Shiva appears on the television screens and a hush falls over the room; someone softly intones "Oṃ, namo Nārāyaṇāya." Picking up the cue, everyone joins in and recites the *Nārāyaṇa Upaniṣad,*[1] as well as several other prayers, either from memory or with the aid of a small text. When this is finished, a video player is switched on and in place of Shiva an older gentleman appears, seated on a cushion in front of a large stylized lotus. He quietly utters a short benediction and then recites three verses from the *Upaniṣad* upon which he will discourse, pausing after each half-line so that those watching can recite after him. The following hour-long "sermon" includes extended commentary on the cited verses, illustrative stories, and religious exhortation. Afterward, an image of Vishnu appears and a concluding *āratī* is sung before everyone disperses. At eight other Chicago locations and dozens of places around the country, the same service is taking place. In the United Kingdom, Kenya, Bahrain, Singapore, and elsewhere, similar gatherings take place weekly.

In India, a few kilometers outside Baroda, at a cooperatively farmed orchard called Patanjali Upavan, the twenty or so villagers who have come to serve as "*pujārī*s for a day" by tending the orchard gather in front of a garlanded television to watch the same videotaped discourse seen by their brethren in Chicago. If not exactly the same discourse, it will be one in a series delivered by the same person, Pandurang Vaijnath Athavale. Throughout the week, at hundreds of other locations in India, people will gather for one of Athavale's videotaped discourses.

Despite India's ancient literary heritage, the vast majority of Indians have traditionally received their religious instruction visually and aurally. The venerable tradition of religious oratory has been faced for some time with such cultural changes as the advent of widespread literacy and technological innovation such as the small printing press. More recently, the arrival of various forms of electronic media has added a new dimension to the situation. Recent scholarship has attempted to discern what these changes mean for Indian oral traditions. Susan Wadley detects signs that the role of oral traditions in popular religious edification is being usurped by the standardizing impact of the popular religious tract: "As oral traditions flounder, written texts published by the thousands . . . will become those traditions known and used by an informed public. Oral traditions . . . often confined to local areas, will be replaced by less malleable, more widely spread written traditions" (Wadley 1983:81). Similarly, the appearance of serialized adaptations of religious epics on Indian national television has led some scholars and social commentators to express concern that this will lead to an impoverishing cultural standardization and homogenization. Examining these concerns in Chapter 9 of this volume, Philip Lutgendorf suggests that new electronic presentations are not overwhelming traditional religious performance genres. Rather, a new layer of interpretation is being added to what will likely remain a vibrant and multivocal cultural tradition. The impact of these technological innovations on Indian oral traditions remains an open question, however. It may therefore be useful to look at how one contemporary religious movement is using electronic texts, or video *vacana*,[2] to enhance a traditional format.

The Swadhyaya movement,[3] founded in Bombay a little over forty years ago and involving at least one million people worldwide,[4] during the last decade has been quick to take advantage of the possibilities offered by the videocassette. Its leader's *pravacan* (religious discourse), delivered in Hindi, Gujarati, and Marathi at his center in Bombay, is distributed within the movement around the world. Whether they live in Ahmedabad, Nairobi, Bahrain, London, or Chicago, the Swadhyayees receive their religious instruction from a single charismatic leader in a traditional oral form, made possible by modern technology. While these videotaped performances have proved to be a valuable aid in proselytizing, both in the Indian countryside and among Indian emigrants worldwide, the most significant feature of this movement's use of video is that it serves as the focal point for a form of group experience that is highly valued in certain Hindu religious traditions.

In the wedding of this modern medium with an old tradition, however, new culture-specific issues and problems have arisen. As the editors of the new journal *Public Culture* have noted, when modern forms of technological representation, consumption, and commodification are adopted in the non-Western world, they are "harnessed to the idiosyncrasies of their own traditions, and to the ways in which indigenous elites reconstruct these traditions" (*Public Culture* 1988:1). In order to explain how video *vacana* has been "harnessed to the idiosyncrasies" of its tradition by Swadhyaya, it will first be necessary to describe the reconstruction of this tradition by Swadhyaya's "indigenous elite." I then argue that the significance of video *vacana*'s use in conveying this reconstruction to an audience scattered around the globe is that video technology allows what was previously impossible — namely, a global religious movement organized around participation in a sacred group experience that traditionally depends on the physical presence of a sacred figure.

Athavale and Swadhyaya: The Restoration of "Vedic Hinduism"

Sri Pandurang V. Athavale Shastri, popularly known as Dada (*dādā*, elder brother / paternal grandfather) is a Maharashtrian Brahman who is the head of the Shrimad Bhagavad Gita Pathshala at Madhav Baug, in central Bombay.[5] There he delivered almost daily *pravacan* from the late 1940s until the early 1980s and has continued to give weekly *pravacan* on the *Upaniṣad*s. During the mild winter months he also continues to give thrice weekly *pravacan* on the *Bhagavad Gītā*. The Pathshala, which is devoted to "nonformal Vedic learning," is part of a Lakshmi-Narayan temple complex where Athavale's father, Vaijnath Laxman Athavale, began preaching in the mid-1920s. In 1955, with the aid of a wealthy bullion merchant, Sheth Sri Goverdhandas Sonawala, Athavale founded his own institution. The Tattvajnana Vidyapeeth is a residential school and temple complex on twelve acres.[6] It was the first of today's half-dozen residential schools in Maharashtra and Gujarat, the largest of which is a twenty-two-acre religious and agricultural school near Ahmedabad. Over a dozen trusts and organizations also oversee Swadhyaya activities in India and abroad. Despite the variety of organizations under the aegis of Swadhyaya, no organization, trust, or institution is formally identified as such. Properly speaking, Swadhyaya, literally "self-study,"[7] is the ideology encompassing all these organizations.

The aim of this ideology is the restoration of what is variously referred to as "Vedic Hinduism," "Vedic culture," or the "Vedic way of life." These are not categories Athavale need define. His audience understands that they refer to the perfectly harmonious society that is supposed to have existed at some point in India's hoary antiquity. Neither Athavale's ideological reconstruction of Vedic Hinduism nor the movement's pragmatic attempts to restore it are entirely unique in the history of modern Indian religious movements. However, the particular configuration of thought and practice that constitutes the Swadhyaya movement is unknown to Western scholarship, other than cursory treatment in two recent books about the religions of Indian immigrants in America.[8] It therefore may be useful to describe several key components of Athavale's theology and social vision and how the movement is attempting to realize them.

One especially important concept is that Swadhyaya constitutes a "family" (*parivār*). In an analogy frequently employed by Athavale, "Vedic society" is in several respects like the extended Indian family. This analogy is used to explain the superiority of Vedic religion, social structure, and economic life. It is always behind the ubiquitous reference to Swadhyaya as a family, by both Athavale and the movement's devotees (Swadhyayees). According to Athavale, only in the family does one ordinarily find the freely given love and loyalty that true *bhakti* ("devotion to God") demands. Swadhyaya is understood to be a movement organized around devotion to God and committed to restoring what Athavale frequently refers to as India's "glorious heritage." Swadhyaya is therefore also understood to be an extended family, one that includes all who wish to join in its collective devotional activity.

The family concept implies, above all, the promise of familial support and fellowship. Swadhyaya ideology places great emphasis on creating *ātmīyatā*. (This is a Sanskrit abstract noun construction that might best be translated as "solidarity"; in English-language publications, the concept is referred to as "we-feeling.") The point is that those who join together to do the Lord's work share a familial relationship. It is claimed, for example, that in India no one goes hungry or without clothing in a Swadhyaya village because a family shares what it has. In the United States, the isolated immigrant family is offered almost instant access to the support and fellowship of the extended family and to such relationships that it knew in India.

If Swadhyaya is a family, then it is natural to ask who is the head. Theoretically, it is God. But here on earth Athavale clearly is the family's Dada (*dādā*). (Regardless of the frequent assertion in English that the term simply means "elder brother," in fact its primary meaning in Indian languages is "paternal grandfather.") The special status accorded to Athavale's taped discourses makes sense only in light of the special status accorded to him. Slogans chanted at gatherings reflect the Swadhyayees' view of him: "Krishna sang the *Gītā*. Dadaji has brought it to the world," and "Dada is our life, for him we'll sacrifice ours."[9] There is nothing new or unique about this, of course. Extreme reverence for a charismatic leader is an old and honored tradition in India. Technically, Athavale is not a guru, however, because he does not give *dīkṣā* (initiation). He is nevertheless revered by his followers and depicted in the movement's literature as a master of Eastern and Western philosophy who has spurned fame and fortune so he might quietly carry on the work of Swadhyaya.[10]

While the goal of Swadhyaya is the recovery of Vedic culture, the means to achieving it is individual self-perfection through devotion to God, which is believed inevitably to manifest itself in social action that will perfect society. This twofold ideal, social perfection following individual perfection, is reflected in a slogan I have seen painted on village walls and heard chanted at gatherings: "Swadhyaya — the mind will be divine; every village will become a paradise."[11] Athavale promotes *bhakti* as the solution to all social problems, but what he means by this is no simple matter, for he attacks and derides the "so called learned amongst us [who] have reduced *bhakti* to a mere ritual of offering a flower at the feet of the Lord and eating the candy that we receive from the priest in the temple" (Athavale 1988a:18). True *bhakti,* according to Athavale, is expressed with a sickle and a spade — that is, in work for the good of others. Selfless service perfects oneself and society simultaneously. Athavale denies, however, that Swadhyaya is a movement created to advance social causes. Its only purpose is to promote devotion to God and universal brotherhood — one family under God. Significant social transformation, however, is expected to take place as a natural consequence of this devotional activity.

The primary means that Swadhyaya has adopted for promoting universal brotherhood is *bhaktipherī*. This compound term ordinarily denotes "begging rounds," in the sense that a *bhakta,* a "devotee," might wander about singing devotional songs or performing penances and giving others the opportunity to express devotion by contributing to his maintenance. But as with so many other terms and concepts, Athavale has reinterpreted *bhaktipherī* — or rather, called for restoration of its "true meaning." He says that *yajña* (sacrifice) originally meant a "noble deed with the higher objective of worship of God" (*Nivedanam* 1975:68) and that a primary way in which the "Vedic Brahmans" performed *yajña* was to go on *bhaktipherī* from village to village, spreading "religion and culture." In many ways, Swadhyaya traces its beginnings to the day in 1958 when Athavale sent nineteen Bombay professionals to tour several villages in Gujarat. A Swadhyaya pamphlet recalls: "Twenty third of March, nineteen fifty eight will be written with golden letters in our cultural history. On that day, nineteen young men marched to villages to carry out the great revolution" (*Nivedanam* 1975:14).[12] In accordance with Athavale's wishes, they refused to accept anything from the villagers. They cooked their own food and washed their own clothes, while going from home to home to meet the villagers and tell them about Swadhyaya. These "devotional visits," as *bhaktipheri* is interpreted, have been institutionalized as a key means of expressing devotion and proselytizing. Athavale would reject the latter term, arguing that these visits are for the sole purpose of "meeting fellow human beings and developing a bond of love and understanding with them without expecting anything but their love in return" (Athavale 1988b:15). This may well be, but it nevertheless has been the primary vehicle by which Swadhyaya has been propagated. Although the arrival of video *vacana* added an important new dimension to *bhaktipheri*—one discussed later in this chapter—this method of personal contact remains fundamental to Swadhyaya proselytization. The point here is that Swadhyaya has adopted an active method of proselytizing that has drawn thousands of villages into the movement. A Swadhyaya village is defined as one in which at least 80 percent of the residents have committed themselves to the practices and aims of Swadhyaya.[13]

These villages are the sites of various activities manifesting devotion to God, simultaneously transforming society and helping to restore the "Vedic way of life." They are *bhakti* manifest as a social force. For example, within the last decade more than three thousand small cooperative farms, nine large orchards, and eighteen deep-sea fishing trawlers have begun operations. These are considered economic experiments in the creation of personal wealth—that is, wealth that is of God, for which no individual can take credit and that therefore can be distributed to the needy as *prasād*, the grace of God, rather than as degrading charity. The farms are known as *Yogeśvar kṛṣī* ("agriculture for God"), the orchards as *Vṛkṣmandir* ("temple of trees"), and the trawlers as *Matsyagandhā* (another name of the legendary Satyavati, who was found and raised by fisherman and later gave birth to Ved Vyas, the legendary compiler and arranger of the Vedas). The farms are two- to six-acre plots jointly rented by the Swadhyayees of several villages.[14] The orchards (also called *upavans*) are larger, up to fifty-five acres, and function as regional centers of Swadhyaya activity. The boats are jointly operated by the Swadhyayees of several villages, just as are the farms.[15] Ideally, each person devotes two days a month to caring for the farm or fishing. This is the true meaning of the *ekādaśī* fast,[16] according to Athavale — donating one day in fourteen to the work of the Lord. The proceeds are divided between the cooperative's savings account and immediate aid to individuals. Senior Swadhyaya leaders in each region distribute this aid, first ritually offering it to God so that it is ideally neither given nor accepted as charity but as a free divine gift that may nor may not be repaid. Those who apply their particular skill in such selfless service are thought to be expressing true devotion to the Lord and are said to be *pujārī*s for the duration of such service.

Another example of the social consequences of devotion as understood by the Swadhyaya family has been the organization of multiple, dowry-free weddings. Athavale encourages these joint ceremonies, in which a dozen or more couples are sometimes married, because they are economically efficient. A well-ordered community does not allow its members to destroy themselves financially by the kind of competition involved in dowry and extravagant ceremony. Swadhyaya ideology strongly emphasizes cooperation, as is ideally found in the family, in contrast to competition, which is said to be the hallmark of a secular society. Athavale emphasizes that the family is a cooperative group united by relation to one father, just as — he says — Vedic society was united by one king. What Athavale leaves unstated, but is implied nevertheless, is that the family and Vedic society "cooperate" by subjection to authoritarian rule.

The Indian family and Vedic society are both patriarchal and authoritarian structures. These are not negative images in Swadhyaya ideology, but positive ones that Athavale uses to illustrate three key themes: the priority of duty over freedom and equality, religion over secularism, and cooperation over competition. First, in the family as in Vedic society, people are and are not equal. All members of a family or a society are equally loved by the father or king, and all equally love and respect one another, but members have different responsibilities according to their position in the family or societal hierarchy. And, like a family, society functions best when individuals realize that their duty to fulfill a given role takes precedence over individual freedom. Second, Vedic society did not distinguish the secular from the religious. Today it is also inappropriate to do so, because one is always a member of the family, whether in the house or out in society. And third, while Athavale does not call for the restoration of monarchy, he does insist that just as the family is a cooperative group united by relations to one father, so society will be made whole again only when all unite in the spirit of "the brotherhood of man under the Fatherhood of God" (Athavale 1988b:8, 10).

This slogan has been embraced by a broad range of people in India, with different understandings of its meaning, since it was popularized over a century ago by Keshub Chunder Sen, the third leader of the Brahmo Samaj. If there was an identifiable "Hindu Renaissance," fertilized by the introduction of certain nineteenth-century Western values and ideals, then this might be taken as its sectarian *mantra*. Today, even in the middle of a Gujarati or Hindi discourse, Athavale will utter this *mantra* in its appropriate language — English. Athavale seems to have inherited some modern and liberal concerns often associated with the Hindu Renaissance — he attacks such practices as untouchability, dowry, and sectarianism as pernicious accretions to Vedic Hinduism; he decries "the superstition and sacerdotalism that have crept into our faith" (Athavale 1987:16); and he embraces the Renaissance *mantra* of universal brotherhood. But blended into these views are concerns often identified as staunchly traditional and conservative, including the attribution of most of contemporary India's problems to secularism, Westernization, and rejection of the caste system. In defense of his traditional and conservative views, Athavale invokes a powerful modern and liberal concern — the claim to science.

What has been tested and proved true in the experience of India's ancient sages is "scientific," according to Athavale. For example, the traditional practice of *mūrti pūjā* (worship of, and meditation on, divine forms) is always referred to as "scientific idol worship" in English publications and described in Hindi publications as the greatest "science" (*vijñān*) of Vedic Hinduism. As described in the opening vignette, both Shiva and Vishnu are worshipped by Swadhyayees. Every Swadhyaya temple has images of Shiva as Mahayogi seated next to an image designed by Athavale, a two-armed Yogeshvara (meant to evoke Krishna and Vishnu) astride a globe of the world. Between them, an image of Parvati with a young Ganesha on her lap represents the Goddess traditions. On the one hand this reflects Athavale's concern to transcend sectarian differences, and on the other it reflects an explicit theme of Swadhyaya ideology: "Inspiration for doing one's work has to be derived from Lord Shri Krishna with the Chakra in His hand, and inspiration for concentrating one's mind has to be derived from Lord Shiva from his pose of meditation" (*Nivedanam* 1975:56). Why is this scientific? Because it works, according to Athavale. The practice of "scientific idol worship" is the best means of perfecting oneself; it is pragmatically true and therefore scientific.

Athavale also invokes science in defense of certain conservative Hindu social views. He describes, for example, the hierarchical structuring of society as expounded by Manu (i.e., the caste system) as the greatest social science of all time. It confirms Athavale's understanding of equality and serves as the basis for his persistent attacks on Western notions of human rights and secularism. These have remained constant themes in his discourses, from the earliest talks to which I have access (an address to a convention in Japan in 1954) to the most recent (*pravacan* delivered to gatherings of several hundred thousand in Ahmedabad and Bombay in January 1988).[17]

To grasp what Athavale means by Vedic society and to understand his assertion that it has been scientifically validated, it is necessary to examine his conception of equality and his rejection of secularism. Equality is positively and emphatically affirmed by Athavale, but he denies that it can be brought about through legislation or the force of law. It is, he says, the "leaders of today [who] raise slogans for equality . . . [and] advocate dismantling of barriers separating us . . . [who] are the very cause of these barriers and no amount of shouting on their part is going to bring them down" (Athavale 1988b:8). The first problem with equality is that it is interpreted to mean equal opportunity, which Athavale rejects because "the capacity to exploit and make effective use of the opportunity being unequal, it will obviously make the rich richer while the poor keep on slipping back and get poorer" (ibid.:9). But even worse is that the secular attempt to bring about equality is done in a destructive manner:

> There are two kinds of people who go to the have-nots in our society. One goes as a social worker carrying help for the needy with pity for them in his mind and, knowingly or unknowingly, belittles them in the process; while the other goes as the politician in power to distribute largesse to them and sows seeds in their mind that it is their birth right to get something for nothing. The former instills the feeling of poverty, helplessness and despair in their mind, while the latter makes them arrogant and aggressive. (ibid.:14)

The theme of secularism leading to moral degeneration and social deterioration is a constant in Athavale's discourses. To understand his analysis, it is instructive to turn briefly to two collections of his discourses in which he considers this issue in detail. The first is a sustained defense of "Vedic culture, civilization and social life," concerned with demonstrating the rational and scientific foundation of the caste system (Athavale 1975). The second is a series of discourses on the social and economic principles of *rāma rājya,* that is, the reign of Rama, as recorded for posterity in Valmiki's *Rāmāyaṇa* (Athavale 1976). This was a historical epoch, Athavale says, during which "society was organized on the principles of (*varṇāśrama dharma*) caste-system which fulfilled all the conditions of an ideal society . . . which was controlled by higher values and religion and not so much by State" (ibid.:39).

Athavale's analysis of caste is different from that of modern Indian religious thinkers and movements generally associated with the Renaissance, who either reject altogether the notion (if not the actual practice, e.g., the Brahmo Samaj and Prarthana Samaj), or interpret *varṇa* ("class") as referring to *svabhāva* ("own-being"), one's natural talents, not one's birth (e.g., Gandhi, Radhakrishnan, and Aurobindo).[18] Athavale's primary argument for *varṇāśrama dharma* (duty according to class and stage of life) is based on the idea that the social hierarchy is "scientific" because its scientific truth has been demonstrated by the premier social scientist of all time, Manu, author of the ancient law book known as *Manava dharma śastra* or *Manu smṛti.*[19] According to Athavale, Manu's organization of society into four "classes" and four "stages of life" (*āśrama*) was designed to avoid the pitfalls into which Western society has fallen and that are threatening India:

> India has her own independent ancient culture which is rich and impressive. She has an excellent and unique social order and caste system. . . . But today the caste system has fallen on evil days because we seek inspiration and education from the west which is oblivious to all that the ancient Indian culture cherished and held dear. (Athavale 1975:76)

The key ideology of the West that has been its undoing and is today threatening India is "the emergence of the rights of man which is like a terrible poison" (ibid.:222). The underlying mistake of the theory of natural rights is the notion of individual freedom. The consequences of this idea, upon which Western social order is founded, are envy, conflict, and the exploitation of the strong by the weak (ibid.:31).

In contrast, Vedic social life is founded on duty, not rights, and on the group rather than the individual. Athavale's arguments in favor of the caste system are detailed and extensive, but his key point is that it is based on birth instead of on acquired merits or attributes (ibid.:106–108); it is prescriptive of one's duties, not descriptive of one's natural abilities, as Renaissance thinkers typically have argued.

Interestingly, Athavale seldom adduces *karma* as a rationalization for caste. Instead, he defends the system on the basis of "scientific" principles of genetics and economics. Relying on obscure late nineteenth-century and early twentieth-century Western racial theorists for his information, Athavale claims that genetic science has confirmed the wisdom of Manu. He repeatedly asserts that Manu's dictates, such as those against intercaste marriage, widow marriage, and divorce, have been scientifically demonstrated and that "the preservation, protection and improvement of inborn racial attributes" is crucial to a "stable social life" (ibid.:77). He also argues that caste affiliation must be determined by birth because of the economic consequences of doing otherwise. The secular notion of individual freedom in choosing one's career leads to social turmoil as individuals compete rather than cooperate. The selfishness that results from an emphasis on individual rights makes the pursuit of wealth the supreme value. In other words, egoism necessarily follows from secularism, and the two combined lead to social dislocation wherein the individual is "thrown to the wolves." Some people are stronger and more intelligent than others and under the banner of rights and equality are able to take advantage of the weaker. The caste system prevented this.

Contemporary rejection of the caste system and the society founded on it has meant that: "Today almost for everything we have to approach government, in temple disputes, charity disputes, in disputes between brothers and in disputes between a husband and a wife" (Athavale 1976:33). In contrast, "There was no social dependence in Rama Rajya. The establishment and propaganda for social services of every type, for example, baby weeks, maternity hospitals, welfare centres, etc., are signs of a degraded society" (ibid.:44).

Athavale is emphatically rejecting what has been called "a new 'Great Tradition,'" embodied in the Indian constitution, wherein justice requires equality of opportunity and equality before the law (see Baird 1981). We have seen that Athavale rejects the former meaning of equality. The obvious question, then, is whether he also rejects the latter meaning. This would seem to follow from his apologia for Manu, as Manu certainly rejected the notion that all are equal before the law (the Brahman and members of the other *varṇa*s being given explicitly unequal punishments for the same crime). On this subject, however, Athavale is ambiguous. He asserts that inequality in society is part of the natural order: "They surely cannot expect the President and the Janitor of a Bank to be equal in all respects. The two will never get equal pay and perks and such has not been the case in any country in the world, communist or capitalist" (Athavale 1988a:15). Before God, however, people are equal, according to Athavale. Vedic society recognized this, and therefore during *rāma rājya* there was no inequality, only a distinction of duties. Today's hatred, hostility, and "undue discrimination" occur because people are selfishly claiming rights. Consciousness of rights leads to conflict, while that of duties leads to harmony.

Despite the clear political overtones to this reconstruction of Vedic Hinduism, Athavale insists that Swadhyaya is simply a *bhakti* movement. Although he denounces politicians, politics, and the secularism of modern India at every opportunity, he has kept Swadhyaya from the kind of political involvements in which other contemporary movements (the Rashtriya Swayamsevak Sangh and Shiv Sena, for example) have become embroiled. Athavale's theology and social vision depend on an ideological reconstruction of an imagined perfect society, but the means to the recovery of this perfection is the individual. Positive social change, Athavale insists, can flow only from individuals who have devoted themselves to God and united in the spirit of a family. Athavale, therefore, describes himself as nothing more than a *bhakta* (devotee), interested only in encouraging others in devotion to God. Nevertheless, as the Dada of a family actively seeking to restore Vedic culture, he is the initiator of what might best be described as a Sanskritic revitalization movement.

Swadhyaya is a good example of the kind of culture-change phenomenon classically described by Anthony F. C. Wallace as a revitalization movement, with revivalistic and nativistic overtones (see Wallace 1956). In the context of India, however, the more important issue is whether or not Swadhyaya is an example of Sanskritization. Since the term was introduced into scholarly discourse more than a generation ago by M. N. Srinivas, it has been widely used and criticized.[20] However, the concept of Sanskritization is useful in the limited sense in which J. A. B. van Buitenen understood it: a process in Indian civilization "in which a person or a group consciously relates himself or itself to an accepted notion of true and ancient ideology and conduct" (van Buitenen 1966:35). Even though Sanskritization is often used to refer to the process by which a lower caste attempts to raise its status through adopting various "Sanskritic" forms, I believe van Buitenen is correct in arguing against building this limited motivation into the conceptualization of the whole process. Athavale takes great pride in hearing illiterate fisherman recite Sanskrit *ślokas*, which he frequently says "many Brahmans cannot do." Yet he is not encouraging them to raise their caste status but to recover what he believes to be an ancient truth, an ancient way of life. As van Buitenen points out, Indian society is pervaded by the notion that knowledge, truth, and a way of life have "been lost, but not irrecoverably . . . somehow it is still available through ancient life lines . . . and . . . the present can be restored only when this original past has been recovered" (van Buitenen 1966:35–36). Athavale's appeal and authority rest largely on the perception that Swadhyaya's mission is the recovery of this original past.

Athavale is in many respects a traditional and conservative Indian religious leader, but he also has incorporated many modern innovations. He certainly has embraced wholeheartedly a new technology that allows him to address very large numbers of people in a traditional format that carries its own special appeal and authority. It is to this marriage of technology and tradition that we now turn.

Sacred Tapes

Two distinct kinds of videos have been produced by Swadhyaya. The first, documentary-style films that serve as an introduction to the movement, are relatively few and not regarded as "sacred tapes." However, they are technically sophisticated, polished videos, filmed on three-quarter inch, broadcast-quality tape. They are professionally reproduced in both American and European/Indian VCR formats for distribution within the movement. Not surprisingly, these are the only Swadhyaya videos with English narration. The half-hour *A Saga of Awakening*, for example, depicts Athavale coming into the life of a poor fishing village. We first see village life as it once was — coarse and hard. We overhear families bitterly squabbling; men drinking, gambling, and smoking; arguments escalating into domestic violence. Then, the narrator tells us, into their lives came a messiah. Strolling along the edge of the surf, barefoot, in *kurtā* and *dhotī*, is Pandurang Athavale. He tells the fishermen that because society does not value them, they do not value themselves. They must recognize their own inherent worth as children of God and, in effect, pull themselves up by their own bootstraps. The way to do so is by recovering their religious heritage, through Swadhyaya. Presently, the video gives witness to a harmonious family sitting down to dinner after praying. *Trikāl sandhyā*,[21] the practice of reciting certain Sanskrit verses in thanksgiving to the Lord at the time of waking, before eating, and at bedtime, is said to be the foundation on which these people are rebuilding their lives. Having abandoned their old ways and practicing devotion to God, they are now secure in the knowledge of their self-worth and — not incidentally — financially more secure. The fishermen ask Athavale how they can return the favor to God. He tells them to do what they know best, to offer their *nipuṇatā* to God.

Athavale uses *nipuṇatā,* a Sanskrit abstract noun meaning, "skillfulness, adroitness," to refer to each person's particular "expertise" or "efficiency," as it is translated in English publications. According to Athavale, this "efficiency" should be offered to God in the form of selfless service. He tells the fishermen to fish, but to offer their catch to God. The *mātsyagandhā* system described previously is thus born of their own desire to serve God. Another video describes the origin of the *yogeśvar kṛṣi* in a similar fashion. It is noteworthy that Athavale's use of *nipuṇatā* subtly reinforces society's structural status quo while simultaneously inspiring self-improvement, or better, group improvement. That is, fishermen should fish, farmers should farm, and when done in a context of devotion, life will be better, physically and spiritually, for the individual and for society. Athavale constantly reassures these low-caste fishermen and farmers that in a context of *bhakti* their lives can have meaning and dignity, regardless of how the larger society views them, and that only through their own efforts will their lives be improved. Their aspirations should not extend beyond their given position in life, however, because that would be socially disruptive. One booklet notes, for example, that although the Swadhyaya agriculture school teaches modern farming methods, which "has immense benefit to the families," the students do not receive a formal degree, which "has a certain advantage for the agriculturist families as a degree provides a temptation to the youth to leave farming and seek a job in over-crowded urban centres away from families" (*Swadhyaya* n.d.:107).

Not all Swadhyaya devotees are farmers and fishermen, however. The movement also has attracted many people from the urban, merchant, and professional classes. These groups were Athavale's original audience and continue to constitute a significant portion of the Swadhyaya family. Such people are certainly not expected to fish or farm; their *nipuṇatā* is different. They can publish Swadhyaya literature, teach in the schools, go on *bhaktipheri,* and so on. But it would be as inappropriate for them to try serving God with a shovel in their hands as it would be for a farmer to transcribe Athavale's *pravacan* for publication.

There are fewer than a half-dozen of the documentary-style videos and, although they are used in *bhaktipheri,* their significance pales next to the hundreds of videos that have been described to me as "sacred tapes." These are videotapes of Athavale's *pravacan,* which he has delivered for many years at his Pathshala in Bombay. The main hall of the Pathshala can accommodate about one thousand two hundred people. In the 1960s, when Athavale began to attract larger audiences than could be accommodated, a loudspeaker system was installed so that an additional three thousand or so people seated in the ground-floor hall and in the courtyard could listen. Around 1975, closed-circuit television was introduced, but still this meant that only a few thousand could actually witness Athavale's *pravacan.* In the early 1980s, video-recording capability was acquired, and today tens of thousands will observe — or better, participate in — Athavale's *pravacan* via videocassette within months of a particular discourse.

To understand how this new technology is used and how it is possible to "participate" vis-à-vis a recorded image, one must know what is being captured on tape and why it has such appeal and authority. I am referring not so much to the content of Athavale's *pravacan* as to its nature, that is, the traditional genre of which it is but a particular instance. Athavale communicates through what is for Indian society a normative framework — oral discourse cloaked in all the garb that indicates special religious significance to his audience. It is noteworthy that Swadhyaya ideology insists that Athavale writes nothing. Although the Swadhyaya publishing trust has produced at least two dozen books, in four languages, that bear only Athavale's names, they are supposed to be just collections of his discourses compiled by anonymous followers.[22] This illustrates the high value placed on oral tradition. Although Athavale is understood to be a great scholar, a master of Eastern and Western philosophy, and although in effect he has his own private publishing house with funds to distribute his words in print, he does not write but only speaks.

The appeal and authority that Athavale's *pravacan* commands can be explained at least partially by reference to contemporary performance theory (see Bauman 1977), especially as it recently has been related to the Indian setting. Lutgendorf (1991) has drawn attention to the specific cultural pattern of framing religious discourse that indicates to an Indian audience that it is participating in a special type of "situated communication," a performance event demarcated from ordinary events and communications by both formal and affective boundaries. These performance events " 'break through' into the mundane context, signaling their presence by formal cues but justifying their existence by their ability to transform and enhance life, often by reference to impersonal values and experiences" (Lutgendorf 1991:34). This is exactly why videotapes of Athavale's *pravacan* are so frequently described as "sacred tapes." They are a vehicle for the projection of, and participation in, the sacred. When shown they constitute a performance event reminiscent of Mircea Eliade's concept of hierophany (Eliade 1959:11). That is, Athavale's *pravacan,* even on videotape, is an occasion for the manifestation of the sacred in the profane world. What, then, are these traditional performance markers that define the boundaries and intent of Athavale's *pravacan* and contribute to its appeal and authority?

First, Athavale's discourse is invariably referred to as *pravacan.* This immediately signifies to an Indian audience that the discourse will not be a lecture (*vyākhyān*), as in a university, nor a speech (*bhāṣaṇ*), as at a political rally, but rather a specifically religious performance. *Pravacan,* from Sanskrit, means "recitation, oral instruction, teaching, expounding, exposition, interpretation of sacred writings" — which is exactly what occurs. Interestingly, *kathā,* a term often used for oral performances involving many of the same activities, is scrupulously avoided. Several times I inquired whether Athavale's *pravacan* also could be referred to as *kathā,* but it always was denied strenuously. The reasons given say something important about how Swadhyayees perceive the purpose of Athavale's discourse. First, it was almost always pointed out that Athavale receives no payment for his *pravacan,* as an ordinary *kathāvācak* does for his *kathā.* Second, I was told that *kathā* is something one goes to primarily for pleasure, for the pure enjoyment of it, whereas one attends *pravacan* for instruction and spiritual guidance. In fact, Athavale's audience does seem to relish his discourse, delighting in his stories and insights. Furthermore, although Athavale may not receive direct payment for services rendered, he is financially supported by some of his followers. While he is not wealthy and appears to be a genuinely "simple" man, a significant core of his followers are wealthy professionals and industrialists. Given the honor and respect they have for him, it is not surprising that they ensure he lives quite comfortably. These apparent contradictions can be explained by reference to Swadhyaya ideology, which stresses that Athavale is selflessly sacrificing to carry on the work of Swadhyaya. The movement's hagiography sometimes emphasizes this by claiming that Athavale has been offered numerous chairs in philosophy and religion at American universities, all of which he has selflessly turned down to pursue Swadhyaya. On the other hand, it is understood that one has to give of oneself to comprehend his message. That is, one has to apply oneself to Swadhyaya ("self-study"), which takes discipline and study. Athavale's *pravacan* is not just to be enjoyed aesthetically; it is to be studied. In fact, at the Chicago meeting described earlier, over half the audience was busily taking notes throughout the discourse, just as if they were attending an academic lecture. But resemble a lecture as it might, it is not; it is *pravacan,* the first clue to an Indian audience of the special nature of the discourse.

Other culturally significant keys to the nature of the discourse were alluded to in the opening vignette — the special "seat" (*pīṭh* or *āsan*) from which the *pravacan* is delivered, the "opening benediction" (*mangalacaraṇ*) and "chant" (*kīrtan*), and finally the traditional *āratī* closing ceremony. The cultural basis of these performance markers and their function in framing oral discourse in India has been described in detail in Lutgendorf's study. Here it need only be noted that the conventional pattern is adhered to strictly, sometimes with revealing enthusiasm. The staging of Athavale's *pravacan* that I witnessed in India was quite conventional, and as might be expected, the more special the occasion, the more elaborate was the staging and the larger the seat from which he spoke. It was in America, however — where his followers have the financial wherewithal to effect their ideal — that this tendency was taken to its logical conclusion. On the evening of September 10, 1988, Athavale spoke (in Hindi) to approximately twenty thousand people at the Rosemont Coliseum in a Chicago suburb. His arrival in a white limousine was witnessed by the assembled audience on the giant overhead television screens normally used for rock concerts and basketball games. But the stage and especially the *āsan* prepared for him really revealed where his followers believe Athavale belongs in the scheme of things. He spoke from atop a large, artfully constructed throne in the form of a lotus. Behind him was the universe — stars and galaxies on a huge blue backdrop. Above him hung the solar system, large brilliantly painted globes sized proportionally. His performance was taped, of course, and already has become another video in the Swadhyaya collection. Regardless of whether it is as elaborate as a lotus throne or as simple as a specially reserved cushion, all the traditional performance markers are invariably present. But these are just the outermost frames, the structure that clues an Indian audience to expect religiously significant messages.

The next and more significant level of framing is the use of a recognized religious text that provides, in Lutgendorf's term, the "seed" to be manifested in performance or the "theme" that is improvised on. Whether it is *kathā* or *pravacan,* an Indian audience expects to hear a classical text explicated. Athavale has delivered long series of discourses on different texts: the *Rāmāyaṇa,* the *Bhagavad Gītā,* and several *Upaniṣad*s in particular. In any individual discourse, however, he is not limited to the "seed" text but can, quite appropriately to the genre, wander far and wide. Lutgendorf has traced the origin of this style to changes in patronage patterns around the turn of the century that gave a speaker only a limited number of opportunities to win over his audience. Because of this change, he explains, performances shifted from systematic narrative exposition to "elaborate improvisation on a very small section of the text — often a single line or half line. The chosen excerpt became the basis for a dazzling display of rhetoric and erudition, involving the citation of numerous works, often in Sanskrit — a practice sure to win approval from the new class of connoisseurs."[23] This is just what occurs in Athavale's *pravacan*. In an hour-long discourse on an *Upaniṣad*, for example, he is sometimes only able to finish explicating a single word or two of the text. Although most of his discourses are delivered in series that are intended to be systematic expositions and that may take dozens of hours to complete, in fact, any one of them can stand alone as a coherent, thematic "sermon." Interestingly, Lutgendorf notes that this style of presentation came to resemble modern academic lectures or sermons, although still delivered extemporaneously, and that the term "*pravacan*" became the preferred label for such performances. There is, therefore, a historical reason behind the Swadhyaya preference for the term "*pravacan*," as well as an ideological one.

Such framing allows Athavale to speak with authority, assuming he can demonstrate to his audience a certain competence. Knowledge of the texts is crucial, of course, as are certain performance skills. In Indian society, this framing and demonstration of competence give the orator a tremendous amount of freedom. Athavale can encode almost any message into his *pravacan*, so long as he can plausibly defend it by citing a supporting passage from a classical text. In fact, what is most important is the implication that what he is saying is not new but simply "the way it was" as regards society and "the way it is" in reference to transcendental truth. This sort of "keying" to tradition is especially important in India, "a 'context-sensitive' society, in which people perceive much of their behavior against the background of social, religious, and historico-legendary contexts" (Lutgendorf 1991:23).

In addition to the authority he achieves by embedding his performance in these traditional frames, Athavale also derives it from a different source. The ability to quote relevant passages from Sanskrit sources is the sine qua non of a traditional Hindu religious orator, a practice at which Athavale is quite proficient. He also displays competence to his audience, however, by frequent reference to Western culture, drawing on its history, science, and a wide array of Western thinkers. In a collection of discourses ostensibly on the subject of the "Vedic caste system," for example, he refers to dozens of Western authors, including Hume, Burke, Darwin, Marx, Russell, and Nietzsche. Although Western science is often cited in confirmation of India's ancient sages, the West generally serves as a foil for demonstrating the superiority of Vedic culture.

In a discussion of the social structure of *rāma rājya,* for example, Athavale considers whether society should "be dominated by wealth, sex or religion" and asserts that: "Freud, Jung, and Adler have been clamouring for a society that is sex predominant since sex urge is dominant in human behaviour" (Athavale 1976:38). Needless to say, Athavale finds the West to be dominated by wealth and sex, while *rāma rājya* was dominated by religion. Athavale does not refer to Western thinkers exclusively in the manner of an academic lecture, however. He frequently illustrates his points in the traditional way any *kathāvācak* would his *kathā,* but substituting a Western "seed" to elaborate upon. That is, in this genre of religious performance, it is entirely appropriate to expand on historico-legendary moments by relating dialogue and telling illustrative stories for which there may be only the slimmest textual basis. In the video *pravacan* described at the beginning of this chapter, for example, Socrates and his wife are the basis for a charming story about a philosopher's dedication. His audience (at least the educated, middle-class members with whom I am acquainted) are awestruck by Athavale's apparent knowledge of the West.

The "textualist" might object that Athavale frequently does little more than invoke famous names, often displaying no more actual knowledge of his reference than does the previous quotation about Freud, Jung, and Adler. That would miss the point, however, and may actually constitute a false judgment about Athavale's knowledge. The "contextualist" recognizes that what is significant is the audience's perception, and that besides the traditional performative and textual frames, Athavale has adopted a significant modern one that lends added authority to his *pravacan.*

The event that is thus framed stands apart from all ordinary ones. It is marked as a special type of "situated communication" in which religiously significant messages are anticipated by the audience. This sort of "performance event" constitutes a sacred occasion in which the performer, as Lutgendorf explains elsewhere in this volume, enters a consecrated condition: "The oral commentator . . . performs rituals before ascending the expounder's dais, where he is garlanded and worshipped as a temporary incarnation of Veda Vyas, the archetypal orator of sacred lore." Participating fully in this tradition, Athavale thus becomes a sacred figure at the center of a sacred event. All the traditional conventions are adhered to in "live" performances, and given the nature of the occasion, the audience inevitably adheres to certain unwritten cultural conventions. To give a simple example, every Indian knows that you do not sit down to participate in this sort of event wearing shoes, nor do you extend your feet in front of you. But what about the video occasion?

When Swadhyayees sit down to a video performance, it makes no difference to them that Athavale is not physically present. They continue to adhere to the traditional rules and observances, although to varying degrees, as if he were there. I have never seen a television garlanded in the United States, but recall the scene at Patanjali Upavan, where the set was garlanded (see also Chapter 9). Athavale's video *pravacan* is a sacred event. The living experience of actually sitting at Athavale's feet is recreated in front of the television screen by the audience's active participation. Of course, devotees cannot interact with a video image. But they can remove their shoes, recite Sanskrit verses, and above all, partake in *satsang,* or companionship with good people.

Recall the emphasis placed on the creation of group solidarity, "we-feeling" (*ātmīyatā*). This is a manifestation of the traditional *bhakti* concept of *satsang,* which extends from the general proposition that it is good to associate with the good to the specific claim that participation in gatherings to hear religious truth is spiritually efficacious. The concept emphasizes "the active, participatory nature of 'being present' at religious performances, as well as the notion that intangible but positive 'impressions' (*samskār*) accrue to one from the companionship of like-minded devotees" (Lutgendorf 1991:111). The Swadhyaya meetings like those described at the beginning of this chapter are *satsang.* This more than anything else reveals how it is possible, through a video image, to recreate the experience of sitting at Athavale's feet — it depends on participation in a group experience. This was made clear to me in a conversation with a devotee who is an assistant professor at an American medical school. Sometimes, he told me, he is called to the hospital on Sunday mornings and therefore misses *satsang* and Athavale's *pravacan.* Although he has the videotape in his possession and a VCR in his living room, he will not watch the tape. He will study his wife's notes and discuss the *pravacan* with others, but the opportunity to participate is gone, and he therefore cannot watch the video.

Participation in various types of organized groups for religious purposes is a common phenomenon in India, especially in the Vaiṣṇava tradition, which emphasizes the importance of *satsang.* People traditionally gather in homes and temples for singing devotional songs (*bhajan*), for recitations of sacred texts, and especially for the kind of performances known as *kathā* or *pravacan.* Swadhyaya, drawing on this tradition, emphasizes the creation of "we-feeling" among an extended "family" that regularly comes together to participate in *satsang*. Athavale's *pravacan,* whether live or on tape, is the central focus of these gatherings.

Not only can Athavale's audience participate in his *pravacan* in group fashion without his physical presence, but Athavale himself sometimes performs without an audience being physically present. Although he delivered *pravacan* almost daily for many years, speaking in different languages on different days, by around 1982, age and the demands of the rapidly expanding movement led him to abandon daily *pravacan.* He still speaks every Sunday when he is in Bombay, in Hindi, and during the winter months he speaks in Gujarati on weekday mornings (usually Monday through Wednesday). This *pravacan* is taped, of course, as is the special twice monthly *pravacan* that he gives in Marathi. The demand for Athavale's video *pravacan* is so large, however, that a recording studio has been constructed in the main offices of Swadhyaya, Vimal Jyoti. There, just a few blocks from the Pathshala, Athavale can record at his convenience, in private. This constitutes a remarkable new blend of tradition and modern technology. In traditional Indian religious discourse, the speaker relies even more heavily on audience feedback than is customary in oral performance generally. But alone, without an audience, Athavale has been busy committing a traditional genre, inherently ephemeral in its particular instances, to the permanency of mylar.

This marriage of technology and tradition has created an interesting problem for Swadhyaya. The movement naturally desires to bring Athavale and his message to as many people as possible. Everyone is welcome to attend Athavale's *pravacan,* and in *bhaktipherī* a specific method has been developed for taking Athavale to people, by videocassette. But then, given the understanding that Athavale's video *pravacan* should only be viewed in "companionship with the good," and that this constitutes a sacred occasion, these tapes cannot be passed around lightly. In fact, their distribution is strictly controlled. It is not possible to buy, rent, or borrow a tape of Athavale's *pravacan.* Even within the movement, their distribution is closely guarded, and only specially selected individuals ever handle them. Once I naively asked why tapes of Athavale's *pravacan* are not distributed — surely every Swadhyayee would like to have his or her own collection. This is not possible, I was told. Think of what might happen — someone might sit in front of the television with shoes on, smoking a cigarette, or maybe even drinking a beer. "No," my acquaintance said, shaking his head, "these are sacred tapes."

The videotapes of Athavale's *pravacan* are not actually sacred objects, in the same sense as a ritually consecrated image in a Hindu temple. They are, however, the medium for a sacred occasion. The sacredness of this event depends on two components: a group of believers and a specially consecrated orator. One without the other does not constitute a sacred occasion, and the tapes' value derives from their ability to make this occasion possible. The explicit reason access to them is restricted is that they exist only to enable this event. Implied in my informant's statement, however, is the fear that it would be somehow disrespectful to Athavale himself if inappropriate behavior were to take place in front of his video image. Access to the tapes is controlled, I believe, for both reasons.

The restriction of these tapes also raises issues of power. The authority of those who control them is certainly enhanced by having this power. Because Athavale's video *pravacan* is shown to thousands of small groups, however, hundreds of people have the authority to possess the tapes. While questions about how these people exercise their authority and about the benefit they derive from control over the tapes are important, I do not believe they have any direct bearing on why the tapes are restricted.

Although the primary function of these "sacred tapes" is not recruitment, they have come to play an important role in the growth of Swadhyaya. Theoretically an individual could be attracted to a movement like Swadhyaya on purely ideological grounds, through a printed medium. Practically, however, a movement that emphasizes familylike relationships and is inspired by oral religious performances is not likely to attract new members solely by means of the printed word.

Furthermore, if active participation in a movement depends on regularly seeing and hearing a single person, then such a practice's capacity to support the growth of a religious movement would seem to be inherently limited. Swadhyaya has always relied on personal contact to attract new members, and video technology has allowed Swadhyaya to overcome the inherent limitation in its *guru-satsang* style of organization. How the movement has integrated video into its recruitment practices is examined in the next section.

Proselytizing via Videocassette

The Swadhyaya form of *bhaktipheri*, as previously explained, began long before the video revolution. It originated in 1958 as a direct response to Communist pamphleteering. The Swadhyaya account is worth quoting:

Rev. Shastriji said: "The Communist ideology is not able to make any headway in India because of the faith of our people in Lord Rama and Krishna. So long as millions of people . . . celebrate Janmashtami and Ramnavami, communists cannot establish themselves in India. The Communists know this fact fully well and that is why they carry on systematic activities to destroy people's faith. . . . They will distribute their literature free of charge in all the villages in order to ridicule Lord Rama and Lord Krishna and this literature will be on fine glossy paper. Even people who are educated will accept this free literature, which will be attractive in appearance. They will read such literature and they will start questioning 'Was Rama like this? Was Krishna like this? If so we do not want such Rama and such Krishna. Do away with them,'" and Rev. Shastriji was overwhelmed with emotions. (*Nivedanam* 1975:14)

In response, Athavale's followers began to take their literature to the villages, and the Swadhyaya family slowly began to expand. Later, audio recordings of Athavale's *pravacan* were taken to the villages, and the movement grew even larger. In the 1980s, Swadhyayees began to take televisions, VCRs, and video *vacana* into the countryside. Although the Swadhyaya family has expanded almost exponentially in the last decade, I do not know to what extent this development can be directly attributed to the use of video technology. The connection is certainly made within the movement, however. Several prominent members expressed their opinion to me that this growth is due to the fact that more and more people can witness Athavale's *pravacan* on videocassette. Their goal, as Athavale's daughter, Mrs. Talwalkar, told me, is to make weekly *pravacan* possible for every Swadhyayee, in every village.

Institutionalized as a major Swadhyaya activity, *bhaktipherī* has come to be intimately associated with and supported by Athavale's video *pravacan*. One indication of the important role that the sacred tapes now play in *bhaktipherī* is that the organization that oversees it also controls their distribution. The trust responsible for publishing Swadhyaya literature, Sat Vichar Darshan (or Exposition on Pious Thoughts, as its name is translated by Swadhyaya), has no connection with the production or distribution of the tapes. The Sanskriti Vistarak Sangh (or Association for Spreading Vedic Culture) controls them. This organization directs the "devotional tours" that have taken Athavale's message into the Indian countryside and around the world.

Bhaktipherī has been imbued with an ideology that, as alluded to previously, in theory cannot be defined as proselytization. The Swadhyaya devotee on *bhaktipherī* is supposed to understand that he or she (women in India and the United States now go an *bhaktipherī* too) has gone out solely to meet fellow human beings and form a friendship based on devotion. Athavale frequently contrasts this ideal with the three kinds of friendship identified by "Western thinkers": friendship for profit, for pleasure, and for principle. Friendship for profit refers to the utilitarian attitude of developing relationships with others only so long as they can be of some benefit to oneself. The distinction between friendship for profit and that for pleasure is not entirely clear, except that mention of the latter gives Athavale rhetorical opportunity to denounce secularism and divorce:

> Today, even the relationship between a husband and a wife has been reduced to this level [friendship for pleasure] and the courts of law have put their stamp of approval on it. If a spouse in marriage is no longer able to get the pleasure he or she expects out of the relationship, both are free to walk out on the other. (Athavale 1988b:11)

The third kind of Western friendship, "for principle," refers to association for the purpose of furthering secular ends, as in political parties. Athavale says that this is too "dry" a relationship to satisfy the psychological and emotional needs of human beings. Beyond these three unsatisfactory relationships is friendship grounded in *bhakti*, which values others simply as children of God. The sole purpose of *bhaktipheri* is supposed to be fostering this divine relationship.

Be that as it may, *bhaktipheri* is an active and well-defined method of proselytization. But while the sacred tapes are the formal means of disseminating Swadhyaya ideology and clearly play a crucial role in maintaining commitment and participation, initial recruitment depends on forging interpersonal bonds and linking up with preexisting social networks. The process of *bhaktipheri* in the United States has been described to me as follows. Once a month, a small group of devotees travels to another city, sometimes several hundred miles away, for a weekend. They may stay with relatives or close friends if they have any in the city, but they will not ask casual acquaintances for shelter. The Swadhyaya devotee on *bhaktipheri* is under strict orders not to accept any gift or aid and is solely responsible for funding his or her own trip. In the new city, the devotees simply look up Gujarati names in the phone book (every American Swadhyayee I know is Gujarati), call, and introduce themselves. They ask if they can come by for a strictly limited, thirty-minute visit, informing their potential hosts that they will not accept so much as a cup of tea. Once invited, they are careful to arrive punctually. They make all the normal inquiries, briefly discuss Swadhyaya, and then leave, after asking if they may return the following month. They continue in this way for several visits, as long as they are welcome. Eventually, some contacts develop into full-fledged relationships, and when enough people to form a small group have expressed sufficient interest, a Swadhyayee entrusted with handling the sacred tapes attends the nascent *satsang,* bringing a tape of Athavale's *pravacan.*

What is important is that the introduction of ideology follows social bridge building. This is consistent with a significant body of literature on the sociology of religion that emphasizes that successful movements rely less on ideological appeal for recruitment than on the development of social relations.[24] For many years, sociological analysis of why people join religious cults and sects depended on "assessment of the particular appeals offered by a group's ideology with an analysis of the kinds of deprivations people suffer to which this ideology offers relief" (Stark and Bainbridge 1985:307). In the 1960s, however, John Lofland and Rodney Stark's study (1965) of the Unification Church indicated that the Moonies (as they are popularly known) succeeded in recruiting only those with whom they first developed strong personal ties and that recruitment often moved through preexisting social networks. Since Lofland and Stark first introduced this interpersonal-bond component to recruitment theory, other studies have supported their thesis; but although social relations play an important role in recruitment, this does not imply that the thesis based on deprivation and ideological appeal is wrong. A more extensive study is necessary to determine the extent to which Swadhyaya attracts new members on the basis of developing strong social ties and the extent to which people are attracted by Athavale's *pravacan.* It is clear, however, that within the movement the importance of developing social relations is not only recognized but given priority.

The history of Swadhyaya in the United States, where the movement has been much more successful in attracting Gujarati speakers than members of other language groups, provides some evidence that social relations have been more important for recruitment than ideological appeal. The North American Swadhyaya organization, Devotional Associates of Yogeswar (DAY), was founded in 1978 by a small group of Gujarati immigrants in Chicago. They began to go on *bhaktipherī* to other immigrant communities around the country and in 1988 held a tenth anniversary celebration in Chicago that dramatized the extent and limits of their success. The September 10 celebration began with a *śobhā-yātra* (religious parade, literally a "journey of splendor") down Michigan Avenue, past a reviewing stand across from the Chicago Art Institute — ten large floats and over nine thousand Swadhyayees, from thirty states, carrying banners with slogans in English: "Devotion is a social force," "Devotion brings the brotherhood of man under the Fatherhood of God," "Devotion generates impersonal wealth," "To be is to be related," "It is not ye that speak, but the spirit of thy Father speaketh in you," "Love reduces friction to a fraction," "Knowing the master is the master key to success," and many others. That evening Athavale spoke in Hindi before approximately twenty thousand people (from the "lotus throne" previously described). Of course, many of these people were not Swadhyayees, but according to the (rounded-off) figures later supplied to me, there were 13,400 Swadhyayees officially registered for this event, 12,700 of whom are listed as Gujarati and the remaining 700 simply as non-Gujarati. Despite a frequently expressed desire to include all Indian language groups, in the United States Swadhyaya is an overwhelmingly Gujarati movement. The most obvious explanation is that because the movement depends on forging interpersonal ties through *bhaktipherī*, it has grown through social networks that are linked by language.

Conclusion

Generally speaking, the printing press may or may not be usurping the role of religious oral traditions in India today. At least one recent large-scale study, Lutgendorf's examination of the *Mānas* performance tradition, has indicated that oral traditions are flourishing, even if changing. Change is, of course, the one constant in the modern world. The advent of video technology may well mark a watershed change for Indian oral traditions. The inexpensive written text's significance — as Wadley notes, it is less malleable and more widely spread than the normally localized oral tradition — would seem to be equally true of video *vacana*. A videotaped performance is fixed, permanent, like a printed text. And video *vacana* can be even more widely disseminated than a printed text because accessing it does not require literacy.

Swadhyaya's use of video *vacana* is surely only the forerunner of an inevitable trend. Video technology is already being widely employed in India and elsewhere to record an astonishing variety of sacred events — christenings, bar mitzvahs, *upanāyana* investitures, and, everywhere, weddings. Once, while staying with a Swadhyaya friend, I noticed another guest putting a videotape into her purse. "Oh," I asked, "is that a copy of Dada's *pravacan*?" "No," she said, "it's my father's funeral." The video record of this sacred event had been sent to her by relatives in India. When people gain access to video technology, they generally begin to record events that are especially meaningful to them. Religious oral performances are especially valued in India, and presumably they will more and more often be taped for posterity.

That a traditionally fluid and ephemeral form is being fixed into permanent video texts is a significant development for Indian oral traditions. However, the immediate significance of how video technology is being used by Swadhyaya does not relate to Athavale's *pravacan* being captured for posterity, although this may become an important issue in the future. After Athavale, will a new leader distribute his or her *pravacan* in place of Athavale's? Or will Athavale continue to speak to his followers through video texts? This remains to be seen. What is immediately significant about Athavale's video *vacana* is that it makes possible what was not before — a kind of global *satsang* that can use a perfectly traditional format but in a way that allows a seemingly personalized mode of interaction with a sacred figure who is multilocational. Like Krishna appearing to each *gopī*, Athavale can be multiplied and yet still be whole and entire to each congregational group.[25]

Notes

1. The *Nārāyaṇa Upaniṣad* is a short, relatively late work, probably "pieced together from passages belonging to different times" (Deussen 1980:803–805). Sometimes known as a *mantra Upaniṣad* (see, for example, Aiyar 1914:128–129), its central theme is the power of the *Nārāyaṇa mantra* used by certain Vaiṣnava sects. It may seem incongruous to recite this before an image of Shiva, but in fact the *Upaniṣad* identifies Nārāyaṇa as Shiva, as well as Brahman, the Rishis, time, etc. All of this movement's temples have images of both Shiva and Vishnu, for reasons that will be explained, but Yogeshvara (Krishna/Vishnu) is clearly given priority.

2. In Sanskrit, *vacana* comes from the root *vac,* literally "speaking, speech, word," but it also implies "advice, instruction, or counsel" and is the basis of the formation *pravacan,* or "religious discourse."

3. Devotees refer to themselves as members of the Swadhyaya *parivār* ("family") rather than members of a "sect" (*sampradāy*).

4. Recent Swadhyaya literature claims there are 10 million Swadhyayees in 100,000 villages. Dr. Raj K. Srivastava, a research fellow at the Centre for the Study of Developing Societies, Delhi, who has been closely observing Swadhyaya for several years, estimates that approximately one million people are actively involved in the movement (personal communication, January 1988).

5. Born in a village (Roha) near Bombay in 1920, Athavale is descended from

a line of Chitpavan Brahmans. His grandfather, a high school principal, is supposed to have withdrawn Athavale from school at the age of ten when he recognized his brilliance and had him educated in English and Sanskrit, as well as both Eastern and Western religions and philosophies. For many years he is supposed to have made daily commutes to the Bombay Asiatic Society Library, and wondrous stories are told about his knowledge of it (e.g., that he knew the library so well that the librarians sometimes had to consult him about the location of a particular book).

6. At the Vidyapeeth, formally inaugurated by Sarvepalli Radhakrishnan in 1956, village youths are brought for six- to twelve-month programs of study in "Vedic subjects," that is, in Swadhyaya doctrine and practice.

7. The Sanskrit term *svādhyāya* means "to study or recite, especially to recite or repeat a sacred text to oneself," but can also be taken as a formation from *sva-√dhyai,* which would be "to contemplate or meditate upon oneself or one's Self." Both meanings are implied in this movement's use of the term.

8. For one-paragraph descriptions of Swadhyaya in Chicago and Houston, see Williams (1988:238, 267). See Fenton (1988:127–130) for a description of Swadhyaya in Atlanta. Fenton also summarizes the larger movement's beliefs and activities, but with several inaccuracies.

9. "kṛṣṇajī ne gītā gāī, dādājī ne jag mẽ pahuncāī" and "dādā hamāre prāṇ hāī, kurbān hamārī jān hai."

10. Sat Vichar Darshan, a trust organized approximately twenty-five years ago to publish Swadhyaya literature, has produced dozens of books and pamphlets in Hindi, Gujarati, Marathi, and English. Athavale's discourses are anonymously collected and published as monographs, along with numerous pamphlets describing Swadhyaya goals and activities. The trust also publishes three versions of a monthly magazine (in Hindi, Gujarati, and Marathi). Data for this chapter are drawn from this literature, from privately circulated translations of some of Athavale's discourses, and from first-person observation in India and the United States.

11. "svādhyāy hogā daivī man, har gāno banegā nandanavan."

12. These "young men" were in their thirties and forties at the time. Today several of them are prominent leaders in the movement.

13. Although over 100,000 Swadhyaya villages are claimed, 10,000 is a more realistic figure (see note 4).

14. Ideally the villagers themselves rent the land, but in fact a great deal of the seed money has been quietly provided by wealthy urban Swadhyayees. Most but not all of these farms are in Gujarat and Maharashtra. There is one small *Yogeśvar kṛṣi* in a London suburb.

15. In January 1988, I attended a celebration in Bombay in honor of the launching of the most recent trawlers. Over 1,800 fishing boats from Porbandur to Goa assembled in Bombay's harbor for a three-day celebration that culminated with over 400,000 people gathering on Chowpatti Beach for Athavale's *pravacan.* See the newspaper coverage in the Bombay editions of *The Times of India* (1988a:5), *The Indian Express* (1988:1), *The Indian Post* (1988:4), *The Daily* (1988:1), and *The Free Press Journal* (1988:1).

16. The eleventh day of the lunar fortnight (*ekādaśī*) is traditionally a day of fasting for many Hindus.

17. In Japan, Athavale addressed a Second World Religious Congress (Athavale n.d.). Concerning the Bombay *pravacan,* see note 15. I also attended the Ahmedabad function, which drew an audience of at least 300,000, the seemingly conservative estimate by *The Times of India* (1988b:1).

18. For example, see Cairns (1983).

19. For a contemporary, scholarly apologia of Manu that is similar in its overall thrust to Athavale's, see N. N. Banerjee (1975). In contrast, for a scholarly critique of Manu's contemporary relevance, which rejects "the evil of casteism," see N. V. Banerjee (1980).

20. See Srinivas (1952), and for an excellent example of the attempt to criticize the term, see Staal (1963).

21. *Sandhyā* generally refers to "evening prayers." *Trikāl,* the "three times," can refer to past, present, and future or to morning, noon, and evening. Swadhyaya literature states that there are three "*sandhī* (meeting) times of God and the soul," that is, "three main activities that take place solely due to God's supreme power . . . waking up in the morning, digestion of food and sleeping at night. We must realize this and remember to pray God with devotional love at least three times a day" (*Balsanskar kendra* n.d.:2).

22. Several of these collections are available in U.S. academic libraries that participated in the P.L. 480 program. All have been published by Sat Vichar Darshan (see note 10).

23. The new patrons that Lutgendorf identifies were the urban merchant classes, as opposed to the rural landed aristocracy who had patronized a more localized and settled form of *kathā* (see Lutgendorf 1991:160–161, 420–426). It is exactly these urban merchant classes who first patronized Athavale and who are the financial base of Swadhyaya today.

24. I am indebted to Lawrence A. Babb for pointing this out to me and for directing my attention to the literature. For a review and analysis of it, see Stark and Bainbridge (1985:307–324).

25. This analogy was suggested by Lawrence A. Babb, to whom I am grateful.

References

Aiyar, K. Narayanasvami. 1914. *Thirty Minor Upaniṣads.* Madras: K. N. Aiyar.

Athavale, Pandurang V. n.d. *Lectures Delivered at the Second World Religious Congress Held at Shimizu City, Japan in October 1954.* Bombay: Shrimad Bhagwad-Geeta Pathshala.

——. 1975. *Thoughts on Glorious Heritage.* Bombay: Sat Vichar Darshan Trust.

——. 1976. *Valmiki Ramayana: A Study.* Bombay: Sat Vichar Darshan Trust.

——. 1987. *Light That Leads.* Bombay: Sat Vichar Darshan Trust.

——. 1988a. Privately circulated translation of discourse (in Gujarati) delivered in Ahmedabad, January 3.

——. 1988b. Privately circulated translation of discourse (in Hindi) delivered in Bombay, January 10.

Baird, Robert D. 1981. "Uniform Civil Code and the Secularization of Law." In *Religion in India,* ed. Baird, pp. 417–445. New Delhi: Manohar.

Balsanskar Kendra Study Course. n.d. Devotional Associates of Yogeshwar.

Banerjee, Nijunja Vihari. 1980. *Studies in the Dharmaśāstra of Manu.* New Delhi: Manshiram Manoharlal.

Banerjee, Nitya Narayan. 1975. *Manu and Modern Times.* New Delhi: Hindutva Publications.

Bauman, Richard. 1977. *Verbal Art as Performance.* Rowley, Mass.: Newbury House.

Cairns, Grace E. 1983. "*Dharma* and *Moksa:* The Highest Values of the Great Tradition in Modernizing India." In *Religion in Modern India,* ed. Giri Raj Gupta, pp. 3–39. New Delhi: Vikas.

Daily, The. 1988. "Fisherfolk, Farmers Flock to Chowpatty" (January 11):1.

Deussen, Paul. 1980. *Sixty Upaniṣads of the Veda.* 2 vols., trans. V. M. Bedekar and G. B. Palsule. Delhi: Motilal Banarsidass.

Eliade, Mircea. 1959. *The Sacred and the Profane,* trans. W. R. Trask. New York: Harcourt Brace Jovanovich.

Fenton, John Y. 1988. *Transplanting Religious Traditions: Asian Indians in America.* New York: Praeger.

Free Press Journal. 1988. "Noted Sanskrit Scholar Gives Discourse on Gita" (January 11):1.

Indian Express. 1988. "Fishermen Converge at Chowpatty" (January 11):1.

Indian Post. 1988. "Lakhs Throng Gita Pathshala Fete" (January 11):4.

Lofland, John, and Rodney Stark. 1965. "Becoming a World-Saver: A Theory of Conversion to a Deviant Perspective." *American Sociological Review* 30:862–875.

Lutgendorf, Philip. 1991. *The Life of a Text: Performing the Ramcaritmanas of Tulsidas.* Berkeley: University of California Press.

Nivedanam [Announcing]. 1975. 3d ed. Bombay: Sat Vichar Darshan Trust.

Public Culture. 1988. "Editors' Comments" 1, no. 1:1–4.

Srinivas, M. N. 1952. *Religion and Society among the Coorgs of South India.* Oxford: Oxford University Press.

Staal, J. F. 1963. "Sanskrit and Sanskritization." *Journal of Asian Studies* 22, no. 3:261–275.

Stark, Rodney, and William S. Bainbridge. 1985. *The Future of Religion: Secularization, Revival and Cult Formation.* Berkeley: University of California Press.

Swadhyaya and Its Activities—A Synopsis. n.d. Bombay: Sat Vichar Darshan Trust.

Times of India. 1988a. "Stress on Value of Equality" (January 11):5.

———. 1988b. "Over 1800 Boats for Pathshala Jubilee" (January 4):1.

Van Buitenen, J. A. B. 1966. "On the Archaism of the *Bhagavata Purana.*" In *Krishna: Myths, Rites, and Attitudes,* ed. Milton Singer, pp. 23–40. Chicago: University of Chicago Press.

Wadley, Susan S. 1983. "Popular Hinduism and Mass Literature in North India: A Preliminary Analysis." In *Religion in Modern India,* ed. Giri Raj Gupta, pp. 81–103. New Delhi: Vikas.

Wallace, Anthony F. C. 1956. "Revitalization Movements." *American Anthropologist* 58:264–281.

Williams, Raymond B. 1988. *Religions of Immigrants from India and Pakistan.* Cambridge: Cambridge University Press.

Contributors

Lawrence A. Babb teaches anthropology at Amherst College.

Steve Derné teaches anthropology at St. John Fisher College in Rochester, New York.

John Stratton Hawley is professor of religion at Barnard College, and director of the South Asian Institute, Columbia University.

Stephen R. Inglis is curator of the South and West Asia Programme, Canadian Museum of Civilization (Ottawa).

John T. Little is currently a graduate student in the Department of Religion, University of Iowa.

Philip Lutgendorf teaches Hindi and South Asian religion and culture in the Department of Asian Studies, University of Iowa.

Scott L. Marcus teaches ethnomusicology in the Department of Music, University of California at Santa Barbara.

Frances W. Pritchett teaches Hindi and other South Asia-related courses in the Department of Asian Languages, Columbia University.

Regula Burckhardt Qureshi teaches in the Department of Music, University of Alberta (Edmonton).

H. Daniel Smith is professor emeritus, Department of Religion, Syracuse University.

Susan S. Wadley teaches anthropology at Syracuse University.

Index

Note: Italicized page numbers indicate illustrations.

Aankhen, 222
"Aarti," 184 n.12
Abhimanyu, 85
Adarsh Chitra Katha, 132 n.7
Adhyātma rāmāyaṇa, 238
Ādi Prakāś (Ravidas), 127
Agni, 103
"Ahen nā bharīn shikwe nā kiye," 151
Ahmed Khan, Syed, 132 n.6
Aiyappan, 70
Aja, 83
Akbar, 113, 115, 118, 122, 123, 157
Akhtar, Begum, 150
Alankarāsana, 39
All-India Radio, 145, 152, 171, 190
Amar Chitra Katha, 8–10, 23, 76–106, 246;
  advertisements in, 80; caste politics in, 78,
  89, 124, 126, 127, 130; children and, 76,
  79, 81, 96, 107, 115, 118, 126, 128; Indian
  history in, 94; marketing of, 77, 78, 129;
  middle-class outlook in, 8, 9, 23; Muslims
  in, 95–96; national integration in, 9, 10,
  93–96, 120–127, 130–131; nationalism in,
  92; poet-saints in, 107–134; publishing
  format, 82, 103–104; saints in, 122–123;
  sales of, 77–80; Sikhs in, 78, 96, 123, 124;
  subscriptions to, 77, 129; taxonomy of,
  81–82; translations of, 78; violence in,
  115, 118; women in, 95
Amman, Sri Senbahavalli, 65
Amonkar, Kishori, 177, 184 n.13
Amrohvi, Iftekhar, 165 n.11
Amusing Ourselves to Death (Postman),
  243
Ānanda Math (Chatterji), 9, 93
Ananda Math (Comic book), 93, 107
Ancestors of Rama, 82, 83
Āratī, 16, 176

Arjuna, 89, 97, 99, 103
Artistic creation, 72
Artistic lineages, 7
Artists, 53, 57, 69; role in society, 65; train-
  ing of, 62–63, 65. *See also specific names*
Art music. *See* Music: art
Art schools, 59. *See also specific names*
Arunachalam, T. S., 60
Aryans, 103
Arzoo, 222
Asari castes, 65
Ashfaqualla, 93
Askari, Thanedar Hasan, 95–96
Athavale, Pandurang Vaijnath, 15, 16, 254–
  280; on equality, 262, 264–65; *pravacan,*
  262, 268–275, 278, 280; on secularism,
  260–262, 264, 265, 277
Athavale, Vaijnath Laxman, 256
Ātmīyatā, 257, 273
Audiences, 2, 4, 5; of Athavale's *pravacan,*
  272–274; film, 13, 190, 193–195, 200,
  207–212, 219, 220; of mythologicals, 13;
  of *nirguṇ bhajan,* 170–171; performer interaction with, 11, 161, 175, 177, 184 n.8;
  of *qawwālī,* 140, 141, 145, 148, 152, 157,
  158, 163; of *Ramayan,* 223, 231, 240, 243,
  246; of recorded music, 176
Audio cassettes, 10–12, 15, 17, 137–138,
  140, 245; of Athavale's *pravacan,* 276;
  companies, 167, 176, 179, 180, 181, 182;
  economics of, 12, 137, 167–168, 179; of
  films, 192; illegal duplication of, 184 n.16;
  impact on recording industry, 12, 137,
  143, 160; of *Rāmcaritmānas,* 176, 245; of
  religious discourses, 12; of religious music, 167–185. *See also* Recorded music
Auliya, Nizamuddin, 144
Ayyappan, 31, 41
Azad, Ismail, 148, 150, 160
Azad, Yusuf, 150, 165 n.7
Azad Hind Fanz, 92

This book has been set in Linotron Galliard. Galliard was designed for Mergenthaler in 1978 by Matthew Carter. Galliard retains many of the features of a sixteenth-century typeface cut by Robert Granjon but has some modifications that give it a more contemporary look.

Printed on acid-free paper.